CAPITALISM
AND THE
INFORMATION AGE

CAPITALISM AND THE INFORMATION AGE

The Political Economy
of the Global Communication Revolution

edited by
Robert W. McChesney,
Ellen Meiksins Wood,
and John Bellamy Foster

Monthly Review Press
New York

Copyright © 1998 by Monthly Review Press
All rights reserved

Library of Congress Cataloging-in-Publication Data
available on request

ISBN 0-85345-989-4 (paper)
ISBN 0-85345-988-6 (cloth)

Monthly Review Press
122 West 27th Street
New York, NY 10001

Manufactured in the United States of America
10 9 8 7 6 5 4 3 2 1

CONTENTS

The Political Economy of Global Communication

ROBERT W. McCHESNEY

Never have so many been held incommunicado by so few.
Eduardo Galeano

Globalization may well be the dominant political, social, and economic issue of our era. Globalization generally refers to the process whereby capitalism is increasingly constituted on a transnational basis, not only in the trade of goods and services but, even more important, in the flow of capital and the trade in currencies and financial instruments. The dominant players in globalization are the world's few hundred largest private corporations, which have increasingly integrated production and marketing across national borders over the past decade.

The extent of globalization should not be exaggerated; it is just one trend—albeit an important one—among many in the complex, rapidly evolving, and not particularly stable worldwide capitalist system. For example, despite the momentum toward the creation of superpowerful "stateless" transnational corporations with investors, managers, workers, and markets worldwide, there is also marked and growing rivalry between the leading capitalist nation-states and regions. This would suggest that any harmonious, integrated world market is going to emerge well off in the future, if it ever appears at all. What is often referred to as globalization is, in fact, a set of neoliberal economic policies that regard profit maximization and the free flow of goods and capital with minimal regulation as the cornerstone principles of an efficient and viable economy. Nation-states still have an important role to play, but largely to advance the interests of business.

There is considerable debate across the political spectrum about just how advanced this globalization process is, or is likely to become, as well as its political implications. Most critics of globalization argue that it favors big business and the wealthy and undermines the capacity of labor, environmentalists, poor people, and just about everyone else, to control their own destiny. Globalization is regarded as having a distinctly antidemocratic edge as it effectively forces national governments to comply with the needs of globally mobile capital or face economic purgatory. In short, more and more of society's basic decisions are made the province of the market and removed from popular consideration. Some argue the term *globalization* is misleading—the real issue is capitalism—and the case for its existence is overstated in historical terms. This line of reasoning tends to discount the aura of "inevitability" that surrounds much of the discussion of globalization, particularly with regard to the alleged inability of nation-states and organized labor to counteract the power of capital. Proponents of globalization do not necessarily disagree with any of these observations; they simply assert that there is no other route to economic growth, and that cautious "business friendly" state intervention combined with the magic of the market will soften the immediate dislocations in due time.

Communication is directly implicated in the "globalization" process in at least two ways. First, due in part to stunning developments such as digital and satellite communication technologies, communication and information are coming to play a larger and more important role in capitalist economies. To the extent globalization does exist as an economic process, it is based to no small extent upon the rise of rapid global communication networks. Some even go so far as to argue that "information" has replaced manufacturing as the foundation of the economy. Second, the commercial media, advertising, and telecommunication markets themselves are rapidly globalizing, arguably even more so than the balance of the political economy. Indeed, global media and communication are in some respects the advancing armies of global capitalism.

This book is dedicated to examining the political economy of global communication in the contemporary era. We wish to evaluate the changing nature of both communication and capitalism, and the nature of their relationship. The essays herein range from broad historical arguments on the role of information and communication in capitalism and democracy to studies of specific topics such as the Internet, telecommunications, education, the labor process, and marketing. All of the essays provide a *critical* perspective, meaning that the market system is viewed skeptically, both for its claims to economic fairness and efficiency and for its ability to provide the basis for a democratic polity. And while we take recent developments in global communication quite seriously, we reject the notion that this is an inevitable process that cannot be changed by organized political activity. There is also a decided emphasis upon the U.S. experience in these essays, and that is not strictly the result of the North American origins of the three editors. U.S. based (though not necessarily U.S. owned) transnational firms are the dominant force in global media and communication; any effort to grasp the emerging global system has to go through Washington, Wall Street, Madison Avenue, and Hollywood.

In the balance of this introduction I provide a brief overview of the field of the political economy of communication, its history, contours, and trajectory. I then sketch out in broad brushstrokes some of the main developments in global media and communication in the 1990s. Although brevity may give the impression that the emerging system is all-powerful and inexorable, in fact it is chock full of problems and is generating widespread resistance. I conclude by outlining some of the forms of this democratic opposition.

The Political Economy of Communication

The scholarly study of the political economy of communication entails two main dimensions. First, it addresses the nature of the relationship of media and communication systems to the broader structure of society. In other words, it examines how media (and communication) systems and content reinforce, challenge, or influence existing class and social relations. Second, the political economy of communication looks specifically at how ownership, support mechanisms (e.g. advertising), and government policies influence media behavior and content. This line of inquiry emphasizes structural factors and the labor process in the production, distribution, and consumption of communication. The political economy of communication cannot provide a comprehensive explanation of all communication activity, but it can explain certain issues extremely well and it provides a necessary context for most other research questions in communication. Although the political economy of communication can be applied to the study of precapitalist and postcapitalist societies and communication systems, it is primarily concerned with capitalist societies and commercial media systems, as these models dominate throughout the world.[1]

It is the combination of these two dimensions that distinguishes the political economy of communication from other variants of communication or cultural analysis. Cultural studies, for example, often is concerned with the relationship of media "texts" to audiences and both of them to existing class and social relations, but it is mostly uninterested in examining the structural factors that influence the production of media content. Media "economics" often provides microanalysis of how media firms and markets operate, but, like the field of mainstream economics, it assumes the existing social and class relations are a given, and a benevolent one at that. Likewise, communication policy studies examine the influence of government policies on media performance, but the work generally presupposes the necessary existence of the market and the broader social situation as the best of all possible worlds. The dominant form of communication research in the United States is drawn from quantitative behavioral social science. This work tends to be the polar opposite of the political economy of communication: it presupposes capitalist society as a given and then discounts structural factors in explaining media behavior. Nevertheless, quantitative communication research sometimes generates valuable findings for political economists.

The political economy of communication is closely related to the classical study of political economy, that blossomed in the nineteenth century and is associated with figures ranging from David Ricardo to John Stuart Mill and, most important, Karl Marx. Like the classical political economists, the political economy of communication views capitalism as a historical process and one in which specific economic issues cannot and should not be separated from related social and political phenomena. In particular, the classical political economists were interested in the relationship of the economy to social classes. This is in distinct contrast to the modern field of contemporary economics, which tends to view modern-day capitalism as history's final and highest possible destination and to regard all phenomena not directly related to market transactions as external to its purview. The issue of social class, in particular, is banished from the range of legitimate inquiry. The structural inequality between capitalists and workers is simply presented as a given and the implications of this striking admission thereafter ignored. The political economy of communication has been strongly influenced by Marx and Marxism, perhaps most important by the notion that the starting point for grasping the nature and logic of a capitalist society is to understand the capital accumulation process. Those political economists—mostly on the left if not Marxist—that continue in the tradition are still of central importance to political economists of communication.

It may seem ironic then that the political economy of communication did not even exist during the heyday of classical political economy. But for most of industrial capitalism's first century, much of what is now considered the communication industry was not part of the capital accumulation process. Much, perhaps most, entertainment and even some journalism were conducted outside of the market or were explicitly subsidized for noncommercial purposes. The great liberal notions of free speech such as the First Amendment or John Stuart Mill's *On Liberty* were decidedly crafted in a world where speech was not regarded as a commercial enterprise. Even the commercial media that did exist in the nineteenth century, most notably newspapers, tended to operate in local and competitive markets and their content was almost always explicitly politically partisan. All of this began to change by the end of the nineteenth century with the emergence of monopoly capitalism. The ascendant economic organization became the large corporation and its playing field was the oligopolistic market. Likewise, the newspaper industry became organized in chains and vastly less competitive as the largest newspapers were able to bury their rivals. This concentration was assisted by the emergence of advertising, which barely existed in competitive capitalism, as the preferred form of non-price competition for large firms in oligopolistic markets. In newspaper industry revenue overall, the share that accounted for advertising increased from 40 percent in 1880 to over 60 percent by 1920.

This was the spawning ground for the political economy of communication in the United States. As communication became integrated into the capital accumulation process, people like John Dewey and Edward Bellamy, among others, began to question how reliable commercial journalism and information could be. By the first decade of the twentieth century there was nothing short of a crisis in U.S. journalism, whereby critics increasingly questioned the legitimacy of newspapers (often in one- or two-newspaper towns) and magazines owned by the wealthy and supported by advertising.[2] The solution to this crisis of corporate media was the creation of professional journalism, which ostensibly assured that trained professional editors and reporters would provide neutral, trustworthy journalism uninfluenced by media owners, advertisers, or the biases of the journalists themselves. A major theme in the research of the political economy of communication therefore has always been to examine this professional journalistic ideology, and attempt to determine how much and what type of autonomy it afforded journalism from owners and advertisers. In general the findings are that it is scarcely neutral and tends to reflect the interests not only of media owners and advertisers, but of business and powerful social forces as well. It is worth noting that the modern public relations industry was born at this exact time. One of P.R.'s primary functions was and is to assist its (usually wealthy corporate) clients surreptitiously to influence the nature of news coverage (and, hopefully, public opinion) by shrewd manipulation of professional news-gathering practices.

Two other issues were central to the research agenda for the political economy of communication from its inception. First, the increasing role of advertising as the main support mechanism for much of the media introduced a new variable for understanding the production of communication. Political economists of communication therefore examine how advertising and commercial values implicitly and explicitly determine or influence the nature of media content. As the old saw goes, (s)he who pays the piper, calls the tune. Moreover, political economists chart the expansion of advertising and commercial values into new areas such as education, politics, public media, and sport.

Second, political economists study the ever increasing concentration of corporate media ownership, a process flowing from the logic of the market. Not far into the twentieth century, capitalist media systems have led to increased concentration, such that a small number of firms dominated each of the major media sectors. This, in itself, has posed a severe threat to the notion of the "free" marketplace of ideas, which is predicated upon low barriers-to-entry, such that it is relatively easy for one to start up a new media channel. In the past generation, however, there has been a marked tendency for the largest media firms in every nation to *conglomerate,* meaning they would have large stakes in several different media sectors, such as movies, television, and publishing. In the United States this process has been especially pronounced, if only due to the scope of the firms involved. In the 1950s most media sectors were dominated by a small number of firms, but conglomeration was just in its infancy. By the time Ben Bagdikian's *The Media Monopoly* was published in 1983, he estimated that around fifty media conglomerates dominated the overwhelming majority of U.S. media. By the fifth edition, in 1997, Bagdikian argued that due to mergers and acquisitions this total was down to around ten firms, with another dozen or so assuming secondary positions.[3]

The other crucial development that stimulated the rise of the political economy of communication was the emergence of new electronic media technologies such as motion pictures, recorded music, radio, and television. These industries were part and parcel of the incorporation of entertainment into the commercial corporate sector. In addition, the emergence of telegraphy, telephony, and telecommunication became an important subset of the political economy of communication. In combination, these developments suggested that in industrial societies media and communication systems were playing a much larger role in people's lives.

Technological change has been a central issue in communication throughout the twentieth century, and is probably more so today in this era of the Internet and digital communication. New communication technologies can upset existing industrial and regulatory regimes and open the door to the possibility of fundamental changes in the media system. Political economists have wrestled with the issue of just how much communication technologies *per se* determine the nature of media content and influence. The general approach by political economy has been to apply the Marxist notion of relative autonomy, i.e., the general course and effects of communication technologies are determined by social factors, particularly the capital accumulation process, but communication technologies have important social effects not reducible to political economic analysis. In these debates, political economists do battle with the strong technological-determinist bent in communication and the intellectual culture writ large.

If communication was only incorporated into the heart of the capital accumulation process in the twentieth century, it has always been a cornerstone feature of liberal democratic theory and practice. As Richard Rosenfeld's recent book on the United States in the 1790s chronicles, the free press played an indispensable role in protecting, preserving, and expanding democracy.[4] James Madison put it succinctly late in his life: "A popular government without popular information, or the means of acquiring it, is but a prologue to a farce or a tragedy, or perhaps both." The political economy of communication takes these provisos seriously; it can probably be distinguished from all other forms of communication research by its explicit commitment to participatory democracy. Research is driven by a central premise drawn directly from classical democratic political theory: the notion that democracy is predicated upon an informed participating citizenry, and that a political culture typified by an active and informed citizenry can only be generated in final analysis by a healthy and vibrant media system.

Accordingly, the political economy of communication has a strongly normative critique of the ways in which state policies and the methods by which media are owned, managed, and subsidized affect the capacity of the media to serve this "democratic function."

But establishing the political economic conditions for a participatory democracy goes far beyond having a viable communication system, its importance notwithstanding. Democracy requires many factors to be successful, but it works best when there is minimal social inequality and when there is a general sense that any individual's well-being is closely related to the welfare of the community. In this light, the workings of capitalism—with its invariable push toward strong class inequality and possessive individualism—has a distinctly antidemocratic edge. In particular, the political economy of communication has focused on how capitalist control and commercial support of media have tended to serve elite interests in a manner that is anathema not only to an informed citizenry but to core democratic values as well.

As a corollary to this, the political economy of communication—like political economy in general—has a prescriptive mission. The purpose of its critique is to assist the process of social change, both in terms of specific media policies within the context of a capitalist political economy and in terms of assisting broader social change toward a postcapitalist and more democratic society. Consequently, it is an aspect of the political economy of communication to study the nature of political debates over communication policy and the efforts to establish alternative media, as well as to participate in them.

A central problem in the political economy of communication has been the matter of determining a more democratic media system than that provided by the market. The problem has been that much more severe because the "really existing alternative" to capitalism and commercial media for much of the twentieth century—the communist systems in Eastern Europe and Asia—were singularly unattractive from a democratic perspective. Much scholarship in the political economy of communication has been influenced by scholars like C. Wright Mills and Jurgen Habermas, whose work aimed at establishing a more democratic media system. In particular, Habermas's notion of the *public sphere,* meaning a place where citizens interact that is controlled by neither business or the state, has provided an operating principle for democratic media. Following this logic, the policy trajectory of much political economic research in communication is to establish a well-funded nonprofit, noncommercial communication sector that is decentralized and controlled in a democratic fashion. Yet even if on principle one aspires to remove communication as much as possible from the capital accumulation process, there are any number of ways to do so, and the final determination should be made through public debate. The political economy of communication, at its best, should develop models for democratic communication that emerge organically from its critique of the commercial media system.

Moreover, the theoretical work of Mills and Habermas as well as others, like C.B. Macpherson, Alex Carey, and Noam Chomsky, has provided a conceptual basis for the consideration of the nature of political culture in advanced capitalist societies. In short, why are such societies, especially those with largely commercial media systems, typified by rampant depoliticization? Macpherson argues that capitalist democracy can only be stable if decisions are made by the few with only superficial mass participation. In this sense depoliticization and cynicism are rational responses by the bulk of the citizenry to their actual amount of power. As Chomsky notes, in mainstream circles it was considered a "crisis of democracy"—with no sense of irony—when formerly quiescent groups like minorities, students, and women became politically engaged in the 1960s and 1970s. Political economy of communication has an important role to play in these debates as much research suggests that the commercial media tend to reinforce depoliticization among the citizenry.

For all the important matters to be studied by political economy of communication, it is a marginal academic enterprise, at least on North American university campuses. In one sense this is part and parcel of the broader fate of communication study, which tends to occupy the low-rent district of the academy. To some extent, communication has been slow to establish a strong institutional presence on U.S. campuses because it is particularly well-suited to interdisciplinary treatment, and many of its leading figures come from fields like psychology, sociology, linguistics, political science, economics, philosophy, and history, in addition to journalism or communication. This marginalization of communication is also due to the tendency—even among those on the left—to maintain the view that communication is a largely dependent variable with little social significance in its own right. This tendency has been especially pronounced in the United States, where, not coincidentally, the corporate commercial model has been most thoroughly ingrained economically, politically, and ideologically. Indeed, it was only in the 1960s and 1970s, due to the trailblazing work of Dallas Smythe and Herbert I. Schiller in particular, that the political economy of communication became widely recognized in the United States as an important area of inquiry in left circles. At the same time, while obviously presuming the importance of communication to social analysis, political economists of communication have battled at their rear flank against the tendency among communication scholars to decontextualize communication from the social framework and thereby exaggerate its explanatory powers.

If the field of communication itself is relatively weak on U.S. campuses, the political economy of communication is arguably its most neglected subfield. This is due to its critical political purview and values. The political economy of communication is an area that will always be discomforting to powerful interests in inegalitarian societies. And since the research is of little use to moneyed interests, it is an area that does not tend to attract gobs of research money. Indeed, in the 1940s there was a conspicuous shift away from dealing with structural factors when researching media and communication, a process encouraged by powerful media interests, university administrations, and foundations, as well as the U.S. government. Thereafter, U.S. communication research revealed an absurd contradiction: in the United States, ownership and subsidy of media were of little explanatory value and, furthermore, media had "limited effects" over the citizenry. In other nations, especially official enemies like the USSR, on the other hand, issues of ownership and control were assumed by mainstream U.S. scholars to be of central importance in evaluating media performance, and the effects were assumed to be immense if not always measurable.

The political economy of communication has always been especially well-suited to examinations of international issues. They have been incorporated into its mission since at least the 1930s, when the rise of shortwave broadcasting made global communication a pressing issue. Then, during the Cold War, the political economy of international communication truly emerged as a sustained area of scholarship. On one hand this entailed charting the growing links between the U.S. government, the corporate communications sector, the military, and U.S. foreign policy. On the other hand, the study of the relationship of media and communication to national development in postcolonial states lent itself to a political economic approach. This invariably required an examination of the role of foreign and transnational communication firms in developing nations, as well as the operations of transnational organizations like the United Nations, the World Bank, and UNESCO.

The political economy of communication arguably reached its high-water mark in the 1960s and 1970s, accompanying the rise of anti-imperialist sentiments worldwide. North American communication political economists such as Schiller, Smythe, Chomsky, and Edward S. Herman were instrumental in revealing how U.S. and Western corporate control over international media and communication systems were central aspects of a neocolonialism that kept much of the third world incapable of genuine self-determination (and much of the U.S. population entirely uninformed or misinformed about U.S. foreign policy and global politics.) This research supported the movement of third world nations in the 1970s to establish a New World Information and Communication Order (NWICO) in conjunction with a New World Economic Order, to rectify the imbalances built into the global political economy after four centuries of imperialism. The movement was squashed for a variety of reasons, not the least of which was adamant opposition from corporate media and the U.S. and British governments. Indeed, the United States and Britain both withdrew from UNESCO in the mid-1980s in large part to express their dissatisfaction with that group's alleged desire to interfere with the operations of the global commercial media corporations.

The aftermath of the NWICO defeat has seen the thoroughgoing demolition of anti-imperialist sentiments in the third world. In their place is the doctrine of neoliberalism, which calls for the fullest possible integration of national economies into the global market system. In addition, the Eastern European Communist bloc has collapsed, leaving no organized opposition to the market system. To the masters of the New World Order there is little need or reason for the political economy of communication; if the market is presumed synonymous with democracy, then what, exactly, is there to study? Yet from the vantage point of those at the bottom of the global social pyramid, for those who continue to regard democracy as distinct from capitalism, and for those who have not lost their historical sensibility, the issues that lie at the heart of the political economy of communication remain as powerful and important as ever. The context is changing but the core issues remain the same. How, exactly, does the global commercial media and communication system work? What is the caliber of its journalism and entertainment? What are its relationship to capitalism and its implications for social, class, and national relations? What is the capacity for the emerging communication system to provide the basis for a democratic polity? What can and should be done to promote a more democratic media and communication system, and, by extension, a more just society?

The Emerging Global Commercial Media System

The most striking development in the 1990s has been the emergence of a *global* commercial media market, utilizing new technologies and the global trend toward deregulation. This global commercial media market is a result of aggressive maneuvering by the dominant firms, new technologies that make global systems cost efficient, and neoliberal economic policies encouraged by the World Bank, IMF, World Trade Organization, and the U.S. government to break down regulatory barriers to a global commercial media and telecommunication market.[5]

A global oligopolistic market that covers the spectrum of media is now crystallizing with very high barriers to entry. National markets remain, and they are indispensable for understanding any particular national situation, but they are becoming secondary in importance. The global media market is dominated by a first tier of some ten enormous media conglomerates: Disney, Time Warner, Bertelsmann, Viacom, News Corporation, TCI, Sony, General Electric (owner of NBC), PolyGram (owned primarily by Philips, the Dutch electronics giant), and Seagram (owner of Universal). These firms have holdings in several media sectors and they operate in every corner of the world. Their annual sales in 1997 range from around $10 billion to $25 billion, placing most of them among the world's few hundred largest firms. Firms like Disney and Time Warner have seen their non-U.S. revenues climb from around 15 percent in 1990 to 30 percent in 1996. Early in the next decade both firms expect to earn a majority of the income outside of the United States. There is a second tier of another forty or so media firms that round out the global media system. Most of these firms are from Western Europe or North America, but a handful are from Asia and Latin America. They tend to have strong regional and niche markets and have annual sales ranging from $1 billion to $5 billion.

A global commercial media system is not entirely new. For much of this century the export markets for motion pictures, television programs, music recordings, and books have been dominated by western, firms, usually U.S. based. But the infrastructure of national media systems—radio, television, newspapers, periodicals—tended to remain nationally owned and controlled. The main development of the 1990s has been the rapid rise of a global commercial television system dominated almost exclusively by the world's fifty largest media firms. There has been a corresponding decline in public service broadcasting, which only a decade ago dominated most points in Europe and many points elsewhere. In Sweden and Germany, for example, the large public broadcasters have seen their audiences cut in half in the 1990s, and these are among the strongest public broadcasting systems in the world. Almost everywhere the traditional subsidies for noncommercial and nonprofit media are being cut. Even the venerable British Broadcasting Corporation (BBC) has acknowledged that its survival as a public service institution depends upon its becoming a significant commercial media force globally. It recently signed major joint venture agreements with the British Flextech and the U.S. Discovery Communications, both of which are either owned outright or significantly by the U.S. TCI.

What stimulates much of the creation of a global media market is the growth in commercial advertising worldwide, especially by Western, usually U.S.-based, firms. Advertising tends to be conducted by large firms operating in oligopolistic markets. With the increasing globalization of the world economy, advertising has come to play a crucial role for the few hundred firms that dominate it. In 1995, for example, the eight largest advertisers spent nearly $25 billion of the $300 billion or so spent on advertising globally.[6] The spending on advertising per capita is increasing at a rate well above GDP growth rates almost everywhere in the world. From this vantage point it becomes clear, also, how closely linked the U.S. and global media systems are to the market economy. Moreover, the global advertising agency market has undergone a wave of consolidation every bit as striking as that in the media industry. In the late 1990s three enormous firms—WPP Group, Omnicom Group, and Inter-public—came to dominate the industry along with another half dozen or so agencies based mostly in New York, but also in London, Chicago, Paris, and Tokyo.

Why exactly do firms like Disney, Bertelsmann, and Time Warner feel the need to get so large? It is when the effects of sheer size, conglomeration, and globalization are combined that a sense of the profit potential emerges. When Disney produces a film, for example, it can also guarantee the film showings on pay cable television and commercial network television, it can produce and sell soundtracks based on the film, it can create spin-off television series, it can produce related amusement park rides, CD-ROMs, books, comics, and merchandise to be sold in Disney retail stores. Moreover, Disney can promote the film and related material incessantly across all its media properties. In this climate, even films that do poorly at the box office can become profitable. Disney's *Hunchback of Notre Dame* (1996) generated a disappointing $200 million at the global box office. However, according to *Adweek* magazine, it is expected to generate $500 million in *profit* (not just revenues), after the other revenue streams are taken into account. And films that are hits can become spectacularly successful. Disney's *The Lion King* (1994) earned over $600 million in global box office, yet generated over $1 billion in profit for Disney.[7] Moreover, media conglomerates can and do use the full force of their various media holdings to promote their other holdings. They do so incessantly. In sum, the profit whole for the vertically integrated firm can be significantly greater than the profit potential of the individual parts in isolation. Firms without this cross-selling and cross-promotional potential are simply incapable of competing in the global marketplace.

In establishing new ventures, media firms are likely to employ joint ventures, whereby they link up—usually through shared ownership—with one or more other media firms on specific media projects. Joint ventures are attractive because they reduce the capital requirements and risk on individual firms and permit the firms to spread their resources more widely. The ten largest global media firms have, on average, joint ventures with *six* of the other nine giants. They each also have even more ventures with smaller media firms. Beyond joint ventures, there is also overlapping direct ownership of these firms. Seagram, owner of Universal, for example, owns 15 percent of Time Warner and has other media equity holdings.[8] TCI is a major shareholder in Time Warner and has holdings in numerous other media firms.

Even without joint ventures and cross-ownership, competition in oligopolistic media markets is hardly "competitive" in the economic sense of the term. Reigning oligopolistic markets are dominated by a handful of firms that compete—often quite ferociously within the oligopolistic framework—on a non-price basis and are protected by severe barriers to entry. The "synergies" of recent mergers rest on and enhance monopoly power. No start-up studio, for example, has successfully joined the Hollywood oligopoly in sixty years. Rupert Murdoch of News Corporation poses the rational issue for an oligopolistic firm when pondering how to proceed in the media market: "We can join forces now, or we can kill each other and then join forces."

When one lays the map of joint ventures over the global media marketplace, even the traditional levels of competition associated with oligopolistic markets may be exaggerated. "Nobody can really afford to get mad with their competitors," says TCI chairman John Malone, "because they are partners in one area and competitors in another." The *Wall Street Journal* observes that media "competitors wind up switching between the roles of adversaries, prized customers and key partners." In this sense the U.S. and global media and communication market exhibits tendencies not only of an oligopoly, but of a cartel or at least a "gentleman's club."

Corporate Media Culture

The global corporate media produce some excellent fare, and much that is good, especially in the production of entertainment material in commercially lucrative genres. But in view of the extraordinary resources the corporate media command, the overall quality is woeful. In the final analysis, this is a thoroughly commercial system with severe limitations for our politics and culture. As George Gerbner puts it, the media giants "have nothing to tell, but plenty to sell." The corporate media are carpet-bombing people with advertising and commercialism, whether they like it or not. Moreover, this is a market-driven system, one based upon one-dollar, one-vote rather than one-person, one-vote. In nations like Brazil or India, this means that a majority of the population will barely be franchised "citizens" in the new global media system.

Yet this will not be a global market where everyone in the world consumes identical media products; it will be more sophisticated than that. Disney, for example, has all of its characters assume local identities and speak local languages. As one executive put it, in an ironic twist on the environmentalist slogan, "the Disney strategy is to 'think global, act local'." But if the media products are differentiated by region, they nevertheless will be linked to global corporate concerns and determined by profitability. In short, the present course is one where much of the world's entertainment and journalism will be provided by a handful of enormous firms, each with distinct, but invariably pro-profit and pro-global market, political positions on the central social issues of our times. Even allowing for the presence of the occasional dissenting voice, the implications for political democracy, by any rudimentary standard, are troubling.

The political and social implications of the global commercial media system become even clearer when viewed in the context of political culture, that is, the type of political culture encouraged by a market-driven, neoliberal environment. It is true that almost everywhere in the world the turn to the market and the celebration of profit produces widening class divisions. Yet ironically such a social order does not work best when accompanied by an explicit police state to protect social inequality. Such political regimes are costly, inefficient, and keep the populace well aware of the grotesque conditions under which they live. Far better is a political culture with elections and formal freedoms, but where the elections are largely meaningless due to the constricted range of debate. A market-dominated political economy tends to produce exactly such a political culture, to some extent because commercial penetration tends to undermine the autonomous social organizations that can bring meaning to public life. Indeed, as noted above, a capitalist society works most efficiently when the bulk of the population is demoralized and effectively depoliticized; when people have abandoned hope that social change for the better is even possible and therefore ignore public life, leaving the decisions to those at the top of the social pyramid. As the *Financial Times* put it, capitalist democracy can best succeed to the extent that is about "the process of depoliticising the economy." (Is it even necessary to note that in a genuine democracy, the matter of who controls the economy and for what purposes would be at the *center* of political debate and consideration?)

The global commercial media are integral to this depoliticization process. Without any necessary forethought and by merely pursuing market dictates, the global commercial media are superior at serving up a depoliticized populace that privileges personal consumption over social understanding and activity, a mass more likely to take orders and less likely to make waves. Hence the global commercial media provide a serious journalism aimed at the elite and the upper middle classes and shaped to its needs and prejudices, and a tabloid news for the balance of the population. The clear focus of the media system is to provide its broadest audience with light escapist entertainment. In the developing world, where public relations and marketing hyperbole are only beginning to be utilized, and where elites are frank about the need to keep the rabble in line, the importance of commercial media is sometimes frankly stated. The late Emilio Azcarraga, the billionaire head of Televisa, Mexico's leading commercial broadcaster which has close ties to the largest global media firms and advertisers, bluntly stated in 1991: "Mexico is a country of a modest, very fucked class, which will never stop being fucked. Television has the obligation to bring diversion to these people and remove them from their sad reality and difficult future."[9]

Matters are rarely put so crudely in the advanced capitalist nations, but are circumstances that different? Indeed, the United States has the most developed commercial media culture and it is the United States that is providing the general model for the global media system. When we look at the U.S. media situation, then, we can get a sense of what the overarching trajectory of the global market is and will be.

By the end of the 1980s, the wheels had come off U.S. journalism. In the new world of conglomerate capitalism the goal of the entire media product was to have a direct positive effect on the firm's earnings statement. The press, and the broadcast media, too, increasingly use surveys to locate the news that would be enjoyed by the affluent market desired by advertisers. This, in itself, seriously compromised a major tenet of journalism: that the news should be determined by the public interest, not by the self-interest of owners or advertisers. It also meant that media firms effectively wrote off the bottom 15 to 50 percent of U.S. society, depending upon the medium. Hence media managers aggressively court the affluent while the balance of the population is pushed to the side. Indeed, the best journalism today is that directed to the business class by the *Wall Street Journal, Business Week,* and the like. We have quality journalism aimed at the affluent and directed to their needs and interests, and schlock journalism for the masses. As Walter Cronkite observes, intense commercial pressures have converted television journalism into "a stew of trivia, soft features and similar tripe."[10]

To do effective journalism is expensive, and corporate managers realize that the surest way to fatten profits is to fire editors and reporters and fill the news hole with inexpensive syndicated material and fluff. The result has been a sharp polarization among journalists, with salaries and benefits climbing for celebrity and privileged journalists at the elite news media while conditions have deteriorated for the balance of the working press. Layoffs among news workers have been widespread in the past decade; one study reveals that there has been an marked decrease in the number of Washington network correspondents alone in that period.[11] With all this unemployment, salaries for nonelite journalists have plummeted, and beginning salaries are so low that young journalists have a difficult time supporting themselves. These developments have contributed to a collapse in the morale of U.S. journalists, a real loss of faith in their enterprise. The past few years has seen several major editors and journalists leave the profession in anger over these trends.[12] James Squires, former editor of the *Chicago Tribune,* argues that the corporate takeover of the media has led to the "death of journalism." And, aside from the pursuit of profit, even business commentators have been struck by how the media conglomerates are willing to censor and distort journalism to suit their corporate interests. Nowhere is this more evident than in the virtual blackout of critical coverage of the operations of the giant media and telecommunication firms, beyond what is produced in the business press and directed at investors.[13]

Tragically, the dominant notion of a "free press" in the United States (and increasingly elsewhere) continues to regard the government as the only organized enemy of freedom. Imagine if the U.S. government had ordered that journalism staffs be cut in half, that scores of foreign bureaus be shut down, and that the news be shaped to suit the interests of the U.S. government. It would doubtlessly constitute the gravest U.S. political crisis since the Civil War, making the red scares and Watergate look like a day at the beach. Yet when corporations pursue the exact same course, scarcely a murmur of dissent can be detected in the political culture.

Nor are newspaper and broadcast journalism the only casualties of a corporate-dominated, profit-motivated media system. The corporate takeover of much of U.S. magazine publishing has resulted in increased pressure upon editors to highlight editorial fare that pleases advertisers or that serves the political agenda of the corporate owners. By 1997 large advertisers like Chrysler and Colgate-Palmolive were successfully requiring that magazine publishers inform them in advance of the magazine's editorial contents so they could pull their advertising if they were displeased with the fare.[14] A similar process is taking place with book publishing. After a wave of mergers and acquisitions, three of the world's four largest media giants now own the three largest global book publishers. Corporatization of publishing has led to a marked shift to the political right in what types of books clear the corporate hurdles, as well as a trend to make books look "like everything else the mass media turn out." Book publishing, which not too long ago played an important role in stimulating public culture and debate, has largely abandoned that function, except to push the ideas of the corporate owners' favored interests. As book publishing has been brought under the control of media conglomerates, *Variety* notes, "even industry mavens decry the glut of mediocre product flooding the market."[15]

Corporate concentration and profit-maximization had similarly disastrous effects upon music, radio, television, and film. The stakes have been raised for commercial success. *Variety* concluded after a 1996 study of 164 films that "Films with budgets greater than $60 million are more likely to generate profit than cheaper pics." One Hollywood movie producer notes that media mergers accelerate the existing trend toward "greater emphasis on the bottom line, more homogenization of content and less risk taking." The one film genre that has proven least risky and with the greatest upside has been "action" fare. This is encouraged by the rapid rise in non-U.S. sales for Hollywood, such that they are now greater than domestic revenues. Violent fare, requiring less nuance than comedy or drama, is especially popular across markets. As one media executive said, "Kicking butt plays everywhere." The other route for the corporate media giants to lessen risk is to specifically produce films that lend themselves to complementary merchandising of products: The revenues and profits generated here can often be equal or superior to those generated by traditional box-office sales or video rentals.[16] The ultimate result of this marriage of Hollywood and Madison Avenue came with the 1996 release of

Time Warner's film *Space Jam*, based upon Nike shoe commercials, starring Bugs Bunny and Michael Jordan and directed by "the country's hottest director of commercials." As *Forbes* magazine puts it, "the real point of the movie is to sell, sell, sell." Time Warner "is looking to hawk up to $1 billion in toys, clothing, books, and sports gear based on the movie characters." The implications for the "art" of filmmaking are self-evident.

Indeed, the commercialism of the media system permeates every aspect of its being. The volume of advertising has increased rapidly in the United States over the past decade; U.S. television networks now broadcast 6,000 commercials per week, up 50 percent since 1983. As *Business Week* observes, "the buying public has been virtually buried alive in ads." Desperate to be seen and heard, advertisers are turning to new approaches, including "stamping their messages on everything that stands still." To circumvent this commercial blizzard, and the consumer skepticism to traditional advertising, marketers are working to infiltrate entertainment. There are more than two dozen consultancies in Los Angeles, for example, just to help link marketers with film and television producers, usually to get the marketer's product "placed" and promoted surreptitiously inside the programming.[17] "The connections between Madison Avenue and Hollywood have grown so elaborate," *Business Week* concludes, "that nothing is off-limits when studios and advertisers sit down to hammer out the marketing campaign." Traditional notions of separation of editorial and commercial interests are weakening. Advertisers play a large and increasing role in determining media content. Media firms solicit the capital and input of advertising firms as they prepare programming. "Networks are happy to cater to advertisers who want a bigger role," one report stated.[18] "We're here to serve advertisers," Westinghouse (owner of CBS) CEO Michael H. Jordan states. "That's our *raison d'etre.*"

The Internet and the Digital Revolution

The rise of a global commercial media system is only one striking trend of the 1990s. The other is the rise of digital computer networks in general, and the Internet in particular. The logic of digital communication is that the traditional distinctions between telephony and all types of media are disappearing. Eventually, these industries will "converge," meaning firms active in one of them will by definition be capable of competing in the others. The present example of convergence is how cable and telephone companies can now offer each other's services. The Internet has opened up very important space for progressive and democratic communication, especially for activists hamstrung by traditional commercial media. This alone has made the Internet an extremely positive development. Some have argued that the Internet will eventually break up the vise-like grip of the global media monopoly and provide the basis for a golden age of free, uncensored, democratic communication. Yet whether one can extrapolate from activist use of the Internet to seeing the Internet become the democratic medium for society writ large is another matter. The notion that the Internet will permit humanity to leapfrog over capitalism and corporate communication is in sharp contrast to the present rapid commercialization of the Internet.

Moreover, it will be many years before the Internet can possibly stake a claim to replace television as the dominant medium in the United States, and much longer elsewhere. This is due to bandwidth limitations, the cost of computers and access, and numerous, often complex, technical problems, all of which will keep Internet usage restricted. Rupert Murdoch, whose News Corporation has been perhaps the most aggressive of the media giants to explore the possibilities of cyberspace, states that establishing an information highway "is going to take longer than people think." He projects that it will take until at least 2010 or 2015 for a broadband network to reach fruition in the United States and Western Europe, and until the middle of the twenty-first century for it to begin to dominate elsewhere.[19] Even Bill Gates, whose Microsoft is spending $400 million annually to become an Internet content provider, acknowledges that the Internet as mass medium "is going to come very slowly." This is the clear consensus across the media and communications industries, and it explains the enormous corporate investments in terrestrial broadcasting and digital satellite broadcasting that would be highly dubious if the broadband information highway was imminent. As Universal president Frank Biondi put it in 1996, media firms "don't even think of the Internet as competition."

It is also unclear how firms will be able to make money by providing Internet content—and in a market-driven system this is the all-important question. Even the rosiest forecasts only see U.S. Internet advertising spending at $5 billion by 2000, representing only 2 or 3 percent of projected U.S. advertising spending that year. The media giants have all established websites and have the product and deep pockets to wait it out and establish themselves as the dominant players in cyberspace. They can also use their existing media to constantly promote their online ventures, and their relationships with major advertisers to bring them aboard their Internet ventures. In short, if the Internet becomes a viable commercial medium, there is a good chance that many of the media giants will be among the firms capable of capitalizing upon it. The other "winners" will probably be firms like Microsoft that have the resources to seize a portion of the market.

While the media firms do not face an immediate or direct threat from the Internet, computer software makers and telecommunication firms do. The Internet is changing the basic nature of both their businesses, and both industries are turning their attention to incorporating the Internet into the heart of their activities. The eventual mergers and alliances that emerge will have tremendous impact upon global media as media firms are brought into the digital communication empires. This is speculative; it is also possible that the Internet itself will eventually be supplanted by a more commercially oriented digital communication network.

Due to the privatization and commercialization that is the cornerstone of the global market economy, we are in the midst of a sweeping reconstruction of global telecommunication from the system of nonprofit national monopolies that dominated only fifteen years ago. The process was formalized in 1997 when the World Trade Organization generated a landmark agreement for telecommunication deregulation signed by sixty-eight firms (accounting for 90 percent of the global telecom market). It will open all markets to foreign competition and permit foreign ownership. In the late 1990s the world's largest telecommunication firms have raced to put together global alliances.[20] When British Telecommunication purchased MCI for some $20 billion in November 1996 to form Concert, it signaled that alliances may turn into formal mergers. AT&T has allied with Singapore Telecom and four major European national firms to form Uniworld or World Partners; Sprint, Deutsche Telekom, and France Telecom have formed Global One.[21] The *Financial Times* predicts the endpoint may be "a handful of giants, straddling the world market." MCI president Gerald H. Taylor concluded in 1996 that "There's probably going to be only four to six global gangs emerge over the next five years as all this sorts out." Each of these global alliances strives to offer "one-stop shopping" of telephone, cellular, paging, and Internet access services to the lucrative global business market.

By the logic of the market and convergence, we should expect that the global media oligopoly will gradually evolve into a far broader global communication oligopoly over the next one or two decades. BT-MCI already owns 13.5 percent of News Corporation and U.S. West has a large stake in Time Warner. The media giants will link with the handful of telecommunication "global gangs," and they all will strike deals with the leading computer firms. As one writer puts it, the goal of all the "info-communication" firms is "to ensure they are among what will end up being a handful of communication monoliths controlling both product and distribution networks in the future. . . . The basic aim of future M&A [mergers and acquisitions] is to control the transmission of three basic telecommunication products—voice, data and video." In short, the Internet and digital communication networks will not undermine the development of a global communication oligopoly; rather, they will be an integral aspect of it. As a market-driven system, it will be built to satisfy the needs of businesses and affluent consumers. This is where the easiest profits are to be found.

Indeed, left to the market, the Internet will as likely increase inequality between the advanced nations (and especially the United States) and the balance of the world. In 1996 only four percent of Internet usage was in the developing world, whereas nearly 75 percent of web users were in the United States.[22] That discrepancy will probably lessen, but there is little reason to believe it will not remain a significant problem. While English is in effect the official web language—thereby playing into the hands of U.S. firms and users—the Internet is being marketed in the developing world, as in the United States, as first and foremost a tool for business and the affluent. In this sense the Internet will probably increase inequality within nations as well as between them. Along these lines, when a Peruvian cooperative attempted to bring Internet access to a peasant community, the recently privatized Peruvian telecommunication service refused to provide them the necessary equipment. It had plans to provide its own commercial Internet access service.[23]

Long ago—back in the Internet's ancient history, like 1994 and 1995—some Internet enthusiasts were so captivated by the technology's powers they regarded "cyberspace" as the end of corporate for-profit communication, because there people would be able to bypass the corporate sector and communicate globally with each other directly. That was then. Perhaps the most striking change to occur in the late 1990s has been the quick fade of euphoria of those who saw the Internet as providing a qualitatively different and egalitarian type of journalism, politics, media, and culture. The indications are that the substantive *content* of this commercial media in the Internet, or any subsequent digital communication system, will look much like what currently exists. Indeed, advertisers and commercialism arguably have more influence over Internet content than anywhere else. Advertisers and media firms both aspire to make the Internet look more and more like commercial television, as that is a proven winner commercially. In December 1996 Microsoft reconfigured its huge online Microsoft Network to resemble a television format.[24] AT&T's director of Internet services says the Internet may become the ultimate advertising-driven medium: "If it's done well, you won't feel there's any tension between the consumerism and the entertainment." Frank Beacham, who in 1995 enthused about the Internet as a public sphere outside corporate or governmental control, lamented one year later that the Internet was shifting "from being a participatory medium that serves the interests of the public to being a broadcast medium where corporations deliver consumer-oriented information. Interactivity would be reduced to little more than sales transactions and email."

Whither Global Communication?

It is tempting to regard the establishment of a global commercial media and communication market dominated by a few dozen enormous corporations as inevitable, much like it is easy to say the same about global capitalism writ large. Yet the emerging communication system, much like the market economy, is fraught with problems and tensions. The limitations of the emerging system, when viewed from a perspective other than that of business or an upper-middle class consumer, are striking. Perhaps no area has seen such a surge in activism in recent years as has the area of organizing for media reform. In almost every nation groups like the U.S. Fairness & Accuracy in Reporting and the British Campaign for Press and Broadcasting Freedom are educating people of the problems of commercial media and organizing for social change. These groups not only criticize commercial media, but they organize to protect public service broadcasting from commercial and bureaucratic encroachment. Scores of similar groups are developing everywhere. Some organizations, like the recently formed Cultural Environment Movement, organize along transnational lines. Organized labor, too, across the world, has become active in issues for public service media and communication. Progressive social movements like the Zapatistas make the dismantlement of the global commercial media system a priority in their programs. Democratic left electoral parties have made media reform a central part of their platforms. The message is increasingly clear: without democratic media, there can be no democracy.

Even more activity is going into the establishment of nonprofit, noncommercial media. The new digital technologies are permitting a vast expansion in the opportunities for activists to launch communication ventures. Indeed, the technological basis now exists for a democratic media unthinkable only a few years ago. Across the world there is an explosion in community and pirate radio, public access television, video and Internet sites. But unless there is organized political force—to demand rights and resources—there is little reason to think these alternative media can ever assume anything more than a marginal role in the global media system. That is the immediate battle for democratic media activists. In the struggle for democratic communication, the political economy of global communication has the indispensable task of grasping and explaining the nature of the emerging system so that it can be changed for the better.

May 1997

Notes

1. For a longer discussion of the history of the field, see Vincent Mosco, *The Political Economy of Communication* (Sage, 1996).
2. See Dan Schiller, *Theorizing Communication* (New York: Oxford University Press, 1996).
3. Ben H. Bagdikian, *The Media Monopoly,* fifth edition (Boston: Beacon Press, 1997).
4. Richard N. Rosenfeld, *American Aurora* (New York: St. Martin's Press, 1997).
5. For a detailed discussion of the current global media situation, see Edward S. Herman and Robert W. McChesney, *The Global Media: The New Missionaries of Corporate Capitalism* (London and Washington: Cassell, 1997).
6. Laurel Wentz and Kevin Bacon, "Global Marketers," *Ad Age International,* November 1996, p. 115.
7. Marla Matzer, "Contented Kingdoms," *Superbrands '97,* supplement to *Adweek,* 7 October 1996, pp. 30, 33.
8. Bernard Simon, "Seagram to hold on to 15% stake in Time Warner," *Financial Times,* 1 June 1995, p. 18.
9. Cited in *Multinational Monitor,* October 1996, p. 13.

10. Dorothy Rabinowitz, "Cronkite Returns to Airwaves," *The Wall Street Journal*, 9 December 1996, p. A12.

11. Penn Kimball, *Downsizing the News: Network Cutbacks in the Nation's Capital* (Washington, DC: Woodrow Wilson Center Press, 1994).

12. See, for example, Mort Rosenblum, *Who Stole the News?* (New York: John Wiley & Sons, 1993); Doug Underwood, *When MBAs Rule the Newsroom How the Marketers and Managers are Reshaping Today's Media* (New York: Columbia University Press, 1993); John McManus, *Market-Driven Journalism: Let the Citizen Beware?* (Thousand Oaks, CA: Sage, 1994); Dennis Mazzocco, *Networks of Power: Corporate TV's Threat to Democracy* (Boston: South End Press, 1994).

13. Elizabeth Lesly, "Self-Censorship Is Still Censorship," *Business Week*, 16 December 1996, p. 78.

14. G. Bruce Knecht, "Magazine Advertisers Demand Prior Notice of 'Offensive' Articles," *The Wall Street Journal*, 30 April 1997, p. A1.

15. Chris Petrikin, "Book Biz: Read It and Weep," *Variety*, 12-18 May 1997, p. 1.

16. Bruce Orwall, "Disney Chases Live-Action Merchandising Hits," *The Wall Street Journal*, 27 November 1996, p. B1.

17. Michael Schneider, "Brand name-dropping," *Electronic Media*, 26 August 1996, pp. 1, 30.

18. Mary Kuntz and Joseph Weber, "The New Hucksterism," *Business Week*, 1 July 1996, p. 82.

19. Raymond Snoddy and Alan Cane, "Full multimedia impact years away, says Murdoch," *Financial Times*, 12 May 1995, p. 1.

20. Tony Jackson, "MCI sees the future in 'one-stop' services," *Financial Times*, 8 August 1996, p. 15.

21. "Global Telecom Alliances," *Information Week*, 13 November 1995, p. 40; Michael Lindemann, "Telecoms operators launch global alliance," *Financial Times*, 1 February 1996, p. 16.

22. Robin Frost, "Web's Heavy U.S. Accent Grates on Overseas Ears," *The Wall Street Journal*, 26 September 1996, p. B4.

23. Calvin Sims, "A Web Entree for Peruvians Without PCS," *New York Times*, 27 May 1996, p. 25.

24. Don Clark, "Microsoft's On-Line Service Goes to a TV Format," *The Wall Street Journal*, 9 December 1996, p. B8.

Modernity, Postmodernity, or Capitalism?

ELLEN MEIKSINS WOOD

Since about the early 1970s, we are supposed to have been living in a new historical epoch. That epoch has been described in various ways. Some accounts emphasize cultural changes ("postmodernism"), while others focus more on economic transformations, changes in production and marketing, or in corporate and financial organization ("late capitalism," "multinational capitalism," "flexible accumulation," and so on). These descriptions have in common a preoccupation with new technologies, new forms of communication, the Internet, the "information superhighway." Whatever else this new age is, it is the "information age." And whatever other factors are supposed to have figured in this epochal shift, the new technologies have been its indispensable condition. All these factors—cultural and economic, with their technological foundations—have been brought together in the concept of "postmodernity" and the proposition that in the past two or three decades, we have witnessed a historic transition from "modernity" to postmodernity.

From Modernity to Postmodernity

I want to consider what is involved in periodizing the history of capitalism into these two major phases, modernity and postmodernity. Then I shall look more closely at what seems to me wrong with the concept of modernity itself. If *that* concept falls, it should follow that there cannot be much left of *post*-modernity. My main objective is to consider whether this periodization helps or hinders our understanding of capitalism.

I had better make one thing clear at the start. Of course it is important to analyze the neverending changes in capitalism. But periodization involves more than just tracking the process of change. To propose a periodization of epochal shifts is to say something about what is essential in defining a social form like capitalism. Epochal shifts have to do with basic transformations in some essential constitutive element of the system. In other words, how we periodize capitalism depends on how we define the system in the first place. The question then is this: what do concepts like modernity and postmodernity tell us about the ways in which the people who use them understand capitalism?

I had better explain, too, that I shall not be talking about the ideas of those people we loosely call, or who call themselves, postmodern-*ists*. My main concern here is the political economy of what some people, including Marxists like Fredric Jameson and David Harvey, are calling postmodernity. So let me sketch out very briefly what they have in mind.[1]

According to theorists like Jameson and Harvey, modernity and postmodernity represent two different phases of capitalism. The shift from one to the other has not been a shift from capitalism to some postcapitalist or "postindustrial" era, and the basic logic of capitalist accumulation still applies. But there has nevertheless been a "sea-change" in the nature of capitalism, a shift from one material configuration to another, expressed in a transition from one cultural formation to a different one.

For Jameson, for instance, postmodernity corresponds to "late capitalism" or a new multinational, "informational," and "consumerist" phase of capitalism. David Harvey, following the Regulation School, would describe it as a transition from Fordism to flexible accumulation. A similar idea occurs in rather less nuanced form in certain theories of "disorganized capitalism."[2] Postmodernity then corresponds to a phase of capitalism where mass production of standardized goods, and the forms of labor associated with it, have been replaced by flexibility: new forms of production—"lean production," the "team concept," "just-in-time" production; diversification of commodities for niche markets, a "flexible" labor force, mobile capital, and so on, all made possible by new informational technologies.

Corresponding to these shifts, according to these theories, there have been major cultural changes. One important way of explaining these changes, notably in Harvey's account of postmodernity, has to do with a "time-space compression," the acceleration of time and the contraction of space made possible by new technologies, in new forms of telecommunication, in fast new methods of production and marketing, new patterns of consumption, new modes of financial organization. The result has been a new cultural and intellectual configuration summed up in the formula "postmodernism," which is said to have replaced the culture of modernism and the intellectual patterns associated with the "project of modernity."

The project of modernity, according to these accounts, had its origins in the Enlightenment, though it came to fruition in the nineteenth century. The so-called Enlightenment project is supposed to represent rationalism, technocentrism, the standardization of knowledge and production, a belief in linear progress, and in universal, absolute truths. *Post*-modernism is supposed to be a reaction to the project of modernity—though it can also be seen as rooted in modernism, in the skepticism, the sensitivity to change and contingency, which were already present in the Enlightenment. Postmodernism sees the world as essentially fragmented and indeterminate, rejects any "totalizing" discourses, any so-called "metanarratives," comprehensive and universalistic theories about the world and history. It also rejects any universalistic political projects, even universalistic emancipatory projects—in other words, projects for a general "*human* emancipation" rather than very particular struggles against very diverse and particular oppressions.

What, then, are the implications of dividing the history of capitalism into these phases, modernity and postmodernity? The first important thing to keep in mind is that modernity is identified with capitalism. This identification may seem fairly innocuous, but I shall argue that it is a fundamental mistake, that the so-called project of modernity may have little to do with capitalism.

The second point is that this periodization seems to mean that there are really two major phases in capitalism and one major rupture. First, modernity seems to be everything from the eighteenth century until (probably) the 1970s

(Harvey actually gives it a very precise date: 1972). We can subdivide the long phase of modernity into smaller phases (as both Jameson and Harvey do); but postmodernity seems to represent a distinctive kind of break. People may disagree about exactly when the break took place, or about its magnitude. But they seem to agree that this break is different from other epochal changes in the history of capitalism. It seems to be a break not just from some immediately preceding phase but from the whole preceding history of capitalism. At least, that seems to be the inescapable implication of tracing modernity back to the Enlightenment. So there is a major interruption in the history of capitalism somewhere between modernity and postmodernity. I shall argue that this interruption, or at least this way of looking at it, is problematic too.

Let me take each of these points separately: first, the concept of modernity and the identification of modernity with capitalism; and then the question of the historic rupture in the latter half of the twentieth century. I shall argue that the theory of postmodernity which emphasizes the discontinuities *within* capitalism is based, explicitly or implicitly, on a theory of history that downplays the discontinuities *between* capitalist and noncapitalist societies, a theory that disguises the historical specificity of capitalism.

Modernity and the Non-History of Capitalism

Let us look first at the identification of modernity with capitalism. For that, we have to begin at the beginning, with the *origin* of capitalism.[3] The main point I want to make is this: in most accounts of capitalism, there really *is* no beginning. Capitalism seems always to *be* there, somewhere; and it only needs to be released from its chains—for instance, from the fetters of feudalism— to be allowed to grow and mature. Typically, these fetters are *political:* the parasitic powers of lordship, or the restrictions of an autocratic state; and these political constraints confine the free movement of "economic" actors and the free expression of economic rationality. The "economic" is identified with exchange or markets; and the assumption seems to be that the seeds of capitalism are contained in the most primitive acts of exchange, in any form of trade or market activity. That assumption is typically connected with another one, namely that history has been an almost natural process of technological development. One way or another, capitalism more or less naturally appears when and where expanding markets and technological development reach the right level. Many Marxist explanations are fundamentally the same—with the addition of bourgeois revolutions to help break through the fetters.

The effect of these explanations is to stress the *continuity* between non-capitalist and capitalist societies, and to deny or disguise the *specificity* of capitalism. Exchange has existed since time immemorial, and it seems that the capitalist market is just more of the same. In this kind of argument, capitalism's need to revolutionize the forces of production is just an extension and an acceleration of universal and transhistorical, almost *natural* tendencies. So the lineage of capitalism passes naturally from the earliest merchant through the medieval burgher to the Enlightenment bourgeois and finally to the industrial capitalist.

There is a similar logic in certain Marxist versions of this story, even though the narrative in more recent versions often shifts from the town to the countryside, and merchants are replaced by rural commodity producers. In these versions, petty commodity production, released from the bonds of feudalism, more or less naturally grows into capitalism. In other words, petty commodity producers, given half a chance, will take the capitalist road.

What gets lost in these narratives is a perception of the capitalist market as a specific social form, the product of a dramatic historical rupture. The capitalist market looks more like an *opportunity* than an *imperative,* a *compulsion,* the imperative of accumulation and profit-maximization, which is rooted in very specific social property relations and which creates its own very specific drive to improve labor productivity by technical means.

The concept of modernity as commonly used belongs to this standard view of history, the one that takes capitalism for granted as the outcome of already existing tendencies, even natural laws, when and where they are given a chance. In the evolutionary process leading from early forms of exchange to modern industrial capitalism, modernity kicks in when these shackled economic forces, and the economic rationality of the bourgeois, are liberated from traditional constraints.

This concept of modernity, then, belongs to a view of history that *cuts across* the great divide between capitalist and noncapitalist societies. It treats specifically capitalist laws of motion as if they were the universal laws of history. And it lumps together various very different historical developments, capitalist and noncapitalist. At its worst, then, this view of history makes capitalism historically invisible. At the very least, it *naturalizes* capitalism.

It is important to notice, too, that even *anti*-modernism can have the same effect of naturalizing capitalism. This effect is already visible in the sociological theories of Max Weber: modern history, he says, has been a long process of *rationalization,* the rationalization of the state in bureaucratic organization and the rationalization of the economy in industrial capitalism. The effect of this process—the progress of reason and freedom associated with the Enlightenment—has been to liberate humanity from traditional constraints; but at the same time, rationalization produces and disguises a new oppression, the "iron cage" of modern organizational forms. Much of this argument depends, of course, on assimilating the various meanings of "reason" and "rationality" (which Weber is famous for distinguishing, though his analysis of modern history arguably relies in large part on their conflation, so that the instrumental "rationality" of capitalism is by definition related to "reason" in its Enlightenment meaning). The paradoxical implication here is that capitalism and bureaucratic domination are just natural extensions of the progress of reason and freedom. In Weber's theory, we can already see one of the characteristic paradoxes of today's postmodernism: in antimodernism there is often no great distance between lament and celebration.

Modernity and the "Enlightenment Project"

I have suggested that the conflation of capitalism with modernity has the effect of disguising the specificity of capitalism, if not conceptualizing it away altogether. Now let me turn briefly to the *other* side of the coin. My point is not just that *capitalism* is historically specific; if this so-called modernity has little to do with capitalism, then the identification of capitalism with modernity may disguise the specificity of modernity too.

I shall illustrate what I mean by going straight to the fountainhead of this so-called modernity: the Enlightenment. Here, again, are some of the main features of modernity which are supposed to go back to the Enlightenment: rationalism and an obsession with rational planning, a fondness for "totalizing" views of the world, the standardization of knowledge, universalism—a belief in universal truths and values, and a belief in linear progress, especially the progress of reason and freedom. These features are supposed to be associated with the development of capitalism, either because early capitalism, in the process of unfolding itself, created them, or because the advancement of these principles—like rationalization—brought capitalism with it.

As we all know, it has become the height of fashion to attack the so-called Enlightenment project. These Enlightenment values I have just been enumerating are supposed to be—and here I quote one of the milder indictments—"at the root of the disasters that have wracked humanity throughout this century"[4]: everything from world wars and imperialism to ecological destruction. There is no space here to pursue all the latest anti-Enlightenment nonsense, which by now far exceeds the reasonable insights that may once have been contained in such critiques of the Enlightenment. So I shall just make one simple point: the conflation of "modernity" with capitalism encourages us to throw out the baby with the bathwater, or, more precisely, to keep the bathwater and throw out the baby.

Postmodernists are inviting us to jettison all that is best in the Enlightenment project—especially its commitment to a universal human emancipation—and we are being asked to blame these values for the destructive effects we should be ascribing to capitalism. Marxist theorists of postmodernity like Harvey and Jameson generally do not fall into this trap, but their periodization does little to avoid it. What I want to suggest here is that it might be useful to separate out the Enlightenment project from those aspects of our current condition that overwhelmingly belong not to the "project of modernity" but to capitalism. This might, by the way, be useful not just in countering anti-Enlightenment postmodernism but also capitalist triumphalism (though maybe they come down to the same thing). Anyway, the obvious way to start is to look at the question historically.

My own argument, to put it baldly, is that much of the Enlightenment project belongs to a distinctly *non*-capitalist society, not just *pre*-capitalist but noncapitalist. Many features of the Enlightenment, in other words, are rooted in noncapitalist social property relations. They belong to a social form that is not just a transitional point on the way to capitalism but an alternative route out of feudalism.

Here is a quick and very incomplete sampling of the kind of thing I have in mind. First, a quick sketch of the relevant historical context, the absolutist state in eighteenth-century France. The main thing about the French absolutist state was that it functioned not just as a political form but as an economic resource for a substantial section of the ruling class. In that sense, it represents not just the political but the economic or material context of the Enlightenment. The absolutist state was a centralized instrument of extra-economic surplus extraction, and office in the state was a form of property which gave its possessors access to peasant-produced surpluses. There also were other, decentralized forms of extra-economic appropriation, the residues of feudalism and its so-called parcelized sovereignties. These forms of extra-economic appropriation were, in other words, directly antithetical to the purely *economic* form of *capitalist* exploitation.

Now think about the fact that the principal home of the so-called project of modernity, eighteenth-century France, is a predominantly rural society (something like 85 to 90 percent rural), with a limited and fragmented internal market, which still operates on noncapitalist principles, not the appropriation of surplus value from commodified labor-power, not the creation of value in production, but rather the age-old practices of commercial profit-taking —profit on alienation, buying cheap and selling dear, trading typically in luxury goods or supplying the state—with an overwhelmingly peasant population which is the antithesis of a mass consumer market. As for the bourgeoisie which is supposed to be the main material source, so to speak, of the Enlightenment, it is *not* a capitalist class. In fact, it is not, for the most part, even a traditional commercial class. The main bourgeois actors here, and later in the French Revolution, are professionals, office-holders, and intellectuals. Their quarrel with the aristocracy has little to do with liberating capitalism from the fetters of feudalism.

Where, then, are the principles of so-called modernity coming from? Are they coming out of a new but growing capitalism? Do they represent an aspiring capitalist class struggling against a feudal aristocracy? Can we at least say that capitalism is the unintended consequence of the project of modernity? Or does that project represent something different?

Consider the class interests of the French bourgeoisie. One way of focusing on them is to project forward to the French Revolution, the culmination of the Enlightenment project. What were the main revolutionary objectives of the bourgeoisie? At the core of their program were civil equality, the attack on *privilege,* and a demand for "careers open to talent." This meant, for example, equal access to the highest state offices which the aristocracy tended to monopolize and which they were threatening to close off altogether. It also meant a more equitable system of taxation, so that the burden would no longer be disproportionately carried by the Third Estate, for the benefit of the privileged estates, among whose most cherished privileges were exemptions from taxation. The main targets of these complaints was the aristocracy, but also the Church.

How did these bourgeois interests express themselves ideologically? Take the example of universalism, the belief in certain universal principles which apply to humanity in general in all times and places. Universalism has certainly had a long history in the West, but it had a very special meaning and salience for the French bourgeoisie. To put it briefly, the bourgeois challenge to privilege and the privileged estates, to the nobility and the Church, expressed itself in asserting universalism against aristocratic *particularism*. The bourgeoisie challenged the aristocracy by invoking the universal principles of *citizenship*, civic equality, and the "nation"—the nation as a universalistic identity which transcended particular and exclusive identities of kinship, tribe, village, status, estate, or class.

In other words, *universality* was opposed to *privilege* in its literal meaning as a special or private law—universality as against differential privilege and prescriptive right. It was a fairly easy step from challenging traditional privilege and prescriptive right to attacking the principles of custom and tradition in general. And this kind of challenge easily became a theory of history, where the bourgeoisie and its organic intellectuals were assigned a leading role as the historic agents of a rupture with the past, the embodiments of reason and freedom, the vanguard of progress.

As for the bourgeois attitude toward the absolutist state, it is rather more ambiguous. As long as the bourgeoisie had reasonable access to lucrative state careers, the monarchical state suited it well; and even later, it was the so-called bourgeois revolution that completed the centralizing project of absolutism. In fact, in some ways the bourgeois challenge to the traditional order was simply extending rather than repudiating absolutist principles.

Take, again, the principle of universality. The monarchical state even in the sixteenth century had challenged the feudal claims of the nobility—often with the support of the Third Estate and the bourgeoisie in particular—precisely by claiming to represent universality against the particularity of the nobility and other competing jurisdictions. The bourgeoisie also inherited and extended other absolutist principles: the preoccupation with rational planning and standardization, for example, something pioneered by the absolutist state and its leading officials, like Richelieu and Colbert. After all, even the standardization of the French language was part of the state's centralizing project—a project of "rationalization" which had its classic cultural expression in the formal gardens at Versailles.[5]

Let me introduce an interesting footnote here: people like David Harvey (and Marshall Berman[6]), who have given us some of the most important treatments of modernity and postmodernity, like to emphasize the *duality* of the modernist consciousness. The modernist sensibility, they say, combines universality and immutability with a sensitivity to ephemerality, contingency, fragmentation. They suggest that this dualism goes back to the Enlightenment. The argument seems to be that the preoccupation with universality and absolute truth was actually an attempt to make sense out of the fleeting, ephemeral, and constantly mobile and changing experience of modern life, which they associate with capitalism.

Berman quotes some passages from Rousseau's *New Eloise,* as one of the earliest expressions of the modernist sensibility (he calls Rousseau "the archetypal modern voice in the early phase of modernity"[7]). The most telling passage comes from a letter in which Rousseau's character St. Preux records his reactions on coming to Paris. What Berman sees here is the modernist sense of new possibilities combined with the unease and uncertainty that comes from constant motion, change, and diversity. It is an experience that Berman associates with an early phase of capitalism.

But something rather different occurs to me when I read the words of St. Preux in the *New Eloise,* or even when I read Berman's own account of the "maelstrom" of modern life: not so much the experience of modern *capitalism* but the age-old fear and fascination aroused by the *city.* So much of what Rousseau's St. Preux, and Marshall Berman himself, have to say about the experience of "modern life" could, it seems to me, have been said by the Italian countryman arriving in the ancient city of Rome. It may be significant that Rousseau himself expresses a special affinity for the Roman philosopher Seneca—quoting him on the title page of *Emile,* on a theme that is central to the *New Eloise,* and to Rousseau's work in general: the need to restore the health of humanity by a return to natural principles. For all Rousseau's so-called romanticism, the sensibility of the *New Eloise* may indeed have more in common with ancient Stoicism than with capitalist modernism. But in any case, it may be no accident that these so-called "modernist" literary tropes— Rousseau's and those of other European writers—come not from a highly urbanized society but from societies with a still overwhelmingly rural population.

At any rate, my main point is that the ideology of the French bourgeoisie in the eighteenth century had not much to do with capitalism and much more to do with struggles over *non*-capitalist forms of appropriation, conflicts over extra-economic powers of exploitation. I have no wish to reduce the Enlightenment to crude class ideology; but the point is that in this particular historical conjuncture, in distinctly noncapitalist conditions, even bourgeois *class ideology* took the form of a larger vision of general human emancipation, not just emancipation for the bourgeoisie but for humanity in general. In other words, for all its limitations, this was an emancipatory universalism—which is, of course, why it could be taken up by much more democratic and revolutionary forces.

Modernity vs. Capitalism

To see the complexities here, we need only compare France with England. England is not generally seen as the main home of "modernity" in the currently fashionable sense of the word, but it certainly *is* associated with the rise of capitalism. England in the eighteenth century, at the height of "agrarian capitalism," has a growing urban population, which forms a much larger proportion of the total population than in France. Small proprietors are being dispossessed, not just by direct coercion but also by economic pressures. London is the largest city in Europe. There is a far more integrated—and competitive—internal market, the first national market in Europe, or the world. There already exists the beginning of a mass consumer market for cheap everyday goods, especially food and textiles, and an increasingly proletarianized work force. England's productive base, in agriculture, is already operating on basically capitalist principles, with an aristocracy deeply involved in agrarian capitalism and new forms of commerce. And England is in the process of creating an industrial capitalism.

What, then, are the characteristic and distinctive ideological expressions of English capitalism in the same period? Not Cartesian rationalism and rational planning but the "invisible hand" of classical political economy and the philosophy of British empiricism. Not the formal garden of Versailles but the irregular, apparently unplanned and "natural" landscape garden. Certainly there is an interest in science and technology shared with England's European neighbors. And, after all, the French Enlightenment owed much to people like Bacon, Locke, and Newton. But here in England, the characteristic ideology that sets it apart from other European cultures is above all the ideology of "improvement": not the Enlightenment idea of the improvement of *humanity* but the improvement of *property,* the ethic—and indeed the science—of *productivity* and profit, the commitment to increasing the productivity of labor, the ethic of enclosure and dispossession.

The idea of improvement and productivity in this sense goes back to the seventeenth century and has its earliest theoretical expression in the political economy of William Petty, and in the writings of John Locke. *This* ideology, especially the notion of agricultural improvement and the improvement literature produced in England, is conspicuously absent in eighteenth-century France, where peasants dominate production and landlords retain their rentier mentality—as, for that matter, does the *bourgeoisie* on the whole. The exception here, by the way, proves the rule: in particular, the Physiocrats, those French political economists for whom English agriculture was the model.

Now if we want to look for the roots of a *destructive* "modernity"—the ideology, say, of technocentrism and ecological degradation—we might start by looking *here,* not in the Enlightenment but in the project of "improvement," the subordination of all human values to productivity and profit. Dare I say that it is no accident that the mad cow disease scandal has happened in Britain, the birthplace of "improvement," and not elsewhere in Europe?

An Epochal Shift?

So much for modernity. Now let me return to the larger question of periodization and to the shift from modernity to postmodernity. I have tried to situate the concept of modernity in a particular conception of history which I think is deeply flawed and which has the effect of obscuring the historical specificity of capitalism, neutralizing and naturalizing capitalism, if not actually conceptualizing it out of existence. But we still have to deal with the *changes* in capitalism. Capitalism by definition means constant change and development, not to mention cyclical crises. But was there a historic rupture of some special kind—perhaps in the 1960s or 1970s?

I have to confess straight away that I am only beginning to clarify my thoughts on this. But the one thing I *am* fairly certain about is that the concepts of modernity and postmodernity, and the periodization of capitalism in these terms, will offer little help in understanding whether there *has* been some historic rupture, and if there has, what exactly it is, how deep it is, how lasting and decisive, or what consequences it might have for any political project. These concepts and this periodization invite us, I think, to look in all the wrong places.

I have been saying here that the concept of modernity as currently used is associated with a view of capitalist development that combines technological determinism with commercial inevitability, so that capitalism is simply an extension of certain transhistorical, almost natural processes: the expansion of trade and technological progress. What kind of periodization of capitalism would we expect from this kind of view? What would be the signposts of major epochal change? We might expect the milestones to mark some major change in the market and/or some major technological shift. That is, in fact, largely what we are offered by current theories of the transition from modernity to postmodernity. And while these theories may tell us many interesting things, they tell us little about any major historical ruptures in capitalism.

Take the so-called transition from Fordism to flexible accumulation. Let us accept, for the sake of argument, that these changes in the labor process and marketing strategies are as widespread as the theorists of "disorganized" capitalism say they are. What exactly is new about this shift? There are no doubt many new things; but what is *so* new that it justifies talking about an epochal transition from modernity to postmodernity, and even from the whole of capitalism up to that point to some really new kind of capitalism?

The old Fordism used the assembly line as a substitute for higher-cost skilled craftsmen and to tighten the control of the labor process by capital, with the obvious objective of extracting more value from labor. Now, the new technologies are used to the same ends: to make products easy and cheap to assemble (how else, for instance, would outsourcing be possible?), to control the labor process, to eliminate or combine various skills in both manufacturing and service sectors, to replace higher- with lower-wage workers, to "downsize" workers altogether—again to extract more value from labor. What is *new*, then, about this so-called new economy is not that the new technologies represent a unique kind of epochal shift. On the contrary, they simply allow the logic of the old mass production economy to be diversified and *extended*. Now, the old logic can reach into whole new sectors, and it can affect types of workers more or less untouched before.

To see these developments as a major epochal rupture, we must focus on the more or less autonomous logic of *technology*, whether the technology of the labor process or the technology of marketing. My emphasis *here* is on the logic of *capitalism*, not some particular technology or labor process but the logic of specific social property relations. There certainly have been constant technological changes and changes in marketing strategies. But these changes do not constitute a major epochal shift in capitalism's laws of motion.

Or perhaps it is possible to say that Fordism itself did constitute some kind of epochal shift, at least in the sense that it represented the completion of the process that Marx called the real, as distinct from the formal, subsumption of labor by capital. In *that* sense, the new technologies represent not an epochal shift so much as an *extension* of Fordism. It is not just that the logic of capitalist accumulation still applies in some general sense to the new technologies or to new forms of production and marketing, but that they are following the logic of Fordism in particular.

On the whole, I am inclined to dismiss the "condition of postmodernity" as not so much a *historical* condition corresponding to a period of capitalism but as a psychological condition corresponding to a period in the biography of the Western left intelligentsia. It certainly has *something* to do with capitalism, but it may just be the theoretical self-consciousness of a generation of intellectuals who came to maturity in the atypical moment of the long postwar boom. For some in this generation, the end of the boom felt like the end of *normality*, and so the cyclical decline since the 1970s has had a special, cataclysmic meaning for them. Others, especially "postmodern-*ists,*" still seem to be stuck in the prosperous phase of so-called consumer capitalism.

If there has been some special kind of epochal change in the latter half of the twentieth century, we have to look for it somewhere else. If we are looking for some change more profound than a change in technology or marketing strategies, then explanations having to do with flexible accumulation, consumerism, information technology, the culture of postmodernism, or any of the usual suspects, are just not good enough.

Eric Hobsbawm, in his recent history of the twentieth century, talks about a monumental change in the mid-twentieth century, in fact what he calls "the greatest, most rapid, and most fundamental (economic, social, and cultural transformation) in recorded history."[8] Its most dramatic symptom, he suggests, has been the massive decline of the world's rural population, and in particular the death of the peasantry. But what underlies this change, I think, is that this is the period when capitalism itself has become for the first time something approaching a universal system. Capitalism, even in so-called advanced capitalist societies, has only now truly penetrated every aspect of life, the state, the practices and ideologies of ruling and producing classes, and the prevailing culture. In *The Pristine Culture of Capitalism* and elsewhere, I have suggested some of the ways in which even in Europe (and contrary to some conventions, more in Continental Europe than in Britain), capitalism has been slow to absorb the state and the dominant culture; but in the past few decades, the process has been all but completed. The issue here is not, for reasons I shall explain in a moment, what is generally meant by that rather tired formula, "globalization." I am speaking here about the universalization (or should I say *totalization*) of capitalism itself, its social relations, its laws of motion, its contradictions—the logic of commodification, accumulation, and profit-maximization penetrating every aspect of our lives.

Globalization or Universalization?

This distinction between "globalization" and the universalization of capitalism needs a bit more explanation. "Globalization" figures prominently in just about every account of the current epoch, but this now all-pervasive concept is problematic for several reasons. There are, first, empirical questions about how "global" the current economy really is. But beyond these specific empirical questions there are larger issues, having to do not only with the *answers* but with the questions themselves and with the assumptions on which they are based.

Here is one concise account of globalization, which nicely sums up the questionable assumptions on which the conventional notion is based and which neatly captures the role of the new technologies in that conventional conception. On the analogy of Marx's famous, and much misunderstood, aphorism that "the handmill gives you society with the feudal lord and the steam-mill gives you society with the industrial capitalist," this definition of globalization suggests that "the microchip gives you society with the global capitalist."[9] The new technologies have inevitably given rise to a new kind of capitalist system, with "global assembly lines," an "international bourgeoisie" and freely mobile capital which can "walk to any part of the world where labor is cheap and captive and plentiful," bypassing the nation-state and leaving in its wake an essentially powerless working class (if, indeed, such a working class can still be said to exist at all).

This account needs first to be put into perspective with a few simple facts about the global economy. Foreign branches of multinational corporations account for about 15 percent of the world's industrial output, while 85 percent is produced by domestic corporations in single geographical locales.[10] While finance capital moves freely across national boundaries by electronic means, industrial capital is less mobile; and such mobility as it does have, does not unambiguously conform to the conventional picture. For instance, in 1993, 78.9 percent of U.S. foreign direct manufacturing investment was in other advanced capitalist countries: Canada, Europe, Australia, and Japan. Investment in pursuit of cheap, unskilled, and unregulated third world labor certainly takes place, and I have no intention of underestimating the importance of this tendency—which, of course, follows the logic of capitalist exploitation as it has operated since the beginning. There may be evidence that this trend has accelerated more recently, but there are also signs that it can recede as well as advance, in accordance with prevailing economic conditions. Nor does even this type of investment neatly fit the "globalization" model. For example, the conventional model seems to assume that investment in cheaper and less regulated labor markets directly replaces production at home. But the majority of the goods produced in such labor markets as a result of U.S. direct manufacturing investment are for local consumption, not sold in the United States. And U.S. manufacturing production occurs overwhelmingly in the United States, on a much larger scale than several decades ago: domestic manufacturing production is five times greater than it was, say, in 1950.

None of this makes capitalism less vicious. Nor does it deny that new technologies, like earlier technological changes, can facilitate new methods of exploitation. And it certainly does not argue against the current crisis and stagnation of capitalism, the destructive effects of deregulation, downsizing, mass unemployment, increasing poverty, or the attacks on social provision. But it does mean that we may have to look elsewhere for an explanation of the long-term structural crisis of capitalism than in simplistic formulas about "globalization." What people are calling "globalization" may be more an effect than a primary cause.

More politically important, however, are the assumptions about state and class power that are typically linked with propositions about the internationalization of production and the mobility of capital. Basically, these assumptions come down to this: the more "global" capital is, the less the state can do;

and, while the working class is ever more fragmented, power has passed to a transnational capitalist class united in a variety of supranational organizations. This new global order, the argument usually goes, has effectively ended the socialist project as anything more than a better and maybe more humane management of "flexible" capitalism.

Let me take the point about international capital first. It is true that there are now more giant corporations with a global reach than ever before, and there are now more international organizations like the IMF or the World Bank serving the interests of capital. But to acknowledge this is very far from saying that there exists a unified international capitalist class or any organization that serves as a kind of capitalist international.

After all, if anything has been "globalized," if there is any truly international economic force, it is the market itself. What does this mean if not the internationalization of *competition?* Like all capitalist processes, this one is contradictory in its effects. "Globalization" in this respect may mean new forms of capitalist integration and cooperation across national boundaries, but it also means that a growing number of national and regional capitalists are compelled to enter into active competition with each other. It even means that, as national economies become more open to capital from outside, domestic capitalists are drawn into new forms of competition with each other, over the benefits to be derived from inward investment.

So the "global" economy if anything may mean less not more capitalist unity. Although it is far too early to make any confident pronouncements about the direction and consequences of "globalization," it seems reasonable to say that, far from integrating capital, it is at least as likely to produce *dis*-integrative effects. At any rate, the internationalization of the market is hardly an unambiguous advantage to capital. The increasing exposure of capital to the international forces of the market is at least as much a point of vulnerability as a source of strength.

The propositions about the state associated with "globalization" take us beyond these empirical problems to more fundamental conceptual problems and to certain underlying assumptions that reveal the affinities between this concept and the historical models I was criticizing before. "Globalization" takes as its starting point the modern nation-state and the national economies associated with it. Globalization, in other words, is in the first instance concerned with geographic space and political jurisdiction. What defines the present historical moment is supposed to be the breaching, transcendence, or obliteration of national boundaries by economic agencies, and, correspondingly, the weakening of political authorities whose jurisdiction is confined within those boundaries—manifest not only in the expansion of markets but in the transnational organization of corporations, the more or less free movement of capital across national borders, and so on.

Questions have been raised about the degree to which the increasingly "global" economy really has weakened the nation-state or diluted local and regional particularities. These are certainly important questions; but equally significant is the fact that the debate is taking place on this terrain at all. What is striking, among other things, is how faithfully the concept of globalization reproduces the question-begging assumptions and procedures associated with the traditional non-history of capitalism.

The traditional models of capitalist development, as we saw, took for granted the logic of capitalism. They concerned themselves simply with its liberation from constraints and its quantitative expansion. Capitalism was simply the extension of a perennial "economic" rationality, a rationality inherent in every act of exchange, even the most rudimentary and primitive. This economic logic inevitably worked itself out, coming to fruition in "commercial society," wherever it was liberated from external constraints, especially from the political parasitism of lordship and the dead hand of autocratic states, advancing in tandem with technological progress. And once certain artificial barriers to the spread of markets were removed (barriers erected, say, by "barbarian" invasions of the Roman Empire, or—as in the "Pirenne thesis"— by the closing of East-West trade routes as a consequence of Muslim conquests), these economic principles moved along a growing network of trade to embrace more and more of the world.

In these accounts, then, the rise of capitalism represents little more than a quantitative expansion of trade, effected in large part by technological advance and the casting off of political fetters. It was only a matter of time before a theory emerged that would do for the current historical moment what old theories of capitalist development had done for the transition from feudalism to capitalism. "Globalization" is just another step in the geographic expansion of "economic" rationality and its emancipation from political jurisdiction. In the long geopolitical process that has constituted the spread of capitalism, the borders of the nation-state appear to be the last frontier, and national-state power the final fetter to be burst asunder.

"Globalization" even has in common with the old non-history of capitalism a kind of technological determinism. Just as in old theories of economic development the ultimate cause of capitalist expansion was an almost natural process of technological progress, now the new information technologies seem to represent not only the necessary conditions of possibility for globalization but its causal *explanation*. Just as capitalism emerged when—and because— it was technically possible, so it has been "globalized" by the simple realization of technical capacities.

This conception of globalization as a kind of territorial imperative and/or an inexorable impulse for liberation from political constraint, driven by the natural laws of technological progress, is ill-equipped to deal with some of the most notable features of today's world order. For instance, by definition "globalization" entails a weakening of the nation-state; and however much this conception may permit us to acknowledge the incompleteness of the globalizing process and the residual powers still left to the state, it has far greater difficulty in accommodating the simple fact that the global economy—the transnationalization of markets and capital—not only *presupposes* the nation-state but relies on the state as its principal instrument.[11] If anything, the new global order is more than ever a world of nation-states; and if these states are permeable to the movements of capital, that permeability has as its corollary, indeed as its condition, the existence of national boundaries and state jurisdictions.

The contrast between today's "global" economy and earlier forms of colonial imperialism should suffice to illustrate the point: the old-style colonies were what they were precisely because they presented no effective geopolitical barrier to imperial power. The movement of capital across colonial boundaries was, of course, not just a matter of paper transfers or electronic transmissions but the bodily movement of coercive force. Geopolitical borders, in other words, were not only notionally but physically permeable. Today, transnational capital may be more effective than was the old-style military imperialism in penetrating every corner of the world, but it tends to accomplish this through the medium of local capital and national states. It may ultimately rely on a new kind of military imperialism—in fact, the military power of a single nation-state, the last remaining "superpower"—to sustain the sovereignty of the market; but it depends on many local political jurisdictions—on, say, the Indian or Chinese state—to maintain the conditions of economic stability and labor discipline which are the conditions of profitable investment.[12] And every new opportunity for transnational cooperation is matched by opportunities for new kinds of inter-imperialist rivalry—in which the nation-state is still the principal agent.

"Globalization," then, is imperfect even as description, but it is more profoundly vacuous as explanation. Really to explain the origins of capitalism it was necessary to give up the habit of assuming the very thing that needed explanation, and to account for the origins of a new historical dynamic—the historically unprecedented imperatives of capitalist accumulation—by explaining the transformation of social property relations that set it in train. Similarly, we must now talk about the new world order not just in essentially geographic terms, nor simply as the liberation and spatial expansion of some perennial "economic" logic, but as a continuing process of social transformation—a social transformation that increasingly subjects human beings, their social relations and practices, to the imperatives of capital accumulation.

For that reason, I prefer to talk about the *universalization* of capitalism—the increasing imposition of capitalist imperatives, a capitalist "logic of process," on all aspects of social life—rather than about "globalization." This means, among other things, that while the process of *globalization* may be limited in various ways, it does not follow that the determinative and transformative effects of *capitalism* are correspondingly limited. For instance, the nation-state may survive, local and regional specificities may persist, and yet the imperatives of accumulation, competition, commodification, and profit-maximization may be no less universal for that.

The universalization of the "economic" logic of capitalism certainly has a geographic dimension, in the sense that parts of the world formerly outside its orbit, or subject to its pressures externally through the medium of imperialist coercion, are now directly governed by it, as it were from within. The substance of yesterday's "interimperialist rivalries" was the division and redivision of a largely noncapitalist world; and classical theories of imperialism seem to have taken it for granted that, the imperatives of capitalist expansion notwithstanding, this would always be so—until capitalism itself had suffered its terminal crisis. Today, the former objects of that rivalry are likely to be not only sources of cheap labor, resources, or growing markets, but capitalist competitors themselves.

The global reach of capitalism in this sense is not, however, synonymous with "globalization." To say that virtually the whole globe is now capitalist is not the same as saying that all capital is now "globalized." It does not, for instance, necessarily imply the dissolution of the nation-state or even a declining role for it. "Globalization"—in particular, the withdrawal of the state from regulatory and social welfare functions in the interests of capital mobility and "competitiveness" in the world market—is the product of policy choices, not the working out of natural laws, not even the inevitable destination of history—however much these policies have spread from neoliberalism across the whole political spectrum.

"Globalization" in this sense is, to be sure, not simply a contingent and arbitrary choice. It is certainly a response to structural changes—in fact, a response precisely to the universalization of capitalism, representing policy choices adopted to meet the needs of capital in a global system where all significant economic actors are operating according to the logic of capitalism, just as old-style imperialism represented policy choices in the interests of capital in a largely noncapitalist world.

But if globalization is capital's political response to structural conditions, it follows that there are alternative, socialist ways of responding to the same conditions. If old forms of political action like yesterday's Keynesian regulation are even less adequate today than they were in a less "global" economy, this surely does not mean that the scope for political action of *any* kind has narrowed. It simply means that political action cannot just take the form of *intervening* in the capitalist economy but must increasingly take the form of *detaching* material life from the logic of capitalism. *That* is the kind of thing the left should be thinking about, instead of allowing itself to be paralyzed by the bogeyman of globalization.

To return, then, to the question of epochal shifts: if there has been a major epochal shift since the 1970s, it is not a major discontinuity in capitalism but, on the contrary, capitalism itself reaching maturity. This is indeed a major change—indeed a more substantial change than is encompassed by the idea of globalization. It may be that we are seeing the first real effects of capitalism as a comprehensive system. We are seeing the consequences of capitalism as a system not only without effective rivals but also with no real escape routes. Capitalism is living alone with its own internal contradictions. It has little recourse outside its own internal mechanisms to correct or compensate for those contradictions and their destructive effects. Even imperialism, which was supposed to be the last refuge of capitalism, no longer is what it was when capitalist powers played out their rivalries and contradictions on *non*-capitalist terrain, in "extra-economic" ways, by means of colonial wars and territorial struggles. Now even *this* corrective mechanism has for the most part been replaced by purely *capitalist* mechanisms of economic domination and financial imperialism.

So this is not just a *phase* of capitalism. This *is* capitalism. If "modernity" has anything at all to do with it, then modernity is well and truly over, not created but destroyed by capitalism. The Enlightenment is dead. Maybe socialism will revive it, but for now the culture of "improvement" reigns supreme. And if *this* is what the story is about, we really have no need for the idea of postmodernity. The only concept we need to deal with this new reality is *capitalism*. The antithesis to that, of course, is not postmodernism but socialism. The universality of capitalism, then, is not grounds for abandoning the socialist project, as capitalist triumphalists would like to believe. On the contrary, the "totalization" of capitalism also means its increasing vulnerability to its own internal contradictions and to oppositional politics.

Notes

This essay began as a talk presented at the Socialist Scholars Conference in April 1996, for a panel organized by Monthly Review. *A somewhat different version was presented a few weeks later at a conference at the University of Sussex on "The Direction of Contemporary Capitalism." A revised and expanded version was published in* Monthly Review *48, no. 3 (July/August 1996). It was further revised and substantially expanded for a special issue of the* Review of International Political Economy, *based on the Sussex conference. (I am very grateful to Andrew Chitty and Hannes Lacher for their very helpful criticisms and suggestions on that version—though I am sure they will feel I did not do enough to meet their trenchant objections.) Finally, some sections of the present article are based on my contribution to "Globalization and Epochal Shifts: An Exchange,"* Monthly Review *48, no. 9 (February 1997), in which I replied to A. Sivanandan's criticism of my* MR *article cited above.*

1. See, for example, Fredric Jameson in "Five Theses on Actually Existing Marxism," *Monthly Review* 47, no. 11 (May 1996); and David Harvey, *The Condition of Postmodernity* (Oxford and Cambridge, MA, 1990).

2. For the theory of "disorganized capitalism," see S. Lash and J. Urry, *The End of Organised Capitalism* (Oxford, 1987).

3. I have developed some of the arguments in this section in "From Opportunity to Imperative: The History of the Market," *Monthly Review* 46, no. 3 (July/August 1994).

4. Roger Burbach, "For a Zapatista Style Postmodernist Perspective," *Monthly Review* 47, no. 10 (March 1996): 37.

5. I have discussed some of the points in this paragraph at greater length in *The Pristine Culture of Capitalism: A Historical Essay on Old Regimes and Modern States* (London, 1991).

6. Marshall Berman, *All That is Solid Melts into Air: The Experience of Modernity* (New York, 1982).

7. Ibid., p. 18.

8. Eric Hobsbawm, *The Age of Extremes: A History of the World, 1914-1991* (New York, 1995), pp. 8, 289.

9. A. Sivanandan, "Globalization and Epochal Shifts: An Exchange," *Monthly Review* 48, no. 9: 20.

10. See Robert E. Lipsey, Magnus Blomstrom, and Eric Ronstetter, "Internationalized Production in World Output," National Bureau of Economic Research, Inc., *Working Paper 5385,* December 1995.

11. See Leo Panitch, "Globalisation and the State," in R. Miliband and L. Panitch, eds., *Socialist Register 1994: Between Globalism and Nationalism* (London, 1994).

12. Aijaz Ahmad has made the latter point in an interview published in *Monthly Review* 48, no. 5: 16-18. For a discussion of the "structural dialectic" of today's imperialism, which includes both the global expansion of capital *and* the "intensification of the nation-state," see also his "The Politics of Literary Postcoloniality," in *Race and Class* 36, no. 3 (1995), especially pp. 10-12.

Virtual Capitalism:

Monopoly Capital, Marketing, and the Information Highway

MICHAEL DAWSON and JOHN BELLAMY FOSTER

One of the great technological myths of our time is that the entire system of organized capitalism is being displaced by a new "electronic republic." The old system dating back to the Industrial Revolution (and even earlier) must give way, Newt Gingrich declares, as

> more and more people are going to operate outside corporate structures and hierarchies in the nooks and crannies that the Information Revolution creates. While the Industrial Revolution herded people into gigantic social institutions—big corporations, big unions, big government—the Information Revolution is breaking up these giants and leading us back to something that is—strangely enough—much more like Tocqueville's 1830s America.[1]

For the new right this means nothing less than capitalism reborn as a world of small entrepreneurs; one in which technology has erased all social barriers to the ideal world of perfect competition. Thus for new right pundit George Gilder, the new information technology is

> hostile to hierarchies, monopolies, industrial bureaucracies, and other top-down systems of all kinds. Just as intelligence and control are moving from gigantic mainframes to personal computers, from centralized databases to desktop libraries, from the central Bell pyramid to a new array of communications tools, and from a few national broadcast networks to millions of programmers around the globe, so is economic power shifting from mass institutions to individuals.[2]

Much of this is echoed in the corporate community, though the emphasis there is not on a world of small entrepreneurs (which after all is hard to imagine when corporations rule the world), but on what Microsoft Chairman Bill Gates has called "Friction-Free Capitalism": a new stage of capitalism, in which perfect information becomes the basis for the perfection of the market.[3]

Progressives and even radicals meanwhile are not immune to such fantasies. Not only is "the end of organized capitalism" frequently seen as an inevitable result of the revolution in computer and communication technology in a "post-Fordist," "postmodern" world, but a new era of electronic democracy is often envisioned as an almost automatic product of the new cyberspace technology. Equality, it is often contended, will reign on the Internet, which is too universal and anarchic to be controlled.[4]

What has nurtured these euphoric visions—more than mere computerization or the advent of digital technology—is the phenomenal growth of the Internet and the prospect of a future information highway. The nature of the former, which has grown by leaps and bounds in the last few years with the rise of the World Wide Web, is by now well-known. The latter refers to an enormously expanded system of interactive communications based on the convergence of three communications devices—the personal computer, the telephone, and the television—within a single, digital network, wired to homes, schools, and workplaces. The expectation of business and government planners is that eventually most personal computers will be connected into an interactive network that far transcends the present Internet; and that television sets (though this is further off in the future) will be made interactive through the introduction of set-top boxes (specialized computer interfaces). Nevertheless, the information highway in this wider sense of the convergence of basic communication devices is still decades away, according to most analysts.[5]

The general technological character of the new system is not in doubt, though the paths to and from the information highway may vary. Nor does anyone doubt the potential of the new technology to revolutionize the field of human communication. Yet, none of this tells us what purposes the system will serve or whom it will benefit. The entire history of communications should warn us against the view that the technology will be determinant; rather, much will depend on the political-economic system and the struggles around it.

Indeed, history has shown that every technological revolution in communications—no matter what its potential for democratization has been—has lent itself to the growth of new monopolies of information when inscribed within existing systems of social and economic power. Whether this will happen once again will be determined not by the nature of the technology itself, but by the degree of determination and organization of popular forces. "The proponents of a forthcoming [information] utopia are correct," Robert McChesney has written, "in that these new technologies do have world-historical potential, in a manner not unlike the printing press or the Industrial Revolution. However, to the extent that these technological enthusiasts believe these technologies override the logic and power of capital, there is little evidence to support such a view."[6]

A struggle will take place over the new information system; but it will have to be more than a battle for the control of technology if popular democratic forces are to triumph. Relations of social control extending beyond communication are involved. In order to understand these relations it is necessary to scrutinize the larger political-economic system and its connection to the emerging information highway.

Monopoly Capital and the Universal Market

Right-wing populists like Gingrich and Gilder are correct in one respect: the economy of the United States (and increasingly the world as a whole) is dominated by a relatively small number of corporations. But while Gingrich and Gilder admit this only to discard it as an outmoded reality, displaced by the technology of the information economy, a more rational approach (one more in accord, as we shall see, with business's own outlook) would attempt to understand how these dominant economic enterprises are currently struggling to utilize the new technology, which they in large part control, in order to amass still greater wealth and power.

Here a brief examination of the nature and logic of monopoly capital and of modern marketing is required. Today's advanced capitalist economies remain highly polarized class systems. In the United States 94 percent of all financial wealth is owned by the top 20 percent of the population, leaving only 6 percent for the bottom 80 percent. In fact the top 1 percent of the population with 48 percent of total financial wealth owns eight times as much as the bottom 80 percent. The main mechanisms for the augmentation of wealth on behalf of the rich are corporations. The top 200 manufacturing corporations in the United States own more than 60 percent of all manufacturing assets, while the top 710, one-fourth of 1 percent of U.S. manufacturing corporations, account for over 80 percent. In the early 1990s the top 600 corporations in the U.S. economy took in more than 80 percent of all sales revenue.

Such concentration is not merely a national phenomenon. The largest 300 corporations in the world now account for 70 percent of foreign direct investment and 25 percent of world capital assets. In the United States a mere handful of firms now dominate the major media, and the same in telecommunications—and are expanding globally. As CEO John Malone of TCI has stated, with only slight exaggeration, "[T]wo or three companies will eventually dominate the delivery of telecommunications services over information superhighways worldwide. The big bubbles get bigger and the little bubbles disappear." Likewise MCI president Gerald H. Taylor observed in 1996 that "There is probably going to be only four to six global gangs" remaining as dominant forces in telecommunications in "the next five years as all of this sorts out." In the words of media mogul Rupert Murdoch, "Monopoly is a terrible thing until you have it."[7]

In the increasingly global monopoly capitalist order of today the role of price competition is much reduced in comparison to the nineteenth-century era of freely competitive capitalism. In the earlier era—when each individual firm accounted for only a small share of the market—the chief weapons of competition were cutting costs and enhancing quality: by such means a firm could hope to survive and even expand its profits and market share. Competition was generalized and anonymous and not confined to the rivalries of a few firms. Ordinarily, no single firm could influence the market as a whole, which meant that price, output, and investment levels were determined by market conditions and not by individual capitals. With concentration and centralization, however, all of this changed. As the number of competitors in key industries shrank to a mere handful (called "oligopolists" in the language of neoclassical economics), competition became "corespective." Serious price-cutting, of the kind that would threaten the existence of firms and thus generate price warfare among the large monopolistic (or oligopolistic) enterprises, came to be viewed as self-defeating and was effectively banned. At the same time competition over market share was magnified, in which the main weapons were product differentiation and a whole panoply of aggressive marketing techniques. Monopolistic competition of this sort, rather than traditional price competition, became the main terrain for intercorporate rivalry. As new industries emerge (such as the personal computer and computer software industries), competition is normally stiff at first, involving serious price-cutting—a process that continues until a shakedown results in the formation of a mature, oligopolistic market.[8]

Under monopoly capital, profit margins in mature industries tend to be high while output is limited to levels below its potential, resulting in endemic excess capacity in plant and equipment. Such a regime of accumulation tends to depress the growth of effective demand and to choke off investment. As Paul Sweezy has put it, "the capital accumulation that would be necessary to sustain an expanding economy is aborted." Corporations are able to generate more surplus than they can profitably reinvest in new productive capacity, making stagnation the normal state of the advanced capitalist economy. One study of the economic surplus generated by the U.S. economy (following the methodology first introduced in Baran and Sweezy's *Monopoly Capital* [1966]) found that gross economic surplus rose from 50 percent of GNP in 1963 to 55 percent in 1988.[9]

The effects of this can be seen in the general state of the economy, which has been characterized by economic stagnation for a quarter-century now, with no sign of full recovery on the horizon. The average annual rate of growth for the U.S. economy dropped from 4.4 percent in the 1960s to 3.2 percent in the 1970s, 2.8 percent in the 1980s, and 1.8 percent from 1990 to 1995—a drop of about 60 percent between the 1960s and the first six years of the 1990s. Nor is the United States alone. Similar statistics can be provided for all of the advanced capitalist economies over the same period. One response of capital to this crisis has been to attempt to restructure the global economy, attacking unions and the state in order to reduce wages and welfare expenditures, and promoting deregulation, privatization, and the removal of barriers to capital mobility throughout the globe.[10]

However, this political-economic response on the part of capital has done nothing to alleviate the general structural crisis in which it is caught. In the wealthiest economies, most markets are saturated and the artificial stimulation of demand through marketing has become a business necessity—a means of partially compensating for the overall deficiency of effective demand. As one marketing specialist noted more than three and a half decades ago, "The problem of business used to be how to manufacture and produce goods; but the principal problem has become now how to market or sell goods."

Increasingly, the center of gravity of the system has shifted from production to sales (and finance).[11]

Of course, this shift in emphasis of the economy, associated with the entire phenomenon of overaccumulation and stagnation characteristic of advanced capitalism, has been developing for decades. Three decades ago, Baran and Sweezy provided a classic account of the role of the "sales effort" in the U.S. economy in *Monopoly Capital*. Advertising, they indicated, had been around on a small scale in the nineteenth-century era of freely competitive capitalism, but had taken on entirely new dimensions both quantitatively and qualitatively with the rise of monopoly capitalism near the turn of the century, reaching its current order of magnitude (as a percentage of national income) somewhere around 1920. Thus by 1962 annual expenditures on advertising had grown to over $12 billion, or around 2 percent of GNP. Large firms, able to exercise a powerful influence on the market, discovered that they could create significant product differentiation in the eyes of buyers by such means as advertising, brand names, trademarks, distinctive packaging, style and model changes, etc. By manipulating the motives of the buyers through such techniques, firms were able to raise profit margins and enhance their growth rates, driving out their smaller competitors. While genuine price competition became rare, competition organized around saleable appearances became pervasive. The sales effort thus emerged as a major means of both surplus absorption and product cycle management in the demand-constrained world of monopoly capitalism.[12]

These changes, as Harry Braverman later noted in *Labor and Monopoly Capital* (1974), were reflected in the organization of firms themselves. Although production continued to constitute the largest section of most manufacturing corporations, and though finance was "the brain center of the entire organism," "the predominance of marketing in all areas of the corporation's functioning" was not to be denied. Within the firm,

> marketing considerations [have] become so dominant that the structure of the engineering division is itself permeated by and often subordinated to it. Styling, design, and packaging, although effectuated by the producing part of the organization, represent the imposition of marketing demands upon the engineering division. The planning of product obsolescence, both through styling and the impermanence of construction, is a marketing demand exercised through the engineering division, as is the concept of the product cycle: the attempt to gear consumer needs to the needs of production instead of the other way around.[13]

Three decades after *Monopoly Capital* was published (and more than two decades after the appearance of *Labor and Monopoly Capital*) this analysis seems more pertinent then ever. Marketing as a whole (as distinct from advertising) has become an omnipresent force within the monopoly capitalist economy. In 1992, U.S. business spent an estimated $1 trillion dollars (one in every six dollars of GDP) on marketing, simply convincing people to consume more and more goods. Advertising itself accounted for only a relatively small part of this, with companies spending about $140 billion dollars on advertising in the United States in 1993, compared, for example, to annual sales promotion expenditures which ran at perhaps three times that level.[14]

Marketing, as practiced in the 1990s, is in essence a system of scientific management, akin to the detailed management of labor power within production, that is aimed at the buyer. It is understood by its leading exponents as consisting of four elements: targeting, motivation research, product development, and sales communication. Targeting is an attempt to ascertain, through demographic information, the prospective "targets" (market segments of buyers) for a marketing campaign.

Nowadays the focus is on "hypertargeting" in which the market segment is frequently an individual household or even an individual. As business consultant Regis McKenna explains in his book *Relationship Marketing* (1991),

> The marketer [in the near future] will have available not only existing technologies but also their converging capabilities: personal computers, databases, CD-ROMS, graphic displays, multimedia, color terminals, computer-video technology . . . a custom processor that can be built into anything anywhere to create intelligence on a countertop or a dashboard, scanners that read text, and networks that instantaneously create and distribute vast reaches of information. . . .The marriage of technology and marketing . . . should be the vehicle for bringing the customer into the company.[15]

The interactive nature of the information highway offers the possibility of detailed information on each potential buyer. Time Warner already has 52 million households in its database, and this is only the beginning.

Targeting is of little value without motivation research, which is the attempt to analyze the potential buyer's motivation for buying, and to manipulate that behavior in order to produce what Veblen once called "a quantity-production of customers." In modern marketing, business historian Daniel Pope explains, "focus strategies, based on segmenting markets" are used to "hone in on consumers whose life-styles and personalities have been carefully profiled."[16]

Product management, the third component of marketing, is the development and packaging of products to conform to the needs of marketing; as Baran and Sweezy observed, this leads to "the interpenetration of the production and sales efforts." Much of product design is concerned with brand positioning and styling geared to marketing rather than the creation of distinct use values. Product obsolescence is often planned as part of a marketing strategy. Above all, product management is the manipulation of the product's external appearance to create stimuli for buying. In the inverted world of marketing, the visual symbol associated with a product becomes the product. In the words of a Pepsi executive, "It is the visual that carries nine-tenths of what it is you're saying. . . . We're in effect creating a living day-dream, and the link to this is the bottle of Pepsi-Cola."[17]

Advertising is the best known element of sales communications. But increasingly sales promotion and direct marketing are taking over. Sales promotion is the attempt to get buyers to buy now, like providing a catalyst in a chemical reaction. It involves such techniques as sports and events sponsorships, rebates, scratch and win games, coupons, etc. With the growth of more and more personalized marketing knowledge, direct mail has proliferated. The number of catalogs distributed to U.S. households increased by an average annual growth rate of 16 percent between 1980 and 1994. In the future, sales promotions and direct marketing will account for much of the traffic on the information highway.[18]

There is no doubt that the main reason for corporate interest in the information highway lies in the fact that it is seen as opening up vast new markets, which also means expanding the range and effectiveness of targeting, motivation research, product management, and sales communication—that is, a total marketing strategy. "[T]here is great pressure from the manufacturing corporations and their allies in government to initiate a new marketing phase," Raymond Williams noted in his discussion of the new information technology. What is emerging, and has been emerging for some time, is a "universal market": "It is only in its era of monopoly," Braverman wrote, "that the capitalist mode of production takes over the totality of individual, family, and social needs and, in subordinating them to the market, also reshapes them to the needs of capital." The prospective information highway offers the most powerful means yet for achieving that.[19]

The emergence of a universal market is evident in all aspects of life, including the realm of entertainment with which people occupy much of their "free time." According to Braverman, "the atrophy of community and the sharp division from the natural environment leaves a void when it comes to the 'free' hours." As a result,

> the filling of the time away from the job also becomes dependent on the market, which develops to an enormous degree those passive amusements, entertainments, and spectacles that suit the restricted circumstances of the city and are offered as substitutes for life itself. Since they become the means of filling all the hours of 'free' time, they flow profusely from corporate institutions which have transformed every means of entertainment and 'sport' into a production process for the enlargement of capital.[20]

In this way mass entertainment is channeled along lines most conducive to the market and becomes the central conduit for marketing throughout the society. Over time the major communications media and entertainment industries have tended to merge and become indistinguishable—a process that is accelerating in the digital age with the promise of a fully integrated and interactive information highway.

"The moment of any new technology," Williams reminds us in *The Politics of Modernism*, "is a moment of choice." But such choices are to a certain extent inscribed within given economic and cultural contexts. Unless current systemic tendencies are in some way checked, he observes,

> New information systems will be dominated by financial institutions, mail-order marketers, travel agencies, and general advertisers. These kinds of content, predictable from the lines of force of the economic system, will be seen as the whole or necessary content of advanced electronic entertainment and information. More seriously, they will come to define such entertainment and information, and to form practical and self-fulfilling expectations.[21]

These conclusions find their strongest confirmation in the business literature, where the more sophisticated analyses recognize that digitalization is not simply a question of technology, but that a new infrastructure of accumulation is being ushered in.

The Fantasy of "Friction-Free Capitalism"

With this background it is possible to look at the ideology of the information age from a more critical perspective. As we have seen, beguiling futuristic visions of the information highway abound. The majority of those disseminated to the general public are devoted to the expected democratizing effects of the new technology. Others celebrate what is seen as the growing economic dominance of small high-tech firms resulting from an information revolution that is supposedly making big corporations and big government increasingly obsolete.

Yet, less noticed in the public discussion is still another vision of the information highway that is largely confined to the corporate community, the vision that fuels what Bill Gates has called "the race for the gold."

Most corporate analyses of the information highway begin by acknowledging the current communications merger frenzy, which, according to Gates, is an attempt on the part of corporations to determine which firms will control the lion's share of the bits of information that will make their way into homes, classrooms, and work sites throughout the society. Already it is clear that the cables for transmitting bits in and out of these sites will most likely be controlled by the phone and cable companies. Yet, "the ambitions of cable and phone companies," Gates writes, "go well beyond simply providing a pipe for bits." These companies are interested in moving up "the economic food chain" from the delivery and distribution of bits at the bottom to computer applications and services and content at the top. Such companies want to own the bits, not simply deliver them. "This is why cable companies, regional telephone companies, and consumer-electronics manufacturers are rushing to work with Hollywood studios, television and cable broadcasters, and other content businesses."[22]

Still, behind this scramble for control of the new communications system, we are led to believe, lies an invisible hand that points in a beneficial direction. The overall corporate vision in this respect is best represented by Gates himself who prophesies that the information highway will introduce a new age of "friction-free capitalism."

For the first time, he argues, Adam Smith's concept of markets in which "every buyer knew every seller's price, and every seller knew what every buyer was willing to pay"—what economists call "perfect knowledge" or "perfect information," a presupposition of "perfect competition"—will become possible, with the arrival of the new technology. "This will carry us," he claims, "into a new world of low-friction, low-overhead capitalism, in which market information will be plentiful and transaction costs low. It will be a shopper's heaven." More than that, it will be a universal, "frictionless" market, in which targeting, motivation research, product management, and sales communication will permeate all aspects of virtual reality. Hence, "the very mechanism of capitalism," according to Gates, "is improved by the electronic market."

The targeting of potential buyers by advertisers, Gates tells us, will be more effective than ever before. "The information highway will be able to sort consumers according to much finer individual distinctions, and to deliver to each a different stream of advertising."[23]

If the information highway is to affect production, in Gates's view, it will be mainly through added capacity to customize products for individual affluent buyers—as a result of increased interactivity. "Computers will enable goods that today are mass-produced to be both mass-produced and custom made for particular customers." Buyers will be able to be able to purchase "custom made" products (say, a pair of jeans) by choosing from a menu of predetermined alternatives—made available to them on their computer screens. Yet, "customized" production of this kind, while superficially more personal and flexible, will mainly be an arm of mass marketing—little more than an additional inducement to buy.[24]

Not only will marketing suffuse the entire information highway, as this is conceived by today's information entrepreneurs, but information itself will in large part be marketed. "There are those," Gates writes, "who think the Internet has shown that information will be free, or largely so. Although a great deal of information, from NASA photos to bulletin board entries donated by users, will continue to be free, I believe the most attractive information, whether Hollywood movies or encyclopedic databases, will continue to be produced with profit in mind."[25]

Gates is not the only one to laud the commercial possibilities of the new system. For Vice President Al Gore, "this is by all odds the most important and lucrative marketplace of the 21st century." After an imaginative discussion of the educational and political opportunities offered by the information highway, *Time* magazine observes: "It's even easier to picture the information highway being exploited to make a lot of money."[26]

In the information highway, advertising will become less distinct from marketing in general. The historical context in which modern advertising developed, particularly in the electronic media, was that unlike previous information transactions—books, newspapers, pictures, etc.—broadcasting offered no direct points of sale. Broadcasters thus came to rely on commercial sponsors. Insofar as the interactivity of the information highway will increase the potential for the proliferation of direct points of sale, while at the same time reducing the opportunities to broadcast to audiences of tens of millions on one channel at one point in time, much of the distinctiveness of contemporary advertising will be lost.[27]

Advertisers will no longer simply solicit responses, they will respond to active solicitations. Ads will become a "medium of collaboration" between buyers and sellers. As *Wired* author Michael Schrage explains, "Advertisements will feel and play like visual conversations, video games, and simulations."[28]

Where is all of this leading? No one knows for sure. But one likely answer is to be found in the phenomenon known as "one to one marketing." The superior ability to track customers based on the individualized data available through "the marketing information revolution" means that traditional mass marketing—and even niche marketing which was based on the segmentation of markets by means of statistical analysis—is now giving way to marketing aimed directly at given households and individuals, sometimes referred to as "narrowcasting." According to the authors of the best-selling marketing tract *The One to One Future* (1993),the primary objects of the new era of marketing are to (1) increase a given firm's "share of the customer" rather than simply the share of the market; and (2) to "collaborate with your customers" through two-way (interactive) communication.

In *The Marketing Information Revolution* (1994), the authors argue that in this new world of "differentiated products in decentralized markets" every customer becomes a market segment. The object then is to make use of the new interactive environment for the effective "control of the customer." This can be achieved through modular product design which gives consumers a menu of options to choose from, while at the same time simplifying the customer's decision-making process. The rewards will go "to those firms that best manage these relationships, in effect controlling the customer through direct contact and the continual exchange of information." In essence, what is being offered is a division of the buyer, to complement the older division of labor, with the object of promoting accumulation under globalized monopoly capitalism.[29]

The underlying assumption in all of this—what can be termed the model of "virtual capitalism" offered by business—is that on the information highway the main information providers, as well as the main collecting centers for information, will be the large communications and entertainment firms.

Within this context of corporate-dominated capitalism, Gates informs us, "the information highway will allow those who produce goods to see, a lot more efficiently than ever before, what buyers want, and will allow potential consumers to buy those goods more efficiently." It is this increased efficiency in selling and buying that more than anything else constitutes the ideal of "friction-free capitalism."[30]

All of this takes on a "virtual reality" character: even as digital technology expands and plays an ever more dominant role in such areas as finance, marketing, entertainment, the media, and communications in general, the underlying system of production continues to stagnate—with low growth rates, high unemployment and idle capacity, and increasing polarization of wealth/poverty. On the one hand, "all that is solid [apparently] melts into air"; on the other hand, material conditions for the great majority of the population are stagnating, and for a large portion of society deteriorating, when viewed in economic terms alone—even apart from the degradation of the environment.[31]

Opposing the System

Even the most superficial analysis of capital's plans for the design of the information highway makes a mockery of George Gilder's contention that "economic power [is] shifting from mass institutions to individuals" as a result of the new technology. Likewise Bill Gates's vision of friction-free capitalism is revealed, in the end, as little more than a vision of a more perfect and universal corporate-dominated market environment—one from which countless numbers of people with meager pecuniary resources will be effectively excluded. "We are all created equal in the virtual world," Gates declares, but "virtual equity," he concedes, "is far easier to achieve than real-world equity." In the age of the information highway, tens of millions of poorer individuals in the United States, not to mention the great majority of the population in the periphery of the world economy, will simply be left behind.[32]

The information highway will be grafted onto a global capitalist system already characterized by vast and growing inequality, economic stagnation, market saturation, financial instability, urban crisis, social polarization, graded access to information, ecological degradation, etc. The combination of marketing and the new information technology will enable certain firms to obtain higher profit margins and larger market shares, and will thereby promote greater concentration and centralization of capital. It will create a wider universe of commodity fetishism. It will not, however, solve the major material crises of capitalist society (not even the deficiency of effective demand), and is indeed likely to make many of these contradictions more acute. Capitalism cannot sustain itself without marketing, but marketing at present levels increasingly threatens to consume the system. The world of perfect information envisioned by Gates is impossible in a social and economic order in which valued information is increasingly controlled and disseminated by monopoly capital.

Yet it would be wrong simply to dismiss the new information technology. "Nothing either way is determined by the technology," Raymond Williams states, "but it is an important feature of the new systems that they offer opportunities for new cultural relationships, which the older systems could not."

The new communications technology, according to Williams, provides "contemporary tools of the long revolution toward an educated and participatory democracy, and of the recovery of effective communication in complex urban and industrial societies." He further suggests that "one of the major benefits of the new technologies could be a significant improvement in the practicability of every kind of voluntary association: the fibres of civil society as distinct from both the market and the state." But these tools can only be put to this purpose as a result of social struggle, since the dominant forces in society propose to utilize the new technology for quite different ends.[33]

The social struggle needs to be conceived and carried out in the largest terms if it is to succeed. The struggle for noncommercial communications must be a core part of the battle waged by each social movement in a broad, radical alliance of social movements. The critique of existing communications must reach beyond a shallow critique of commercialization and extend to monopoly capital and the global system itself. Above all it must be realized that nothing can be won, nothing of any genuine value saved, except by opposing the system itself. For capital, left to itself, nothing is sacred, not even the bones of the saints: all is reduced, as Marx once noted, to a mere cash nexus.[34]

The worst fear of capital in the new information environment is that citizens will become informed and interactive in ways that go against plans for a commercialized I-way, and that challenge the entire political-economic universe as it is now constituted. They are right to be scared. For the power to change society radically will continue to reside with the currently marginalized majority. The rule of capital is rooted as much in the capacity to gain the consent of the governed—to obtain their collaboration in their own margi-nalization and exploitation—as it is in the actual material means of control. If virtual capitalism—the dream of Bill Gates—is an inverted world in which all of human culture increasingly serves the market, the mere possibility of resistance holds out the hope that it can be set right-side-up again, or better yet transcended altogether.

Notes

1. Newt Gingrich, *To Renew America* (New York: HarperCollins, 1995), p. 57.

2. George Gilder, *Life After Television* (New York: Norton, 1992).

3. Bill Gates, *The Road Ahead* (New York: Viking, 1995).

4. See Scott Lash and John Urry, *The End of Organized Capitalism* (Madison: University of Wisconsin Press, 1987), and *Economies of Signs and Space* (Thousand Oaks, CA: Sage, 1994); Lawrence Grossman, *The Electronic Republic* (New York: Viking, 1995). The *Whole Earth Review*, with its endless hype of cyberspace, is the best example of the new age populist approach to the information highway. Constant references to the democratic possibilities of the new information technology are coupled with a very limited and superficial criticism of the commercialization of the Internet.

5. Here the "information highway" refers to both the Internet and the expected conver-gence of basic communications technologies, such as the telephone, the personal computer, and television. We are expressly concerned with the relation of these transformations to the sales effort under monopoly capitalism. Recently, the concept of the information highway has been greatly expanded in the work of Heather Menzies, to encompass the wider digital revolution occurring through the agency of corpora-tions, including major changes within production—and within relations of exploita-tion; see Heather Menzies, *Whose Brave New World? The Information Highway and the New Economy* (Toronto: Between the Lines, 1996). A full political economy of the information highway requires the integration of these levels of analysis—a task accom-plished, we hope, in this volume as a whole.

6. Robert W. McChesney, "Public Broadcasting in the Age of Communications Revolu-tion," *Monthly Review* 47, no. 7 (December 1995): 18-19.

7. Edward Wolff, *Top Heavy* (New York: Twentieth Century Fund, 1995), p. 7; *Statistical Abstract of the United States, 1986* (Washington, DC: U.S. Government Printing Office, 1986), p. 524; Richard DuBoff, *Accumulation and Power* (Armonk, NY: M.E. Sharpe, 1989), p. 171; Robert Heilbroner, *The Making of Economic Society* (New York: Prentice Hall, 1992), p. 117; John H. Dunning, *Multinational Enterprises and the Global Econ-omy* (Reading, MA: Addison-Wesley, 1993), p. 15; Richard Barnet and John Cavanagh, *Global Dreams* (New York: Simon and Schuster, 1994), p.15; Grossman, *The Electronic*

Republic, pp. 173-74; Robert W. McChesney, *Corporate Media and the Threat to Democracy* (New York: Seven Stories Press, 1997), p. 32.

8. Paul M. Sweezy, "Competition and Monopoly," in John Bellamy Foster and Henryk Szlajfer (eds.), *The Faltering Economy: The Problem of Accumulation Under Monopoly Capitalism* (New York: Monthly Review Press, 1984), pp. 27-40.

9. Paul M. Sweezy, "Can Capitalism Be Saved?" *The Nation*, 9 July 1984, p. 704; Michael Dawson and John Bellamy Foster, "The Tendency of the Surplus to Rise, 1963-1988," in John B. Davis (ed.), *The Economic Surplus in the Advanced Economies* (Brookfield, VT: Edward Elgar, 1992), pp. 42-70. Stagnation, it should be noted, does not result simply from the monopolistic character of the economy, but also (and perhaps even more importantly) from the related tendency toward the maturation of industry. See Harry Magdoff and Paul M. Sweezy, *The Irreversible Crisis* (New York: Monthly Review Press, 1988); and John Bellamy Foster, "The Long Stagnation and the Class Struggle," *Journal of Economic Issues* 31, no. 2 (June 1997): 445-451.

10. *Economic Report of the President, 1997*, p. 303; John Miller, "Is the Boom and Bust Cycle Over?" *Dollars & Sense* no. 211 (May/June 1997): 10-12.

11. Steuart Henderson Britt, *The Spenders* (New York: McGraw Hill, 1960), p. 52. Quoted in Paul A. Baran and Paul M. Sweezy, "Theses on Advertising," in Baran, *The Longer View* (New York: Monthly Review Press, 1969), p. 224.

12. Baran and Sweezy, *Monopoly Capital* (New York: Monthly Review Press, 1966).

13. Harry Braverman, *Labor and Monopoly Capital* (New York: Monthly Review Press, 1974), p. 266.

14. Kevin J. Clancy and Robert S. Shulman, *Across the Board*, October 1993, p. 38; *Marketing Myths that Are Killing Business* (New York: McGraw Hill, 1994), pp. 140, 171.

15. Richard McKenna, *Relationship Marketing* (Reading, MA: Addison-Wesley, 1991), p. 18.

16. Daniel Pope, *The Making of Modern Advertising* (New York: Basic Books, 1983), pp. 288-90.

17. Baran and Sweezy, *Monopoly Capital*, pp. 131-33; Michael Dawson, "The Consumer Trap: Big Business Marketing and the Frustration of Personal Life in the United States Since 1945," Ph.D. dissertation, University of Oregon, Eugene, 1995, pp. 300-305.

18. Clancy and Shulman, *Marketing Myths*, pp. 171-72, 221.

19. Raymond Williams, *The Politics of Modernism* (New York: Verso, 1989), p. 122; Braverman, *Labor and Monopoly Capital*, p. 271.

20. Braverman, *Labor and Monopoly Capital*, pp. 278-79.

21. Williams, *Politics of Modernism*, pp. 134-35.

22. Gates, *The Road Ahead*, pp. 241-42.

23. Ibid., p. 171; Bill Gates, "Keynote Address," in O'Reilly Associates (ed.), *The Internet and Society* (Cambridge, MA: Harvard University Press, 1997), p. 32.

24. Gates, *The Road Ahead*, pp. 166-67.

25. Ibid., p. 100.

26. *Time*, 12 April 1993, pp. 52-54; *Business Week*, 5 September 1994, p. 61.

27. Williams, *The Politics of Modernism*, p. 126; Nicholas Negroponte, *Being Digital* (New York: Vintage, 1995), p. 170.

28. Michael Schrage, "Is Advertising Finally Dead?" *Wired*, February 1994, p. 124.
29. Don Peppers and Martha Rogers, *The One to One Future* (New York: Doubleday, 1993); Richard Blattberg, Rashi Glazer, and John D.C. Little (eds.), *The Marketing Information Revolution* (Boston: Harvard Business School Press, 1994), pp. 17-29.
30. Gates, *The Road Ahead*, p. 183.
31. Karl Marx and Friedrich Engels, *The Communist Manifesto* (New York: Monthly Review Press, 1949), p. 7.
32. Gates, *The Road Ahead*, p. 258.
33. Williams, *The Politics of Modernism*, pp. 135-38; *Problems in Materialism and Culture* (New York: Verso, 1980), pp. 170-95, and *Television* (New York: Schocken, 1974), pp. 151-52.
34. Marx, *Capital* I (New York: Vintage, 1977), p. 229.

Global Village or Cultural Pillage?

The Unequal Inheritance of the Communications Revolution

PETER GOLDING

In May 1997, the incoming Labour government in the UK announced that it intended to rejoin UNESCO the following year, after more than a decade of criticism and detachment following its withdrawal in 1986. The announcement attracted little attention; few saw it as the clarion call to a new and harmonious global cultural order by a new British government—much less as a conversion to the heroic demands for a new world information order, demands which had been the original pretext for the withdrawal of the UK and the United States in 1985.

For in truth, little changes. Just outside the industrial midlands city in which the author lives, sits a sparkling new "leisure park," complete with a multiscreen cinema complex and bowling alley. On the perimeter of the vast parking lot which is the main feature of the park is an array of fast food shops and ethnic eateries entirely derived from, and indeed franchised from, the chains that have become familiar to UK vacationers who have made it to the playgrounds of Florida and California. Forget the temperature outside and the lack of air conditioning in the car, and one could easily imagine having been suddenly and dramatically beamed cross-Atlantic. On offer at the multiplex are the *Star Wars* retreads and the familiar blockbusters off the Hollywood production line, while the ersatz New York delis and burger bars are as internationally interchangeable as all the other now familiar icons of global merchandising.

Such common observations have troubled observers for decades. After all, resentment of "Americanisation" was a forceful current in public antipathy to the arrival of commercial television in Europe, initially in the UK in the early 1950s. Two simple models have emerged from these concerns, neither of which is any longer satisfactory as a way of understanding how recipient cultures have responded to the massive flows of media and cultural products from dominant producers in the post-imperial world. One is the attractive but entirely fanciful celebration of the "global village" in which nations speak peace unto nations, and the shrinking virtual globe in which a common culture is created by flourishing interchange, producing an entirely benign common order, beyond babel and chaos. The other model has recognized the inequities and pernicious effects of domination inherent in the "one-way traffic" in cultural goods, but in its narrow focus, either on the media, or on a very truncated model of "cultural imperialism," has set up a simple David and Goliath caricature which is neither analytically nor politically sufficient.[1]

In this chapter I wish to review some of the characteristics of the global cultural system, inevitably in a very superficial way, to suggest that its massive inequities remain both potent and deeply rooted in more general economic inequalities, and then briefly to assess some countertendencies in the current situation.

Convergence: More Fiscal than Digital

We hear a lot about the convergence of the communications and information industries. What is meant by this is the technological dissolution of distinctions among, especially, telecommunication, computing, and broadcasting, that is made feasible by digital technology. Thus the distribution and delivery of previously distinct forms of communication become fused, potentially, into a single form and format. While a significant and potentially revolutionary feature of communications technology, this aspect of convergence is, thus far, less manifest than the convergence effected by the large global companies that produce and supply much of the cultural material that makes up the symbolic landscape in which most of us live.

Some 500 corporations control about 70 percent of world trade. This is reflected especially in the production and control of cultural products like television programming, films, records, and advertising. The key corporations in the cultural sector have become all too familiar, and have declined in number as the mergermania of recent years has self-reinforced, with more and more investment capital chasing fewer and fewer stock opportunities. News Corporation, with the extraordinary figure of Rupert Murdoch at its helm, is of course archetypal. With well over a hundred newspapers worldwide, including the hugely profitable *Sun* in the UK as well as the *Times* and *Sunday Times,* News Corporation also embraces Twentieth Century Fox, HarperCollins publishers, and the Fox TV network and cable channels. It also controls of a large slice of U.S. local television, and major interests in satellite television through BSkyB, Asian Star television, Sky Latin America, and Japan Sky Broadcasting. It holds major stakes in a vast array of other global communications activities.[2]

Beyond Murdoch's emblematic empire-building, however, lie others who have emerged from the spate of mergers in recent years. Disney's union with the ABC network, the Time Warner (itself a couplet created in 1989) linkup with CNN, and a variety of telecommunications marriages, have bequeathed a structure of awesome corporate concentration. Time Warner, the largest purely media corporation on the planet, includes in its activities *Time* magazine, Warner music and Warner Bros. studios, the Home Box Office cable TV channel, and major holdings in cable systems and channels, as well as the mammoth operation in bookselling operated by Time-Life Books. Disney, still rooted in theme parks and film, grew from giant to colossus in 1995, with its acquisition of Capital Cities/ABC, and also has operations in cable stations, sports and children's channels, newspapers, and baseball teams.

The conglomeration, of which these megacorporations are both typical and exemplary, is complemented by the changing structure and function of cultural and communications organizations which have their roots outside the private corporate sector. Particularly in Europe this would be represented by the PTTs, the post and telephony structures, and by public service broadcasting organizations. In the last two decades, aggressive privatization and commercialization of both has meant that public regulation or intervention has been inhibited by the displacement of such organizations into the commercial

sector, with the wholesale or partial abandonment of the public service aspi-
rations and commitments which were the historical mission of both telecommunications and broadcasting throughout much of Western Europe and
elsewhere.

The domination of the entertainment giants in global markets remains
impressive. As the conglomerates consolidate their grip on the world's most
lucrative market, the United States, investors search overseas for rewarding
opportunities. The low risks involved in start-up ventures in new markets can
reap large returns. To lower the costs, governments in countries like Taiwan
and the Philippines are persuaded to facilitate foreign investment in initiatives
such as cable TV. Partnerships are forged, as for example between Latin
American cable and telecommunication operators and U.S. partners, and links
such as the tie-up between TV Globo, Televisa, and Venevision with Hughes,
News Corporation, and TCI in the United States. Cable TV and production
houses are also moving into growing markets in the Far East and Australia.

U.S. entertainment products continue to secure high returns in international markets, despite the enthusiasm for local products among national
television audiences. *Baywatch, The X-Files,* and *ER* feature strongly in global
programming, though even more impressive is the commercial globalization
of children's programming. In a global children's TV marketplace estimated at
$100 billion, Nickelodeon and other players, such as Disney and Fox, com-
mand center stage. The multinational potential of cartoons and adventure-ac-
tion series, together with the merchandising opportunities they afford, is
immense. Some 65 to 70 percent of all merchandising from "entertainment
properties" comes from children's material, encouraging entertainment corporations quickly to set up consumer products divisions which significantly
drive the programming. Notes a former director of Mattel toys, now with
MTM entertainment: "Launching products in concert with entertainment
makes it a more pervasive brand. It has become important to weave the tenets
of product licensing and merchandising into the creative process early on."[3]
TV spin-offs from action movies offer the same economic synergy, with the
book and the computer game never far behind.

One of the problems for local producers in poorer countries in trying to
compete with imported U.S. entertainment has always been cost. The attraction of much imported fare is its high production values available at a price
local producers cannot possible emulate, since they do not have access to the

scale of market required. The large U.S. studios can also churn out the long-running series that build and sustain audiences in the predictable patterns that advertisers require.

Thus across the cultural industries the structural shift that matters has not been so much digital as financial, and we can turn now to the consequences for recipient, and especially "third world" societies.

At the Receiving End

Following the "lost decade" of the 1980s, subsequent years have been no kinder to the poorer nations of the globe. Some 1.4 billion of the world's 5.3 billion population live in poverty, of which 1.2 billion are in the least industrialized countries.[4] The gap continues to widen. On average GNP per person grew by 2.4 percent in industrialized countries between 1965 and 1989, but remained more or less static in the least industrialized. Efforts to effect a transformation in the international economy have foundered on the dams of self-interest. Aid, itself firmly locked into policies molded by economic interest, has in any case declined, especially from the wealthiest nations (aid dropped as a percentage of GNP from 0.56 to 0.19 between 1960 and 1990 in the United States, for example).

The trend has intensified since the 1980-1983 recession, propelled by protectionism, massive debt growth, and a fall in direct investment. For the poorest countries debt burdens grossly distort their economies. The clarion call in 1974 for a "new international economic order" had been muffled utterly, first by the oil price surges of the 1970s, then by soaring debt mountains, and finally by falling primary commodity prices, which by the late 1980s were at their lowest for fifty years. Since 1980 debt to multilateral organizations like the World Bank has increased five times, and countries like Nicaragua, Congo, and Mozambique carry debt burdens several times larger than their gross national product. Despite recent attempts to ease the burdens on the "HIPCs" (heavily indebted poor countries—no disaster lacks its acronym), the long term consequences remain dire. Since 1995 the World Trade Organization, enforcing free trade agreements, has reinforced the competitive struggle which the "structural adjustments" imposed within indebted nations were presumed to prepare them for.[5] We remain inhabitants of a world in which a quarter of the population consumes nearly 80 percent of world production.

More recently the rising stars of world capitalism, the countries of the Asian "economic miracle," have also begun to falter. The strength of the dollar, and the global recession of the early 1990s, severely hit their export growth, not least in the new technology goods which had been so crucial to the boom of the previous decade. Long term forecasters of the impending Asian century begun to reconsider prospects, and turn to Latin America. The truth was that world inequalities remain as firmly entrenched as ever.

Communications and information technologies increasingly sit at the core of these economic shifts and structures. The pace and scale of technological innovation in the rich industrialized countries has altered the nature of production and the comparative advantage of the more highly technologically advanced centers of production. Information technology has reduced communications and transaction costs, and enhanced the tradability of services. However, three myths have tended to be nurtured by the glamour and glitz of high-tech advances.

The first is the myth of globalization, which suggests a world in which nation-states have all but succumbed to the electronic displacement of national boundaries and statutory regulation. Although the power of global companies to ignore the nation-state is palpable, nonetheless the nation-state remains a tangible factor, both culturally and fiscally, in the material experience of most people. The United States, in particular, remains a singular capital entity. Despite its massive attractiveness to inward investment this remains only 6 percent of total U.S. stocks and bonds, and the ratio of exports and imports to GDP has been unchanged since 1980.[6]

The second myth is the magic power of new technologies to boost productivity. The failings of computers in this regard are often noted—the travel agent can book your flight ticket via ever more elaborate networking, but the trip takes just as long if not longer. Despite massive investments in IT (rising in the United States from 7 percent of firms expenditure on equipment in 1970 to 40 percent in 1996) productivity gains are limited. Almost all growth since the 1970s is due to increased inputs of labor and capital.[7] What IT can do is reduce the trading advantage of low labor cost economies, if richer countries can circumvent labor costs with the efficiencies that do accrue from IT, or can use IT to relocate their production to low labor cost areas without significant increases in communications costs resulting from this move.

The third myth is that IT has created a new "information economy." There is not the space here to argue through this complex debate. However, the notion that the increased use of IT, and the appearance in the labor force statistics of more and more "knowledge workers" has somehow engineered a new form of society, has become a seductive one in recent years. It is difficult to see how the word-processing clerk at General Motors is engaged in anything other than the manufacture of motor cars, and the confusion between work methods and economic order is one among many that befuddle this debate.

The net consequence of these shifts has been to produce massive global inequities in access to and ownership of communication facilities. Table 1 shows, broadly, the relative access of different regions of the world to newspapers, books, and broadcasting.

In many parts of the world, and especially in Africa, little movement has been evident over the past two decades. Africa has just 3 percent of the world's

Table 1. Communication Facilities in the Main Global Regions

REGION	BOOKS PUBLISHED PER MILLION INHABITANTS		DAILY NEWSPAPERS PER 1,000 INHABITANTS		RADIOS PER 1,000 INHABITANTS		TV SETS PER 1,000 INHABITANTS	
	1970	1991	1980	1992	1980	1993	1980	1993
AFRICA	22	20	16	16	104	173	17	39
NORTH AMERICA	366	365	159*	143*	926*	982*	331*	406*
ASIA	59	70	56	63	96	179	37	69
EUROPE	515	802	193	267	604	628	350	390
DEVELOPED COUNTRIES	428	513	242	279	879	968	422	494
DEVELOPING COUNTRIES	39	55	37	44	98	178	25	60
WORLD	182	160	88	96	294	350	125	154

*America as a whole
Source: *UNESCO Statistical Yearbook 1995*. Tables 6.1 to 6.9

television sets, 2 percent of the world's daily newspapers, and 6 percent of the world's radio receivers. These proportions are scarcely changing as the world's richer countries pull further ahead in the technology race. Even using UNESCO's crude categories, which lump together in the rubric "developing countries" both the rapidly industrializing tigers of Southeast Asia and the impoverished wastelands of sub-Saharan Africa, the gulf between the two worlds is stark. The developed regions produce ten times as many books per capita, have six times as many newspapers, five times as many radios, and eight times as many televisions per capita as the developing countries as a bloc. Table 2 shows, at a national level, the sheer range of experience among the world's nations in access to the main traditional communications facilities. The figures illustrate, using the United States as a base, the relative positions of some of the poorest and richest states. While these basic facilities suffuse and define the daily lives of much of the world's richer populations, they scarcely register in the environment of much of the poorest.

Of course, given the pap and advertising fodder that constitutes the largest proportion of media fare, it is easy to conclude that these are deficits which should be welcomed as a blessing in disguise. But the technologies do not determine their use, and the massive technology gap illustrated by these figures does not merely signal the emancipation of poorer nations from the yoke of Disney and Murdoch. It also forecloses the communication and democratic potential which information technologies can provide, especially among large dispersed populations in which education and political infrastructures are costly to provide, and require every accelerating aid available.

This contradiction is important. It is certainly true that much of the globe has "been conquered by that fatal cocktail of blood, valium and advertising dictated by the norms of private television in the United States."[8] This is true most obviously in Europe. More than a quarter of the output of the UK's Channel 4 depends on U.S. products, but in much of the rest of Europe the proportion is substantially higher. On Germany's private channels, U.S. production accounts for from 32 percent (RTL) to 56 percent (ProSieben) of acquired material. Nonetheless European networks retain autonomous production capacity, and local programming is enduringly popular. Elsewhere this is less so. The vibrant Latin American market is fertile soil for U.S. television exporters. With a large, and largely monolingual market, the potential is enormous. Most pan-Latin satellite services are run by major U.S. studios, in

Table 2. The Unequal World of Communications: A Comparative Analysis

The table shows communication facilities in a selected range of nations as an index based on the United States as 100. Thus the figures illustrate the relative character of these facilities. The figures are calculated from data in the *UNESCO Statistical Yearbook 1995*. The actual year to which the data refers varies from country to country, but is mostly 1992 to 1994.

COUNTRY	DAILY NEWSPAPERS PER 1,000 INHABITANTS	TV SETS PER 1,000 INHABITANTS	RADIOS PER 1,000 INHABITANTS	BOOKS PUBLISHED
BOTSWANA	12	2.1	5.6	0.3
BENIN	0.9	0.7	1.3	1.3
ETHIOPIA	0.4	0.4	9.3	0.5
MALI	1.7	0.2	2.1	—
NIGERIA	7.6	47	9.2	3.2
ZAIRE	1.3	0.1	4.6	0.1
UNITED STATES	100	100	100	100
NICARAGUA	9.7	8.2	12.3	—
BRAZIL	23.3	26	18.3	55.9
PERU	30	12	11.9	4.3
AFGHANISTAN	5.1	1.2	5.6	—
CHINA	18.2	4.6	8.7	189
INDIA	13.1	4.9	3.8	26
IRAN	8.5	7.7	10.8	13.8
PAKISTAN	2.5	2.2	4.2	0.6
ALBANIA	37.8	11.4	8.3	0.8
GERMANY	137	68.5	42	136
SWEDEN	217	57.6	41	26.2
UNITED KINGDOM	162	53.3	54	193

a market expected to grow 26 percent between 1996 and 2005. The studios have increased their direct involvement substantially. Sony Entertainment Television (SET) is available in about 1 million homes in Latin America, drawing on the vast resources of Sony's library. WB—the Warner network—launched its first twenty-four-hour entertainment channel in Latin America and the Caribbean in 1995, to ensure the global reach of "Looney Tunes." Foreign ownership restrictions are circumvented by partnership deals, such as that between Country Music Television and TVA Brazil. On many channels U.S. imports dominate, such as Mexico's TV Azteca, in which close ties with NBC ensure 40 percent of output is U.S. originated.

In Asia the picture is similar. SET has moved fast into India, with its 16 million cabled homes. Between 1990 and 1995 TV revenue in the Asia Pacific region's top thirteen countries grew 50 percent. With what is often a weak press sector, broadcasting has a comprehensive capture of the advertising steaming up from the bubbling economies of Asia.[9] But, of course, here China is the big catch. With more than 230 million television homes, the growth of consumer spending in China is a mirage of temptation for any entertainment conglomerate. Yet the downside to this consumer explosion is palpable, including mass unemployment, appalling work conditions, pollution, and growing inequality.[10]

Despite these seemingly inexorable trends, however, the alternative potential of communications technologies must be recognized both analytically and politically, a point to which I return later.

As with newspapers and broadcasting, so with telecommunications. The huge opportunities afforded by developments in this field, both for personal communication and liberation from constraints of time and place, and for the acceleration and facilitation of commerce, are distributed with massive inequities. Telecommunications trade grew from less than $50 billion in 1990 to $96 billion in 1995. The telecommunications services market has grown from just under $400 billion to over $600 billion in the same period. In terms of market capitalization, the telecommunications industry ranks third in the world behind health care and banking, and it is growing at twice the rate of the global economy.[11]

The routing of telecommunications is a simple reflection of the global capital structure. Four of the five top international telecommunication routes have the United States as one partner, and the United States is partner to 51 percent of international telephone traffic in the top fifty routes.[12] Japan and the United States dominate world telecommunication equipment exports, accounting for 48 percent of the value of exports by the top ten nations.[13] Even within the developing world the overwhelming volume of traffic is among and between the major trading elites, with the top twenty-five routes including those between Hong Kong, China, Singapore, and Malaysia. No African country features in the top international routes among developing nations until we get down to number fifteen (Namibia and South Africa). Yet, paradoxically, the biggest users of international telephony are a small number of affluent sub-Saharan subscribers, living in a continent where there is not even one line per hundred people. More obviously, however, "twenty-four OECD countries, while containing only 15 percent of the world's population, account for 71 percent of all telephone lines."[14] While half the world's population have never made a phone call, a fraction are on line and in touch to great effect and benefit.

New Technologies: Old Forces

The arrival of new communication and information technologies has offered the promise of more egalitarian, participatory, and progressive structures. Yet, in practice, the reality has been of their rapid incorporation into familiar structures of inequity and commercial exploitation. The Internet repeats this picture only too clearly. By 1994 not a single Less Developed Country had a computer network directly connected to the Internet. Packet switched data networks existed in only five LDCs. The Internet Society estimate that in 1994 there were 0.002 Internet users per 1,000 inhabitants in India, compared to 48.9 in Sweden. Most African nations still have no Internet access, yet the possible uses for such networks, for example in electronic health and education services, are enormous. Africa One, the fiber-optic undersea cable which will create a communications ring around the continent, will not be complete before 1999 at the earliest, and it remains to be seen if it is better news for AT&T Submarine Systems, the company who developed Africa One, than it is for the potential users. No African country was involved in the development stages of the US$2.6 billion project.

Once again the convergence we look to is organizational and commercial rather than just technological. One or two of the key players illustrate this trend. America Online, the world's largest provider of on-line services with 1996 sales of $1,094 million, has deals with media companies like Knight-Ridder, Time Warner, and Turner Broadcasting. In Europe it is teamed with publishing conglomerate Bertelsmann to increase the attractiveness of services on offer. Its nearest competitor, CompuServe, with 1996 sales of $793 million, is the leading on-line service provider in Europe. Other companies have moved in from elsewhere in the information firmament. Reuters, the press agency, relays news and financial information to computer terminals in 154 nations. It also provides data feeds to financial markets. Since 1973, when it launched its Monitor electronic marketplace, the company has acquired various on-line services including the real time stock quote vendor Quotron, and has developed the Reuters Money Network. Total sales in 1995 were $4,198 million, 70 percent derived from information products.

The commercial drives now rapidly transforming the internet intensify its growth as a marketing medium in richer parts of the globe. One consequence is the so-called balkanization of the Internet, in which service providers insert proprietary features into their browsers and servers to ring-fence users into their patch on the web. Convergence is the key. "The convergence of the telecommunications sector with the computer and broadcasting world is creating new synergy, most evident in the exponential growth of the Internet. . . . The significance of the Internet lies not in what it is but in what it will become" (ITU press release 97-2, February 1997). Not surprisingly "broadcasters, producers and distributors are setting up stalls in cyberspace to market their wares and increase viewer loyalty."[15] CNN launched an on-line service in 1995, which will eventually carry not only advertising, as it does now, but added-value services. Sony has arrangements with credit card company Visa for on-line transactions for viewers wanting to buy merchandise.

Inevitably this attracts the big players. Microsoft, the Godzilla of software, with sales of $8,671 million in 1996, has moved fast to ensure the growth of the Internet does not leave it stranded. The company has integrated its own web browser into its Windows operating system and has aggressively pursued diversification into contents companies. During 1996 Microsoft acquired Dimension X to bring interactive media to the web browser, and WebTV Networks, who deliver the internet via television set-top boxes. In 1994 Microsoft invested $420 million jointly with NBC in MSNBC, a twenty-four-hour cable television channel. Microsoft CEO Bill Gates also has his own company, Corbis, which has bought up the digital rights to paintings and photos from some of the world's top collections, including the Smithsonian in Washington and the National Gallery in London.

Coming from the opposite direction, so to speak, Rupert Murdoch, after some stumbling entries into IT, has discovered the immense possibilities inherent in new, cheap, integrated distribution. News Corporation's TV Guide Entertainment Network is a relatively modest site following previous, less than wholly successful ventures. Bigger adventures are the test-bed initiatives in the UK and in China. ChinaByte offers a full range of western Internet services translated for the Chinese market, all part of Murdoch's careful positioning of News Corporation for the anticipated boom of the China marketplace. News Corporation is ensuring convergence of broadcasting and the Internet through its global digital television services. Providing interactive services via telephony, however, is essentially a cost-effective and profitable way forward, rather than the most progressive and socially diverse, using high capacity fiber-optic links. In the UK, in 1997, Murdoch launched LineOne, in an attempt to take over the embryonic British on-line market place. Content comes from Murdoch's newspapers, and is designed not only to appeal to new users attracted to on-line popular journalism, astrology, and entertainment, but to retain users within its confines, with few opportunities to leave the service via conventional links.[16] Thus the new technologies are fast being commandeered by the forces of global inequity which have carved the communications architecture of the past century.

On Pessimism and Modes of Resistance

Cataloguing the daunting calculus of global imbalances in the production and distribution of cultural goods can be depressing. Meander through the glossy pages of international business magazines and one navigates a breathtaking wind of confidence, control, and expansion that can blow any sense of alternatives and progressiveness way off course. But pessimism is not determinism, and the picture is neither politically nor analytically complete without some sense of the "prefigurative forms" inherent in various efforts to construct a more equitable and democratic order.

In the 1970s, in the wake of rapid decolonization, third world anger at the increasing evidence of cultural imbalances led to much debate about "cultural sovereignty" and the need for a new world communication order to complement the new world economic order. The high point came with the publication, by UNESCO, on whose stage much of the rhetorical action had been played out, of the "MacBride Report," *Many Voices, One World,* in 1980.[17] The report crystallized much of the indignation that had been expressed at a sequence of global conferences, and which became the force behind a series of declarations, proclamations, and manifestos under the broad rubric of the "New World Information and Communication Order." It was a brave and not insignificant effort, but one which has left much anguish, regret, and missed opportunities in its wake. Belatedly, in the 1990s, the banner has been unfurled, not least because some richer nations recognize their own vulnerability to the dominant forces of global information and communication control.[18] But macro-regulation by the well-meaning structures of international collaboration have yet to prove effective. Indeed one of the more telling transformations of the global arena is the incorporation of such organizations into the project of international capital. The International Telecommunication Union is at one and the same time a cooperative regulatory body, but increasingly also a solidly commercial power in endorsing and enforcing a free-market infrastructure to global telecommunications. It may be that we need to turn elsewhere to examine the potential of alternatives and modalities of resistance. We can very briefly list five such approaches here.

1. *The impassive audience.* Much has been made in recent cultural theory and discussion of the capacity of audiences to resist the messages they receive. Thus, far from worrying about the impact of endless deluges of *Dallas* and *Star Trek*, we should have faith in the active interpretative capacity of consumers to impose their own meanings on such material, in playful, ironic, postmodern, and subversive manner. The massive flows of material exported by the corporate cultural giants thus, whatever their limitations, become the accessories in a victimless crime.

There are two versions of this analysis. One simply asserts the active capacity of audiences, in an attempt to question the determinism inherent in accounts of the political economy of communications which can be construed as detecting a simple equation between ownership, content, and effect. The debate, and the evidence, for this approach have been hotly contested.[19] Mattelart rejects the "ethnographic" account by suggesting that "this new version of empiricism brings us receivers so concrete that one forgets which society they live in, thus concealing both the tree and the forest," a vision, he contends, which imposes a new relativism utterly and willfully ignorant of global inegalitarianism.[20]

The second variant often has a more progressive implication, and revolves around the notion that there is no pristine cultural purity which is tainted by invasion. Rather, cultures are dynamic and thus permanently hybrid. The assumed relation between culture and territory is dismissed, and cultures are conceived as individually molded by personal choice and taste.[21] This analysis leads to the rejection of rigid class and structural determinants of cultural domination, and to considerable faith in the creation of permissive spaces for cultural determination by individual consumers.

Such an analysis—that audiences are not *tabula rasa* for the absorption of imported and commercially manufactured ideology—is a necessary corrective to overly deterministic thinking. However, the degree of interpretability of texts and the finite limits to consumer autonomy are still highly significant. Resistance by audience autonomy is frequently romanticized excess, and is, at most, some form of indirect autonomy over consumption, but never production.

2. *Local power.* Many centers in the third world have become important sources of influential and widely distributed material, films, television programming, or music. Egypt, Brazil, India, and Mexico are all major producers, for example. Some third world urban centers have become telecommunications centers—Bombay, Shanghai, and Jakarta among them. At the same time, at the intranational level, autonomous centers of local radio or video production have played an important role, not only in meeting immediate needs for culturally relevant material, but in skilling local people, and in demystifying the process of cultural production.

3. *Regionalism.* In the wake of the MacBride Report one of the great hopes was for regional collaboration, especially in the world of news agencies. In the Caribbean, Africa, and the Middle East important initiatives were established to provide the kind of flow of relevant news, undistorted by the perceptions of western news capitals in New York, Paris, and London, which third world audiences felt cheated of by the all-embracing power of the big international agencies. Their fate was less than compelling.[22] Nonetheless, the potential for non-national, but nonglobal cooperation in cultural and linguistic space, for example in Latin America, remains underexplored.

4. *Communication Policy.* In a simple world all that would be necessary to resist the conglomerate incorporation of global culture would be the democratically effective implementation of relevant policy by legitimate national

policy forums. In the real world communication policy has been more chimera than panacea. Many third world states have been oppressive in character and effect, and have rapidly recognized the key role of control of the cultural apparatus. Local elites, integrated into a cosmopolitan culture of easy superiority and rule, created communication policies more concerned with the sustenance of power and privilege than with resistance to cultural imperialism.

In many countries the state became the key mechanism of global incorporation. McDowell examines the evolution of communication policy in India, and shows how it was crucial in the establishment and expansion of the private sector, setting in train "long-term forces contributing to the contemporary transition from national broadcasting to the commercialization, privatization, and transnational integration of audio-visual service production and distribution."[23] The role of policy is thus not neutral—it depends entirely on the political forces which generate policy. Communication policy must be understood as a potential force for the democratic control of the sector, but not as intrinsically and ubiquitously a benign one.

5. *Doing it differently*. Alternative media, under local or democratic control, have been an ever-present in the history of modern communications. The use of video by the Indians of the Amazonian forests to focus attention on the pillage of their environment has been potent and brave. Alternative journalism in apartheid South Africa, Internet campaigns by the resistance movement in Chiapas, samizdat and e-mail politics in Eastern Europe, community radio in South and Central America—the list is, happily, endless. In Australia the National Indigenous Media Association coordinates an impressive network of radio and television, as well as newspaper and book presses, in the fight for Aboriginal rights.[24] Radio broadcasting among the Bolivian mining communities has been crucial in the struggle for trade union rights and representation.[25]

Alternatives such as these not only function to provide a complement to the mass-produced and ideologically saturated output of global corporate culture. They also provide alternative and exemplary models for the structure of relationships between cultural producers and consumers. To exaggerate their impact and extent would be a dangerous conceit. To ignore their lessons would be myopic negativism.

Each of these forms of resistance offers hope, but also salutary lessons of limits and reality. The helm is firmly in the grip of commercial and corporate greed. To move forward we need to recognize the human and social capacity of communications, its institutional centrality to the continuing project of modernity in the search for the creation of an international order retaining some sense of and commitment to liberty, equality, and community. Otherwise, the legacy of technological advance will be to further disconnect the impoverished and rejected of a globe in eternal conflict.

Notes

1. P. Golding and P. Harris (eds.), *Beyond Cultural Imperialism* (London: Sage Publications, 1997).
2. For details of these and other corporate structures, see Herman, E.S. and McChesney, R.W., *The Global Media: The New Missionaries Of Corporate Capitalism* (London: Cassell, 1997).
3. Cited in Johnson, D., "TV Toy Story: Kids' fare drives international merchandising bonanza," *Broadcasting and Cable International* 8, No. 2 (April 1966): 30-34.
4. See Townsend, P., *The International Analysis of Poverty* (Sussex: Harvester Wheatsheaf, 1993).
5. Brazier, C., "State of the World Report," *New Internationalist* No. 287 (1997).
6. Piven, F. Fox, "Is it Global Economics or Neo Laissez-faire?" *New Left Review* no. 213 (September/October 1995): 107-14.
7. Woodall, P. "The hitchhiker's guide to cybernomics," *The Economist,* 28 September 1996.
8. Galeano, E., "Notes on inequality and incommunication," *Media Development* 1/96, p. 22.
9. Johnson, D., "Asia Pacific and revenue booms," *Broadcasting and Cable International* 8, no. 3 (June1996): 7-8.
10. Bin Zhao, "Consumerism, Confucianism, Communism: making sense of China today," *New Left Review* no. 222 (March/April 1997): 43-59.
11. ITU, *World Telecommunication Development Report* (Zurich: International Telecommunications Union, 1997a).
12. Calculated from ITU/TeleGeography Direction of Traffic database (1997b), available on-line at http://www.itu.int/ti/industryoverview/top50int.htm.
13. ITU, *World Telecommunication Development Report* (Zurich: International Telecommunication Union, 1997a).
14. Winseck, D., "Contradictions in the democratisation of international communication," *Media, Culture and Society* 19, no. 2 (1997): 234.
15. Scott, T., "Broadcasters, producers, go online to increase brand recognition," *Broadcasting and Cable International* 8, no. 2 (1996): 42.
16. Bracken, M., "Gotcha! Murdoch Online," *Internet Magazine* no. 29 (1997): 63-67.
17. See Hamelink, C., "MacBride with hindsight," in P. Golding and P. Harris (eds.), *Beyond Cultural Imperialism.*

18. Schiller, H., *Information Inequality* (New York: Routledge, 1996), p. 121.

19. See several chapters in Ferguson, M. and Golding, P., *Cultural Studies in Question* (London: Sage Publications, 1997).

20. Mattelart, A., *Mapping World Communication: War, Progress, Culture* (Minneapolis: University of Minnesota Press, 1994), p. 237.

21. Garcia Canclini, N., *Hybrid Cultures: Strategies for Entering and Leaving Modernity* (Minneapolis: University of Minnesota Press, 1995).

22. Musa, M., "From optimism to reality: an overview of third world news agencies," in P. Golding and P. Harris (eds.), *Beyond Cultural Imperialism.*

23. McDowell, S.D., "Globalisation and policy choice: television and audiovisual services policies in India," *Media, Culture and Society* 19, no. 2 (1997): 162.

24. Pattel-Gray, A., "Australian Aboriginal communication as resistance," *Media Development* 2/1996: 18-19.

25. O'Connor, A., "The miners' radio stations in Bolivia: a culture of resistance," *Journal of Communication* 40 (1990): 102-10.

Challenging Capitalism in Cyberspace:

The Information Highway, the Postindustrial Economy, and People

HEATHER MENZIES

"All that is solid melts into air" has never rung so true. Capitalism's structures are being digitized: dematerialized from file folders into electronic bits in global communication networks. With this, corporate operations are being drastically reorganized in space and time. They're being scaled up into "virtual" corporate alliances and joint ventures.[1] They're being accelerated into "quick-response" retailing and "just-in-time" manufacturing. And they're being re-engineered into almost cybernetic systems of centralized financial and managerial control, permitting in turn an intensified commoditization of activity as well as an unprecedented fragmentation of work, performance measurement, and related compensation.

In short, it's business as usual with a vengeance. Beneath the rhetoric of the "information" society, and the cowboy frontierism ("frictionless capitalism" and such) of Internet enthusiasts, the ideology of monopoly capitalism is being consolidated (and hegemonized) in forms that are all the more total and totalizing for being invisible and ubiquitous.

The challenge is to come to terms with these developments in ways that make sense of what they're doing to people, and what people can do about them. I hope to at least try to do this here. I'll begin with a short description of the technology behind the restructuring, then explore some of the implications of this restructuring and the ways we can understand and analyse it, and end with some thoughts on the language we use to construct, or confound, our perceptions and our sense of the alternatives.

The Information Highway as Axis of the New Economy

It helps to start with the information highway, since the "highway" is at the center of this vast technological restructuring, and since its infrastructure of interconnecting networks is becoming the axis of the new economy: the site where business deals are forged, where work is dispatched, and where "flexible accumulation" is calculated and managed. The term "information highway" was coined by U.S. Vice President Al Gore in 1993 when he introduced his $2 billion-a-year National Information Infrastructure Program, a sequel to his 1980s High Performance Computing Act geared to retooling U.S. industry with super-fast computers and networks "to enable this country to leapfrog the Japanese."[2] As in Canada, where the federal government launched a similar information-infrastructure boosting program in 1994 (through a largely private-sector consortium called CANARIE), "economic renewal" has been the priority. From the outset too, the focus has been on business, not on multimedia marketing, distribution, or even teleshopping. A 1994 publication called *The Canadian Information Highway: Building Canada's Information and Communications Infrastructure* was unequivocal: "The key to competitiveness will be the ability of firms to develop, acquire and adapt . . . the tools that will be available on and through the information highway."[3]

As for the highway imagery itself, Gore in fact recycled it from his senator grandfather's initiative to build a network of superhighways across the United States in the 1950s, as a way to boost the country's economy and defense capabilities. But the metaphor is actually misleading. It suggests just another line of communication running by outside all the institutions of our lives, when in fact this electronic highway is running right through them and transforming the very ground they stand on. With computerization, much of the information underpinning work and the management of work is being digitized. With networking—i.e., computers combined with communications—all that data and all that managerial control can then be shifted away from grounded institutions into the high-capacity networks of the information highway. It can be deinstitutionalized from bricks and mortar and fixed geography, and reinstitutionalized in the global networks of the information-highway infrastructure. It can go global.

Work can be contracted out through a new global and local division of labor constituted through at-home teleworkers and call centers, through "agile" factories, labs, home and satellite offices, and workshops. Once they are plugged into the information highway, all these production modules can be managed remotely through the networked organizational structures of virtual corporations, virtual colleges and universities, virtual hospitals and government departments. The highway's networks provide a ubiquitous corporate operating environment through which any physical place—from high-rise apartment to suburban basement or garage and any car or truck—can become a virtual workplace or a customer-service and delivery site, at any moment in time.

With the information highway signaling the network-integration phase of a computerized restructuring which dates from the 1970s, the industrial paradigm is shifting. National machine-based economies are being restructured into a global postindustrial systems economy. It's an economy dominated by global-scale corporations, particularly in the information, financial-information, and communication business, which can exploit the highway network as a "unified system" of production, marketing distribution, and consumption.[4]

This isn't a strictly technological development, nor a deterministic one. A host of ideological and historical choices are at work, including deficit cutting and government downsizing; privatization, free trade, and deregulation, plus the downward ratcheting of social and labor standards. All of these play a part in the larger restructuring process: through the uncoupling of economic units from the social constraints of local and national communities; the downward leveling of standards and expectations; the transfer of assets from the public sector to the private, and the consolidation of power into the hands of larger corporate units. The latter two trends apply particularly in the area of communication. As the tools of communication have become both the postindustrial tools of production and its prime tools of regulation, the corporate sector has made it a priority to bring communication under its control.

What's emerging in this global systems economy is a variation on a Lego set, with interchangeable production units operating on a standardized set of pay and performance criteria, where investments and contracts can be activated at a press-enter cue, and terminated just as fast. It's a game plan being actively promoted in the United States by a government-industry think tank called the Agility Forum. Founded in the late 1980s with funding from the U.S. Defense Department, the forum has brought together senior executives from the major military industrial suppliers, plus the major companies in computers, communications, and the auto industry.

Its publications don't talk about monopoly capitalism having reached an omega point through the virtualizing infrastructures of the highway networks, where monopoly corporations, cartels, and conglomerates vanish as structures altogether. They don't say that the invisible electronic structures of the virtual corporation and "federated . . . virtual enterprises"[5] are the perfect vehicle for the kind of "flexible accumulation" which David Harvey describes as capitalism's "solution" to its crisis tendencies—whereby "the financial system has achieved a degree of autonomy from real production unprecedented in capitalism's history."[6] Instead, they mildly predict that virtual joint ventures will become "routine,"[7] with one dissolving today and a different one formed tomorrow, and many happening simultaneously, linking different parts of different corporations in parallel research, product development, and other product-cycle activities for different periods of time. The alliances—called "the new intimacy" between "erstwhile competitors"[8]—represent what they expect will be "the dominant world industrial order of the Twenty-first Century."[9] These alliances are made possible by "streamlined legal practices," "standardized interfaces" and a "pervasive connectivity"[10] through the increasingly standardized networking systems which the forum is promoting, including through a customized express lane on the information highway called the Factory America Network. Integration is "electronic": companies agreeing to act as suppliers or consultants or distributors on this or that "product" or "service product" are given access to certain data files, software, and other technologies, to allow close project-centered cooperation—for the life of the project.

One document, *Key Need Areas for Integrating the Agile Virtual Enterprise,* offers a game plan for streamlining everything from technology and legal protocols, to modules of people and their skills—a global "contingent labor force"—so that technological and human modules can be plugged into any collaborative combination for work along the information highway at minimal start-up costs to the company involved. This means just-in-time suppliers of car parts to GM, or of sweaters from self-employed knitters for Benneton clothing stores. It also means the kind of quick-response in retailing which has allowed Wal-Mart to bulldoze more traditional retailers aside, and made it the fourth largest communication user in the United States.[11]

The game plan also calls for more and better computer "metrics," so each corporate module's "value-added" contribution, or each individual's hourly performance can be measured for "value-based compensation"[12] and profit-sharing. It also envisages further deregulation—a relaxing of antitrust laws, minimum-wage and equal-employment standards, and a fragmentation of product liability so that every participating production unit shares the "liability risk."[13]

This "Lego set" of costlessly interchangeable global production units, operating entirely on its own self-styled rules, has all the markings of a perpetual-motion machine. It's equally a technological extension of the international investment market, with its endless appetite for quarterly profit margins driving up decision-making rates, pushing up turnover rates, accelerating turnaround rates, and driving people to the point of burnout—or out of the economy altogether. It's a fully realized time-space compressed simulacrum, with people and place left holding the bag.

Yet increasingly, this new economy is beyond the reach of voters and of the policymaking restraints of all but the largest national governments. In Canada, a 1994 report on Canadian foreign policy began with a tacit capitulation to global corporate power: "Globalization is . . . making borders porous. . . . [N]ational sovereignty is being reshaped and the power of national governments to control events, reduced."[14] The World Trade Organization, the OECD (with its planned Multilateral Agreement on Investments, or MAI), the World Bank, and IMF, plus the formalized meetings of world bankers are emerging as a new form of "invisible government" on a global scale.[15] WTO Director General Renato Ruggiero has described the MAI as "the constitution of a single global economy."

None of these institutions is accountable to people constituted as democratic communities. At best, they're responsible to investors, to people defined through ownership or assigned role in a corporatist society, not through rights of citizenship.[16]

Grasping Capitalism in Cyberspace

It's hard to make sense of these developments even on their own terms: to parse the political economy of cyberspace with its networked forms of organization which are part structure, part dynamic process, and which increasingly form the environment within which we seek work, perform work, learn, and live. Communication scholar Vincent Mosco supplies some helpful new tools for developing the kind of critical insiders' perspective that seems to be needed. One is his concept of *spatialization,* which opens up Harvey's concept of space-time compression by focusing on structures for crossing geographic space quickly.[17] Virtual corporations and virtual co-venturing seem to embody this concept, combining economies of scale with economies of scope (multi-product, multi-genre, etc.) and economies of speed, through their dynamic networked operations. His notion of *structuration* is also helpful. It seeks to bridge the gap between analyses of structures and analyses of agency by emphasizing the dialectic interaction between them "in the ongoing patterning of social life."[18] This dialectic suggests that people aren't passive parts of the new systems economy. They have agency, and can use it to resist the corporate agenda and to negotiate the terms of their participation, if they can define those terms for themselves outside the social field determined by the corporate networks. However, Mosco's third concept, *commoditization,* which extends Marx's analysis of commoditization and the fetishism of commodity, sheds some light on how difficult this is. Not only do digital networks permit the intensification of capital accumulation by fragmenting various communication services into commodity-like pay-per units (such as local-measured telephone service and pay-per program television viewing).[19] Not only do they permit the Taylorist fragmentation of work, as work intensified into commoditized tasks contracted out via digital networks to home-based or foreign-factory workers. They also obscure what is lost in the transformation from an ongoing relationship and community of employment to a just-in-time job-task, by enclosing people in an entirely commoditized expression of the work to be done. The digital systems which monitor and measure the performance of their work, then print it out as x (commoditized) calls processed per hour, x (commoditized) patient-care orders executed per shift, or cars assembled, and so on. With pay directly hinged to performance—especially as perform-ance-based compensation has become widespread in North America in recent years—workers start to identify with this commoditized expression of their work, and to drive themselves faster and faster. They almost have no choice as the context of their work is stripped of any meaning except the fragmented task and its statistical measures of performance. The new context, the new social field, is whatever the employer chooses to project on (or to bar from) the computer screen in any particular workstation.

The identification is further encouraged through Total Quality Manage-ment and other "cultural training" programs, which have been introduced everywhere, from car factories to hospitals and municipal government of-fices.[20] Through "communications" sessions, pep rallies, and in-house produc-tion-team competition, they encourage employees to identify with management's productivity and performance goals, and to internalize its corporate mission statement. I've called it "training for compliance"[21] after Ursula Franklin's insightful assertion that prescriptive technologies are "de-signs for compliance."[22] It could equally be called the hegemonizing phase of technological restructuring. Once people have been cut off from the old context of work and enclosed in a digital context entirely defined by manage-ment, these management programs encourage them to identify with their role as servo-mechanisms of the technological system,[23] and to embrace the pursuit of microwave ovens, holiday cruises, and other rewards for meeting production targets. In the process, they align themselves with the corporate values of competition and productivity growth as the meaning of their work.

Equally, however, the enormity of this transformation is obscured by the commoditized terms of reference—and by the way these terms are used even by researchers and thinkers wishing to ally themselves with workers in their efforts to name and resist these social forces. These commoditized terms—*contingent labor force, skill sets,* and even "workers"—commoditize perception, and stifle the urgency of human communication and community building here.

Grounding The Discussion In People And Place

For me, the term *deskilling* has never touched the enormity of what's going on. It's asset-stripping applied to the social environment at large. People's knowledge and experience is being appropriated, taken away from them and "black boxed." Their wisdom is being arbitrarily trashed, devalued like a third world currency. Similarly, the "two-tiered" and "contingent" labor force doesn't begin to evoke the social dislocations being imposed. The reserve army of the unemployed is being augmented by a new reserve army: of the self-employed, the contingent part-timers.

The challenge of solidarity lies, it seems, in being simultaneously insiders and outsiders. This involves both bringing one's own personal agency to the task of professional knowledge work (as a member of a larger human community as well as of an incorporated discourse) and finding useful precedents for critiquing cybernetic capitalism within the larger context of real space and time—i.e., people and place. One such precedent is in the language of development as colonization which, Marx himself argued, epitomized capitalism as a social system of exploitation.[24]

Ecofeminist Maria Mies puts her finger on it in describing this type of development as a polarizing process involving the active underdevelopment of people (forced alienation from the land) and places (deforestation, pollution, etc.). In short, where some people get richer and some people get poorer.[25]

These terms are useful in assessing the full meaning, and cost, of global digital networking and time-space compression for people, place, and community. They're useful for taking into account the increased pollution associated with relocating industrial production to places with no regulations to protect the natural environment, and the increased transportation costs (and pollution) involved in ferrying globally produced goods to globally distributed markets.

Seen in the context of the larger social environment, digital globalization also represents a massive underdevelopment of the old social environment, with its sociotechnical infrastructure of people, machines, and bureaucracy. Machines are replacing people. Machine calculation is replacing human intelligence, judgement, and involvement. This explains the stubbornly high levels of unemployment and underemployment in North America and Western Europe in the late 1990s. There's economic growth, but it's largely a jobless economic growth. Or it's growth as short-term contracts, part-time or temporary work—often working as a mere adjunct to sophisticated production and information-management systems which handle all the planning, administration, and other support automatically. In Canada, "nonstandard" (part-time, temporary) jobs accounted for all the new employment growth in 1995.

The evidence for this connection between technological restructuring and un- and underemployment lies in the detailed case studies and stories, intelligently mapped against the larger statistical trends.[26] Networked computer management, administration, and production is not only permitting the production of new goods and services with little or no human involvement. It's also permitting the digital delivery of services. Everything from registering for courses at colleges and universities to ordering customized merchandise, arranging for a bank loan, and making reservations is being privatized—in a special new meaning of that word. It's being transferred from the paid hands of workers to the unpaid hands of consumers who work their way through computerized voice-clip mazes at the other end of 1-800 numbers, only speaking to a teleworker in contingencies the system hasn't yet standardized into software. Finally, it's permitting—or at least providing the rationale for—the replacement of full-time staff with part-time staff, everywhere from factories to hospitals, insurance companies, and subcontractors for privatized government services. The idea is that the computer networks and related data files provide the continuity and institutional context, where a local community of local people known to each other over time provided this in the past.

However, it takes stories—the grounded language of people and place—to convey this larger erosion of the social environment. Where people used to share workspace and operate in an informal work community, more and more now work in isolated work stations, or what I call silicon work cells—in call center cubicles or as teleworkers at home. Not only are they isolated from each other, they're increasingly polarized in terms of income, job stability, hours of work, and level of involvement. On one end, there are the overworked rich with a host of powerful information tools at their disposal, driving them to work at peak-performance pace for ten and twelve hours a day. The barely working poor on the other side of this income and digital divide work marginally, as the hands and voice box of intelligent systems which dictate everything about the job to be done, and monitor every aspect of its performance.

Carol Van Helvoort works for the Pizza Pizza chain, processing orders from a computer and modem hooked up in the bedroom of a one-bedroom apartment on the fringes of Metro Toronto. It doesn't bother her that the computer monitors everything she does. What bothers her is that what she does is so little worth monitoring. For two four-hour chunks every day, she repeats the same few phrases again and again, and goes through the same few actions on her keyboard.

She talked about the inconvenience of having the family phone line taken over for eight hours a day, as Pizza Pizza turns her home into a virtual workplace. She talked about how young mothers have had to get their kids to keep quiet. "But why should they? What does it do to family life?"[27]

She also worried about women's increased vulnerability in abusive relationships, going nowhere when they go to work; being trapped inside the home all the time.

It was the loneliness and isolation that bothered her the most. She used to do her hair all the time; she used to do her nails, but now why bother? "You don't even bother getting dressed half the time," she said, as though she's disappeared that much as a social being.

She'd quit tomorrow, she told me, "but there's nothing out there. If I want to work, I have to pay the price."

High unemployment, declining social benefits (resulting in only 47 percent of Canada's unemployed being eligible for unemployment benefits in 1997, compared to 87 percent in 1993), plus workfare are muting opposition to the restructuring agenda. Adjusting to underdevelopment, which appears to be globalization's agenda for people, seems the only option. But its hegemony can be challenged at the level of language and frame of reference: by recovering the voice of experience, and making it the center of a new critical discourse on globalized capitalism where the priorities of particular people, places, and communities are paramount.

Notes

This essay is largely based on the author's Whose Brave New World? The Information Highway and the New Economy *(Toronto: Between the Lines, 1996).*

1. I will be using the terms *virtual corporation* and *virtual workplace* throughout this paper. It refers to the capacity of corporations to create an electronic simulation of their legal existence through electronic files, access protocols, and a digital address, and to extend this via computer, modem, and communication networks to create a virtual extension of itself anywhere with compatible equipment.
2. Peter Coy, "How do you build an Information Highway?" *Business Week*, 16 September 1991.

3. Industry Canada, *The Canadian Information Highway: Building Canada's Information and Communications Infrastructure* (Ottawa: Supply and Services Canada, 1994), p. 8.
4. Dr. Steven Goldman, *Agile Manufacturing: A New Production Paradigm for Society* (Bethlehem, PA: The Agility Forum, 1993), p. 110.
5. Ibid., p. 27.
6. David Harvey, *The Condition of Postmodernity* (Cambridge, MA: Blackwell Publishers, 1992), p. 194.
7. Ibid., p. 5.
8. Davidow & Malone, 1992. 140.
9. Goldman, *Agile Manufacturing*, p. 1.
10. Steven Goldman, *Key Need Areas For Integrating the Agile Virtual Enterprise* (Bethlehem, PA: Agility Forum, 1994), p. 41.
11. *Information Week,* 10 October 1994, p. 38.
12. Goldman, *Key Need Areas*, p. 17.
13. Ibid., p. 26.
14. A. MacEachen & J.R. Gauthier, co-chairs, "Canada's Foreign Policy: Principles and Priorities for the Future," Report of the Special Joint Committee of the Senate and House of Commons Reviewing Canadian Foreign Policy, Ottawa, November 1994, p. 1.
15. Economist Tom Naylor used this phrase in reference only to the world banking network. I have expanded it to include the WTO, etc. See *Bleeding the Patient: The Debt/Deficit Hoax Exposed* (Ottawa: Canadian Centre for Policy Alternatives, 1994), p. 6.
16. John Ralston Saul, *The Unconscious Civilization* (Toronto: House of Anansi Press, 1995). This is an excellent critique of an emerging corporatist society in our times.
17. Vincent Mosco, *The Political Economy of Communication* (London: Sage Publications), p. 175.
18. Ibid., p. 212.
19. Ibid., p. 153.
20. See Chap. 5, "Panopticons and Telework: The New Cybernetics of Labour" in *Whose Brave New World?* I focus a lot on the social engineering of perception, both through the corporate control of the media and through more directed communications of corporate training and employee-involvement programs, which have eclipsed skills training in the workplace. These trends confirm both Noam Chomsky and Edward Herman's propaganda model of media analysis and Jacques Ellul's more comprehensive analysis of a "propoganda of integration" model operating through a range of communication and knowledge structures in society, including education and training. See also Jacques Ellul, *Propaganda: The Formation of Men's Attitudes* (New York: Random House, 1973). For a reference on the eclipsing of skills training, see also G. Betcherman et al, *The Canadian Workplace in Transition: the Final Report of the Human Resources Management Project* (Kingston: Industrial Relations Centre Press, Queen's University, 1994), p. 82.
21. *Whose Brave New World?*, p. 122.

22. Ursula Franklin, *The Real World of Technology* (Toronto: Anansi Press, 1990), p. 31.

23. Two Canadian thinkers, Marshall McLuhan and George Grant, have used the servo-mechanism metaphor to capture the involuntary nature of people's actions once they are inside a closed system. In the closed system of a household thermostat, a servo-mechanism is programmed to turn the furnace off when the temperature rises above a certain point, and to turn it on when the temperature drops below a certain point. See Marshall McLuhan, *Understanding Media: The Extensions of Man* (New York: McGraw Hill, 1964), p. 51.

24. Karl Marx, *Capital* I (New York: International Publishers, 1967), p. 766.

25. Maria Mies, "Liberating the Consumer" in Maria Mies & Vandana Shiva (co-authors), *Ecofeminism* (New York: Zed Books, 1993), p. 251.

26. See *Whose Brave New World?* for a Canadian analysis.

27. Ibid., p. 127.

U.S. Rules. OK?

Telecommunications Since the 1940s

JILL HILLS

Today the telecommunications sector is in transitional mode. Since the immediate post-World War II period, telecommunications operation has gradually moved from being a security-related, primarily state-owned monopoly of supply of equipment and network, to being a partially privately owned, company-based service industry. Particularly over the past twenty years, three parallel changes—in the technology available, in the structure and regulation of markets, and in corporate strategies—have altered the focus of the sector to customer rather than engineer's satisfaction. However, the customers that have benefitted most are the large multinational users, and the corollary developments have been a greater division between rich and poor, increased concentration internationally, and less ability for governments to control their own telecommunications networks.

Important to these developments in the telecommunications sector have been general changes in the international political economy and concurrent shifts in power between states. Changes in the sector mirror a resurgence of power in the North, particularly for the United States, and a diminution in the power, resources, and sovereignty of the South following the Gulf War and the break-up of the USSR. Recession in the North has renewed mercantilism, reduced aid, and increased demands for the South to provide markets for the

Northern multinationals to exploit. The institutionalization of the rights of multinationals over the sovereignty of states form the rationale for multilateral agreements such as NAFTA, the WTO, and, in 1997, the multilateral agreement on foreign direct investment being negotiated in the OECD. Changes in the sector are a microcosm of these general economic and political trends that reverse the international rules codified in the 1940s that signified respect for sovereignty and greater equality between rich and poor, back towards the colonialism and dependencies of the 1890s.

The declining costs of technology have afforded opportunities for the sector to move from being predominantly nationally based to being international. On the one hand, maturation and emerging competition in the domestic markets of Western network operators have lowered margins and produced an incentive to look overseas for higher profits. On the other, multinational companies have created the demand for operators to provide one-stop shopping in globally constructed networks, and for defensive investments to ensure a "stake" in the strategic markets of the United States, the European Union, and the Far East. Industrialized government policy has encouraged this internationalization. In the West, the policy mechanisms of liberalization and privatization have become a source of revenues from which to ease budgetary constraints and, in the South, have been forced on developing countries and post-Communist countries by multilateral lenders and decreases in bilateral aid.

This increase in private ownership of network operators is the second major trend, paralleling internationalization. However, whereas in the industrialized West such privatization has normally constituted government sale of equity, in developing countries management has often been transferred to a foreign operator. And following the relaxation of the bar to private ownership of international facilities in the 1980s, it has become increasingly necessary for privately owned operators to invest in international infrastructure—satellites and cable—so as to ensure that they are not discriminated against by rivals. Private ownership by foreign enterprises of both developing countries' domestic networks and the international facilities that link them to the outside world is also reminiscent of a return to the prewar days of neocolonial relations between North and South.

The third parallel strand of change has been provided by changes in international regulation. These changes in the rules of international communication have both reflected and reinforced the move towards private ownership of facilities. There is nothing new in countries utilizing bilateral and multilateral regulation to gain advantage for their companies. Since the 1860s the United States has used both techniques for corporate advantage. But the period since the 1980s has been particularly marked by pressure from the United States, not only to alter the international regulatory scheme, but also to alter the institutions from which such rules emanate. In successfully shifting the locus of international regulation away from the International Telecommunications Union (ITU), a European and developing-country power base, to the World Trade Organization (WTO), where its power reflects its huge, high-income market, the United States has also fundamentally shifted the conceptualization of telecommunications away from the postwar public utility, security related, monopoly model, to that of a customer driven, trade-related, service industry.

By involving the WTO, the U.S. multinationals and government were aspiring to universalist rules enforced on other countries. As Hampden-Turner and Trompenaars point out in their study of varieties of capitalism, "No other culture is so keen to make rules for everyone to live by."[1] Yet, in a Catch-22 situation, because of its own tardiness in liberalizing its domestic network to foreign operators—indeed, that prospective liberalization being the main feature of its bilateral and multilateral bargaining position—the United States is currently in a position of weakness in attempting to impose its preferred "universalist" rules on the rest of the world. Its domestic system of regulation in something akin to stand-off, with the Federal Communications Commission and the States locked in jurisdictional disputes, the FCC is being told to put its own house in order before preaching to the rest of the world.[2] The tenor of this article is to argue that the latter 1990s will witness a retrenchment of the United States in the international telecommunications sector, with an increasingly mercantilist attitude as it deals with the domestic restructuring it has so often urged on others—but that this weakness will be compensated for by the further institutionalization of general international economic agreements that favor its multinationals.

Technology and Economics

From the immediate postwar period until the 1980s, telecommunications in the industrialized countries was primarily a national affair. Foreign investment there was made by manufacturers, such as Ericsson of Sweden or Philips of Holland, both with a small home market. The telecommunications technology of this postwar period varied little from that of the 1920s. Strowger and Crossbar—both mechanical forms of exchange-switching technology—dated from that period, together with coaxial cable and wireless.

In terms of markets, technology, and institutions, the period until the late 1970s was one of maturity and some stagnation. Each of the major industrial countries had their own manufacturers supplying their Posts and Telecommunications Operator (PTO), itself often a government department responsible both for network operation and regulating itself. National standards acted as nontariff barriers to foreign equipment. The network was seen as a natural monopoly under which customers' equipment was perceived as an integral part of the local and long-distance networks. Engineering-driven, with low rates of investment, the networks of the 1960s in Europe featured long waiting lists and a uniform service to large and small customers alike. In the United States the vertical integration of AT&T and its manufacturing arm, Western Electric, took the place of the corporatism between government, network operator, and manufacturer evident in Europe and Japan.

In its organization and institutions, the telecommunications sector reflected the postwar emphasis on state-based solutions to recuperation and economic development, as well as state·security. In the immediate post-World War II period, as previously colonized countries gained their independence and multilateral agencies were established on the basis of "one nation, one vote," so the concept of sovereignty gained increased international recognition. To fledgling nation-states, often with boundaries carved according to their colonizer's convenience rather than according to ethnic cleavages or access to natural resources, the state itself had to control broadcasting and telecommunications. Broadcasting, often in a *lingua franca,* provided a means to create national unity from disparate regions or ethnic groupings, and a channel of direct communication between ruling elites and their populations. Telecommunications, traditionally linked with security, was important to those states perceiving themselves as vulnerable to potentially hostile neighbors.

Resulting from these considerations, as countries became independent, so they moved to exclude the foreign operators from colonizing powers that had run their domestic and international networks. British colonies and dominions nationalized the previous holdings of the British private company Cable and Wireless. In Latin America, ITT's hegemony over most countries' telecommunications operation was replaced by national ownership. Only in French African colonies, after independence, were international telecommunications still provided by a subsidiary of the French PTO, France Radio and Cable. Nevertheless, despite the changes in ownership, infrastructure reflected previous colonial priorities, with cables running from colony to Britain, France, Portugal, or the United States; and within countries, network infrastructure served areas of colonial investment. In both formal and informal colonial empires, little if any communications infrastructure linked the new states with each other. So whereas the political control of these countries altered between the 1940s and 1960s, and the majority nationalized their telecommunications operator, the actual infrastructure remained as it was, reflecting prewar economic relations. In the case of the USSR these colonial relations were taken to further, repressive extremes. Satellite states in Central and Eastern Europe were denied any direct external telephonic access.

In both industrialized and nonindustrialized countries, within the networks themselves, high charges on international and long-distance lines paid towards low residential rentals and low local call tariffs. Averaged tariffs (the same charge whatever the distance) kept tariffs in rural areas on "thin" traffic routes, the same as those between urban centers on "thick" traffic routes. In the nonindustrialized countries, telecommunications revenues were not reinvested in capital-intensive networks demanding foreign exchange, but went to support health, water, and education. Where there was vertical integration between private companies, as in the United States between AT&T and Western Electric, or where there was a "national" champion manufacturer as in Britain, France, Germany, and Italy, operating tariffs contributed to high prices for equipment. Eli Noam referred to this arrangement as the "Postal-Industrial" complex, in reference to the additional cross-subsidization of postal workers by the network revenues of telecommunications.[3]

But a number of factors came together to alter this symbiotic relationship between PTOs and manufacturers. First, technology gave PTOs the opportunity to upgrade their networks. The memory microchip and microprocessor introduced in the 1970s had revolutionized computing. A convergence between computing and telecommunications had begun with the digitalization of exchanges, whose introduction into the network first came in France in the latter 1970s. Costing enormous amounts of money to develop, these new exchanges needed to be amortized over larger markets. Exports became essential. Oversupply in turn fueled rationalization, mainly in favor of those with the largest home markets. Then liberalization of network operation undermined the previous cost-plus basis of equipment purchase. Instead operators looked for the cheapest available.

In Europe, by the mid-1980s, Britain's manufacturing companies, GEC and Plessey, had been taken over by Siemens of Germany, and as margins dropped and research costs rose, so ITT's European manufacturing facilities went to Alcatel of France, thereby making it into a larger telecoms manufacturer than AT&T's Western Electric, whose domestic market had been eroded by Canadian-owned Northern Telecom. Only in France, West Germany, and Italy did the old system of subsidized manufacture remain. Yet in some developing countries the system was replicated to create national control over their own technology. Both India and South Korea developed their own electronic switches at much cheaper cost than European suppliers.

The Cold War, stretching with varying degrees of intensity from the 1950s to 1990, divided the world into the Soviet camp to the East versus the U.S.-led West. The emphasis on military security and the arms race led to increasing links between the electronics industry, including computer and communications companies, and the defense establishment. Satellites were part of this military-industrial complex. They provided the potential for the United States to challenge the submarine cable hegemony of the British.[4]

Comsat was set up in the 1960s by President John F. Kennedy, officially to act as a cooperative means of bringing the benefits of satellite communications to all, but also as a means of creating a legitimate, government-backed cartel of the American international common carriers, AT&T, ITT, GTE, and RCA. The international Intelsat consortium, established outside the United Nations and governed by its users, was therefore initially open to control through Comsat, as the United States' representative. The first transatlantic telephone cable had only been laid in 1957, so at first Intelsat was primarily geared to meeting demand for transatlantic point-to-point communications. However, because averaged pricing kept down the tariffs for "thin" routes in the same way as did PTOs in domestic networks, Intelsat soon became dominant in the external communications of developing countries in Africa and in the international communications of Australasia.

Although Intelsat revolutionized transatlantic communications and opened up long-distance television transmission, despite earning them a 15 percent return on capital invested, it was never popular with PTOs. They could not use the leasing of transponders to count towards the capital base they claimed for rate of return regulation. Instead they preferred to lay and own their own submarine cables. A number of accidents on launch, a shortage of launch facilities, and escalating costs of insurance all drove satellite costs up and made them uneconomic, except over rough terrain and for mobile communications. Inmarsat—modeled on Intelsat—was created by the European PTOs in the 1970s to provide mobile communications to shipping and later airplanes. Intelsat itself failed to invest sufficiently in new technology and failed to anticipate the economic growth and boom in intraregional communications, first in Europe and then in the Asia-Pacific. It thereby gave a market opportunity to regional, national, and privately owned satellites.

Attempts by IBM in the early 1980s to market satellite transmission within the U.S. domestic market for business communications, using small receiver dishes, failed when data traffic proved insubstantial. Spare capacity on telecommunications satellites both in the United States and Europe allowed the launch in the United States of satellite broadcasting to cable headend (as for instance Home Box Office) and then satellite direct-to-home television broadcasting (as for instance BSkyB) in Europe. Yet private satellites could not be used internationally without changes in the Intelsat constitution to allow such competition. Drawn up originally to protect the technological leadership of the United States, the Intelsat treaty could only be altered by a two-thirds majority of its members. As the Intelsat consortium's orders for satellites began to dry up in the 1980s, so it seemed that nationally owned satellites could provide a useful market for the U.S. industry's overcapacity. Hence the U.S. Federal Communications Commission attempted to unilaterally open the international telecommunications market—both satellite and submarine cable—to U.S. private companies. Beaten off by European PTOs on the cable issue, it was able to press within Intelsat for a reinterpretation of its constitution, that then allowed private satellite operators into the international market, first for "enhanced" services—a U.S. term meaning data transmission—and then, in the 1990s, into the transmission of voice services. In turn there has been an explosion of satellites in the Asia-Pacific, catering for voice, data, and image markets.[5]

Private satellites have never been the competition to Intelsat once feared. Instead the major economic impact has come from submarine optic fiber across the Atlantic. During the 1980s optic fiber began to be economic over long distances. Made from glass fiber and using laser beams to transmit digitalized messages, optic fiber could transmit massive amounts of information without the repeaters necessary for coaxial cable. Manufactured in the United States and Japan, as its capital costs came down, so it allowed spatially distributed companies to invest in their own private networks within the United States and, for the first time since the 1930s, the possibility of international communications infrastructure becoming predominantly owned by private companies. Massive investment in capacity took place on the transatlantic route, so that it has been estimated that only one-tenth of that capacity is being used.[6] As a result Intelsat moved into loss in the 1990s to which the response of the industrialized West was to press (unsuccessfully as yet) for its privatization, a move that would in turn make "thin" routes to the South more expensive.

Cellular radio-based technologies, introduced during the 1980s, became in some countries, such as Sweden and Australia, an adjunct to the fixed network. In others, such as the United States and Britain, the fixed network operators were allowed into the market only in competition with a non-fixed network operator and, in Britain, only via a separate subsidiary. The ITU estimated that the demand for cellular services increased by 45 percent per annum between 1991 and 1993. The imminent saturation of analogue networks and the proliferation of standards in turn led to the development of digital cellular with increased capacity.[7]

In Europe in 1987, in order to allow EU-wide roaming, the European Commission asked national governments to reserve spectrum space for the Europe-wide introduction of Groupe Special Mobile (GSM) technology. In contrast, in the United States, the fragmentation of the domestic market between the RBOCs and non-wire-line companies, coupled with disputes over a digital standard, led to delays in its introduction. The EU decision resulted in the early introduction of GSM and its export overseas. A worldwide battle has ensued between the three digital cellular standards of the United States, Japan, and Europe. GSM is dominant, with about 80 percent of the world market, the major market where it is hardly represented being that of Latin America.[8]

In the 1990s the technology of satellites has been brought together with that of cellular radio by a number of consortia to offer global mobile personal communications by satellite. In this proposed service, cellular phones will uplink to satellites to allow the bypass of national networks. The consortia include Iridium (U.S.), led by Motorola; Globalstar (U.S.) with Loral of the United States as the main investor; Odyssey (U.S.), and ICO, the privatized offshoot of Inmarsat. Although there are bullish estimates as to the number of potential customers worldwide, the tariff of upwards of one dollar per minute and the handset price of $700 to $2,000 means the service will hardly appeal to developing country populations, but may well reduce international traffic revenues to the PTO by filtering out traffic from multinationals.[9] Many governments of the emerging economies of Asia are frightened of the implications and of the lack of international regulation.

Finally, in the search for cheap international communications, the Internet has developed from its original base among academics and research institutions, into a distributed computer network utilizing telecommunications infrastructure to transmit packet-switched data. Historically outside the telecommunications sector, the Internet has benefited from non-distance-sensitive usage charges and the avoidance of bureaucratic mechanisms of cost-sharing. Its development has thrown up problems of international regulation of content and has highlighted how, in a network with no overall central control that crosses state boundaries, regulations made in one country impact on others.

Liberalization and Privatization

In the industrialized West, following what seemed to be the "good times" of the 1950s and 1960s, the 1970s brought a combination of stagnating economies and high inflation, exacerbated by the OPEC price rises for oil in 1973 and 1979. The recession of the early 1980s saw Western companies desperately laying off workers and cutting costs in order to remain profitable. Whereas the cost of computing had decreased dramatically with the mass production of the microchip during the early 1980s, that of communications had not. In order to increase their own internal efficiency, major users required not only low cost, but customized communications, differentiated from those available to small business or residential consumers. The traditional PTOs with their slow depreciation of technology and low capital investment in infrastructure were not meeting these needs.

In the 1970s, as the United States saw its world share of exports fall, so it moved into deficit and debt. Coincidentally, the stagflation of the 1970s reduced the faith of economists in Keynesian solutions to the recession of the 1980s. Instead, monetarist solutions were advocated, and a return to free market competition. In the United States this free-market ideology, while officially endorsed and promulgated, was tempered by a massive Keynesian program of investment in defense. The reincarnation and reinvigoration of the Cold War under Reagan gave defense interests a greater say in domestic policymaking. Hence, when the erosion of AT&T's network monopoly, first begun in the 1970s, was completed in the Antitrust Consent Decree of 1984, defense interests fought to see that it did not lose either its research facilities or its manufacturing base. The Consent Decree, by separating AT&T's long-distance market from its local network monopoly, split between seven regional Bell Operating Companies, gave it the ability to move overseas for the first time since its overseas manufacturing facilities had been bought by ITT in the 1930s. At the same time, an FCC-mandated depreciation regime, coupled with competition between AT&T, Sprint, and MCI, provided the stimulus to introduce digital switches and optic fiber into the long distance network. A period of massive investment—arguably overinvestment—in long-distance infrastructure followed.

In Britain the free-market ideology of the Thatcher administration translated into proposals for privatization of public assets. Liberalization of the network, with the introduction of a second network operator, Mercury, owned by Cable and Wireless, preceded privatization and was pushed by the financial services sector. Similar changes also took place in Japan, where manufacturing and finance capital wanted entry into the telecommunications sector.

The liberalization of the sector at this point in time can be seen as a means of redistributing resources away from residential customers, the labor force, and manufacturers, to large business. Increasingly, large users became the movers and shakers of the sector as the operators in liberalized markets competed for their custom. Increasingly, it was the needs of the large multinationals rather than those of the developing countries that held sway within international organizations such as the ITU.

The recession of the 1980s preempted the success of the nonindustrialized countries in pressuring for a more equitable sharing of world resources. By the time that the ITU published its *Maitland Report* in 1984, detailing the distribution of telephones in a world where Tokyo had more telephones than the whole of Africa, and calling for increased resources for developing countries, the tide of international finance had already turned against the developing world.[9] Latin American countries, owing most money to commercial banks, were the first to succumb.

Faced with escalating debt, in the 1980s, a number of the major Latin American countries sold their telecommunications operators to consortia made up of U.S. banks and mainly U.S. or Spanish operators. Backed by the World Bank, these consortia were able to buy the assets cheaply in a highly advantageous debt-to-equity exchange, in which nonperforming debt was swapped for the asset base and revenue stream of the telecommunications operator. Control changed hands to the foreign operators. By the mid 1980s, as increasing numbers of countries (fifteen in Africa by 1985) had to restructure their debt, so any attempts by the nonindustrialized South to make demands in multilateral institutions had ceased. A rebalancing of power began, back to the North and to the United States in particular, culminating in the Gulf War and the fall of the Berlin Wall at the turn of the decade. The ITU reflected this rebalancing with institutional changes formalized in the early 1990s that gave increased influence to private companies.[10]

During the 1980s, beset by recession and structural unemployment, European governments had begun to see in telecommunications the potential for countries to drag themselves out of recession. Technology was pushed as the means of achieving a unified market to rival the United States and to combat the computer- and electronics-based resurgence of Japan. The liberalization of telecommunications in Britain and the prospect of a common European market had begun to alter PTO stances. Even the most monopoly-conscious, such as West Germany, agreed to open up the network to value-added data services, and this domestic decision affected perspectives on international regulation. The European Commission in its Green Paper of 1987 codified these ongoing changes in preparation for the European Single Market of 1992.[11] Nevertheless the Commission, responding to its member nations' concerns, was still primarily focused on the equipment industry and the opportunities that a single market would give.

Hence the Commission saw in the concept of the Integrated Services Digital Network the potential for a unifying technology within Europe. ISDN was first proposed by the Japanese within the ITU in the early 1980s as a means by which PTOs could cut the costs of providing separate networks for voice, data, and facsimile. The original intention was to develop worldwide standards so that equipment could be plugged in wherever needed and would be able to communicate globally. This concept of a unified standard fell to national and company interests opposed to the idea of ITU prorogation of national sovereignty by the determination of equipment standards within domestic markets. The United States went its own way, with an ensuing fragmentation of domestic standards and noncompatibility of equipment. Even in Europe, PTOs, varied in their interpretation of market demand and high prices, have limited access. In contradiction to the ITU's or Commission's hopes, technology could not replace political will for a unified global or European market.

Nevertheless, as the costs of optic fiber decreased, so the possibility of linking the European Union in one "broadband" highway, transmitting voice, data, and images over an interactive network, took the place of ISDN as the technological utopia. A new set of actors entered the telecommunications market in the form of cable TV companies. As it became possible for companies to supply both television and telephone connections to residential customers, so network operators argued that they should be allowed into television carriage. Again regulatory changes were needed to allow the technological convergence of the previous separate markets.

In the United States the regulations that kept cable TV and telecommunications apart were not lifted until the 1996 Telecommunications Act. It was no coincidence that the concept of the "information superhighway" was born at a time of lobbying by the industry for market liberalization. Its hype provided ideological legitimation for the convergence of long-distance, local, and cable TV that the industry wanted.

In contrast, in Britain in the late 1980s the government lifted the regulatory barriers to cable TV companies providing telecommunications. The resulting entry of U.S. and Canadian companies into British cable TV, to gain experience before regulatory liberalization at home, created competition to BT in the local loop. But initial projections of penetration were optimistic. Capital cost of infrastructure, together with resistance to TV packages and the prospect of competition at home, has induced takeover and concentration of the largest companies, now joined to the long-distance operator Mercury in Cable and Wireless Communications. The number of cable companies has fallen from thirty-six to twelve in ten years and U.S. investors, such as NYNEX, have withdrawn.

Subsequently, learning from this British experience, the European Commission has issued a directive that liberalizes the network infrastructure throughout Europe, allowing cable TV companies to supply telecommunications services.[12] Liberalization has become the major policy mechanism of the European Union, and basic services will be opened to competition in 1998. Yet in a rerun of previous technological utopias, and in response to the concept of the "global information highway" promulgated by U.S. Vice President Al Gore, the European Union also adopted the idea of an information superhighway. However, in traditional EU fashion, the Bangemann Report, adopted by the European Council, written by a group of industrialists, presses the case for a liberalized highway, with a plurality of operators, thereby providing a huge market for equipment in the 1990s.[13]

Most European countries now have at least two mobile operators, providing competition with the fixed network in the local loop and kept separate by regulation based on technology. But fixed-link operators increasingly seek to take advantage of new wireless-based technology that can deliver the last mile to the home cheaper than that of the fixed link. In the United States, using this potential to its advantage during the 1990s, wireless technology once more allowed AT&T, through acquisition, back into the local loop, and once more into the potential provision of the nationwide network from which it had been excluded by the 1984 Consent Decree. In turn, that potential entry led to pressures for a rewrite of the 1934 Communications Act and to a revamp of domestic market structure. The immediate impact has been increased concentration as companies restructure to include geographical or technologically constructed markets from which they were previously separated.

To a large extent liberalized markets have been constructed by governments to satisfy competing companies wishing to enter the market. Often technology-based, such market separation has had to be achieved by regulation. Yet such regulation, based on artificial barriers, succumbs to the economics of the technologies. In a digital age it makes little sense to divide the transmission of image from voice or data, or to prevent the use of low-cost wireless technology by fixed network operators. Economic pressures to internationalize exacerbate the tendency to offset risk by merger and concentration into domestic and global consortia, alliances, and companies. Hence there is an irony—liberalization of individual national networks has increased the concentration of the industry internationally, thereby making it more difficult to regulate on a national basis.

Domestic and International Regulation

During the period of the last ten years in industrialized countries where liberalization of the network has been pursued, despite the 1980s expectation that competitive markets required less regulation, the trend has been towards deepening regulation, with price controls, interconnection agreements, and technological roll-out policed by an "independent" regulator, separate from the network operator. Despite the agreement within the WTO in 1997 that member countries agreeing to liberalize their networks should create such an "independent" regulator, the model has its problems. Without the legitimacy of election, and because discussions are often covered by commercial confidentiality, it is easy for regulators to be captured by the dominant operator. Regulators have to rely on creating the legitimacy they need in order to stand up to industry pressure by calling on public opinion through the mass media. In turn, as in the case of NTT in Japan or that of BT in Britain in the 1990s, the dominant operator may be demonized by the regulator in order to gain public backing.

Regulation is an ongoing political process that distributes costs and benefits throughout the sector. In liberalized industrialized markets, it seemed that the initial liberalization would threaten universal service. But competitors found it difficult to make inroads into the dominant operator's market, as increased traffic and new technology allowed tariffs to fall. In particular in the United States, the limited liberalization, the retention of cross-subsidies between AT&T and the RBOCs through access charges to the local network, and various social welfare-type packages ensured that universal service was protected at the cost of higher than necessary prices. In Japan heavy regulation of NTT prevented it from raising its local call rate beyond the ten yen set in the 1970s, and declining revenues impacted on shares. Shareholders (mostly private individuals) were sacrificed to universal service. In Britain in particular, the original claims of the dominant operator for price rises in order to meet the "costs" of universal service were met with sympathy. But then the political costs of high rental charges were too great and costing studies were used to undermine BT's arguments. Ongoing debate over the definition of "costs" has become part of the political process of regulation, each definition favoring a different group of operators or users. Most recently the British regulator has argued that if compensatory gains are taken into consideration, BT's provision of universal service costs it almost nothing.[14]

Where the network infrastructure required expansion to meet universal service targets, in the past access charges were seen as the means to pay for the capital cost of the local loop. Access charges were levied in addition to those charges made for actual interconnection. As cable operators in Britain, the RBOCs refused to pay access charges in order to compensate the dominant operator, BT, for universal service. As a result, there are no access charges in Britain for long distance companies. In contrast, in the United States, such charges totaled $24 billion in 1996. If AT&T and the other long-distance companies were to pay no access charges, then some of the RBOCs would lose 25 percent of their revenue.[15] But in the latter 1990s, as competitors are becoming more successful, the long-distance operators such as AT&T are threatened with a diminution in their long-distance revenues, and the prospect of heavy investment in the local loop to combat threats from providers of integrated telecommunications and TV. It therefore seems unlikely that access charges to the RBOCs can remain in anything like the current form, and it remains to be seen whether their profits or customers will suffer.

Despite the dominance of white, young, male users, its limitation to industrialized countries where infrastructure is available and to those who can speak English and afford a computer, the Internet has been hyped as a means of universal access to communications. A further problem has arisen in the industrialized countries in terms of who should resource the infrastructure for the Internet. Although local phone revenues are boosted by the increased demand for second and third residential lines to accommodate Internet and facsimile, it seems likely that some form of tariff restructuring will need to take place in order to adjust tariffs to costs. The problem is particularly acute in the United States where local infrastructure has not been revamped; but the demands of Internet users may also affect capacity on the transatlantic route. In Britain use of the Internet is growing at 10 percent per month and makes up 10 percent of local calls.[16] Particularly since international telephone calls via the Internet are now a technological possibility, thereby threatening the dominant operator's revenues, it seems likely that where control of infrastructure rests with the telecom operators, so also eventually will control of the access. Already in Europe the operators are moving to become Internet access suppliers. It is exactly for this reason that Bill Gates of Microsoft is proposing to launch satellites to bypass telecommunications networks for Internet users, in much the same way as IBM attempted to become a satellite carrier in the 1980s.

The traditional concept of the international network was of national networks joined at the borders by international gateways. But that concept began to change in the 1980s as multinationals demanded seamless networks. Instead there arose the concept of a network comprising a cobweb of connections between companies straddling state borders. However, for this seamless network to take effect required changes in international regulations.

The regulations on international communications agreed by members of the ITU in the immediate postwar period protected the international traffic of PTOs by banning other companies from providing international service to the public. The only exceptions were SWIFT, the airline network, and SITA, the banking network. These regulations came under scrutiny for the first time in twenty years at a meeting of the ITU in 1988. Termed WATTC 88, conflicting views emerged on how international communications should be structured and regulated in the future. On the one side stood those, such as France and Spain, wishing to retain the previous system of control by PTOs and wanting any private networks provided by multinationals to come under the same system of regulation. On the other were those such as the UK and United States, who wanted the freedom for their multinationals to invest in international infrastructure without being subject to the regulations of the ITU. In the end a compromise was reached that effectively opened the door to international resale by private networks of spare capacity to third parties. Only the United States, still demanding complete freedom for its multinationals to override the sovereignty of states, voted against the final proposals.

WATTC 88 was the turning point in loosening the control of PTOs over international communications. Within a short time the United States began to push international resale as a means to combat the accounting rate system. This system of bilateral charges originated in the 1860s for the telegraph. Under its aegis the cost of an international telephone call is split fifty-fifty between the sender and deliverer, with the sender paying. Although construed as a charge related to costs, as those technological costs have become distance-insensitive, the system has not responded with decreased charges. Instead, because Americans, in general, make more outgoing telephone calls, the system has been used both by the European states and by developing countries to gain a payment from the United States towards their networks. Following lack of success at negotiating a reduction in accounting rates within the multilateral ITU, and a $5 billion outgoing payment for the previous year, in 1996 the FCC reverted to bilateral pressure. Arguing that the rates were currently three times costs, the FCC proposed a ceiling on the bilateral accounting rates that U.S. operators could agree to with their counterparts overseas. Among a range of proposals for these new rules, in time-honored fashion the FCC suggested that market access to the United States be dependent on whether the operator agreed to these lower rates.[17]

Some of the resistance to a renegotiation of these rates on the part of developing countries stems from their experience of "call-back," a system by which a customer in a high-tariff country can obtain dial tone in a low-tariff country, such as the United States. A feature of overcapacity in international facilities and also arbitrage in tariffs, "call-back" has increased the outflow of U.S. accounting rate payments while providing smaller U.S. companies with the mechanism to enter previously closed foreign markets. The FCC was asked to intervene, by AT&T among others, but acted only to limit those varieties of the service that harmed the network. Some developing countries have banned "call-back" because it bypasses their own international network and thereby reduces revenues.

Similar fears were evident in many developing country responses to the network liberalization proposals of the United States in the GATT negotiations that ended in 1992 with the formation of the WTO. In the recessionary environment of the 1980s, the discussions under the GATT regime to introduce trade in telecommunications services began to be pushed by the U.S. financial service companies. The "big bangs" of financial liberalization in America and Britain fueled overseas investment and the demand for instant electronic communications. American Express in particular was vociferous about the need for international rules that would enforce the rights of multinationals to invest over the rights of states to exclude that investment.

But the WTO trade agreement of 1992 did not include telecommunications or broadcasting. The French, desiring to protect their language and culture, blocked EU agreement to liberalization of broadcasting. Basic telecommunications services were pulled out of the agreement because the United

States was not satisfied with the liberalization offers then being made and, in particular, the closed nature of the Asia-Pacific countries. In fact, because financial services in the 1990s were pulling back from overseas expansion in the face of losses, the U.S. trade officials were under pressure to respond to fears of foreign entry to the U.S. market from AT&T.[18] Subsequently the United States demanded side talks, which were held under the WTO's Group on Basic Communications. Four years later, in 1996, the United States once again pulled out of an agreement on the grounds that it was now not satisfied that its new satellite/mobile companies were being given access to enough countries.

During 1996 considerable pressure was brought to bear on nonindustrialized countries to open access to these satellite companies, both in the WTO negotiations and in the ITU's World Telecommunications Policy Forum, where a Memorandum of Understanding was negotiated between them and the satellite operators.[19] The Policy Forum brings together private companies and representatives of governments to discuss international regulatory matters, but it has no regulatory force. The general principles agreed at the meeting included demands that the satellite operators should work to bring prices down so as to serve rural areas in developing countries, and that sovereignty of regulation should be respected. Some developing countries, such as Malaysia and India, were not swayed, however; they refused to agree to the MOU.

Full liberalization of the U.S. market to foreign operators is hardly likely to make much difference to developing countries. One wonders therefore whether the motivation of those signing up to the agreement is more related to fear of bilateral reprisals. However, as the 1997 U.S. refusal to allow two operating licences for the major Japanese carriers to begin service in the United States indicates, even items negotiated within the WTO and accepted by the United States there will still be the subject of bilateral pressure—the problem in this case being the Japanese refusal to allow more than 20 percent of their dominant operators to be foreign-owned.

Corporate Strategies

Since the first liberalization of networks in the mid-1980s, PTOs that were once national in their focus have become international in their corporate strategy. Lying behind these changes in strategy have been not only the economic opportunities offered by technology and alterations in domestic regulatory arrangements, but also the needs of major users. As the expertise to run international corporate networks has increased in cost, so companies have turned to outsourcing—that is, the provision of their international communication by specialist companies. Strategies involve the establishment of "nodes" for customers to link into, the takeover of existing companies—such as BT's takeover of Tymenet in the United States and merger with MCI—or alliances between PTOs. Although termed "global" networks, these alliances are not global, the largest currently being available in eight industrialized countries. BT and MCI joined by Telefonica have formed one grouping; Concert, Deutsche Telecom, France Telecom, and Sprint have come together in Global One; and AT&T, KDD (Japan), Singapore Telecom, and Unisource NV (a grouping of smaller European operators) form World Partners—each vying for multinational customers.

The investment in international facilities by private companies "overlays" existing facilities owned jointly by national PTOs. Private submarine cables allow the bypassing of the bilateral accounting rate system when used for resale, and private networks and satellite ownership allows the bypassing of the PTO monopoly of uplinks to Intelsat. In addition, satellite transmission to small aperture terminals allow business communications to bypass PTO networks in developing countries. Pressure to own facilities is such that, for instance, Cable and Wireless now has investments in about eighteen submarine cables and at least two satellites. Particularly in the Asia-Pacific region, private ownership of facilities is increasing very fast.

The second kind of investment is that directly into other states—foreign direct investment (FDI). Here, if it followed the pattern of FDI in general, one would expect telecommunications investment to be mainly between industrialized countries. However, because of regulatory difficulties in most of the major industrialized countries—only about 20 percent of the world market is truly open—FDI by telecommunications operators has primarily taken place in developing countries. In particular American operators invested in Latin America in the 1980s, and then, following the break-up of the USSR, in Central Europe during the early 1990s. Where developing countries have required loans from either multilateral or commercial institutions, the World Bank has insisted that the telecommunications operator should be privatized. As a result, foreign companies have entered the market in Africa and India. In fact the African market, often shunned by the West as too risky, has become a major forum for investment by Malaysia Telecom. In total in 1996 the value of equity offerings, privatization sales, and mergers involving telecommunications companies reached over $120 billion in 1996.[20]

It is becoming increasingly evident that the profits for Western companies are to be made from integrating the control of domestic operation and international linkages—as in prewar times. For instance Telefonica, the Spanish operator that runs a number of Latin American domestic networks, has joined Concert so as to exploit the routes between North and South America. It is this increasing penetration of international capital into the national telecoms market, and the channeling of revenues overseas, that is difficult to regulate so that telecommunications can serve national priorities.

Conclusion

Fueled by the falling costs of technology and by the mercantilist competition between governments and companies in the industrialized world, telecommunications is a sector witnessing increasing divisions between rich and poor. It is becoming difficult for those governments representing the majority of the world population to hope that they can construct networks with new technology to meet the needs of their populations. Technology may be cheaper, yet the possibility of gaining enough revenues to finance expansion becomes less feasible where countries are loaded with debt and hard currency is expensive. In any case the World Bank, serving Western interests, will not loan for any purpose without privatization of the telecommunications operator. Foreign investment is the only route. Yet foreign investment is actually a very expensive way for developing countries to borrow money, both in economic and political terms. In telecommunications, network operation, when handed over to a foreign company without proper regulation, involves the loss of ongoing network revenues and capital outflow in the repatriation of profits. Where private companies own both the domestic infrastructure and international links developing countries are returned to their pre-war situation of colonial appendages. And even where PTOs are retained, "call-back," satellite mobile services and lowered accounting rates threaten international revenues and potential expansion to meet even a minimum standard of universal service.

Free trade has always benefited the strongest. The massive increase in liberalization and private ownership of telecommunications operators and of international facilities has been pressed by the United States and Britain on the rest of the world, both in bilateral negotiations and in multilateral institutions. Both look to their multinational companies as large users and to the internationalization of their national operators. In particular the FCC, since the 1980s, has taken upon itself to unilaterally impose liberalization of market structure on the rest of the world—liberalizing submarine optic fiber and satellites in the 1980s; preempting radio spectrum allocation for its global mobile satellite operators in the 1990s; refusing to regulate "call-back," and most recently seeking bilateral limits on accounting rates. The result is an increasingly privatized international network, a fragmentation of ownership and standards, and domination by large consortia.

The United States has been particularly successful in transferring telecommunications regulation from the ITU to the WTO, where it is most powerful. Ironically, while urging liberalization on others, the U.S. network has not been liberalized. Instead the monopoly profits of the RBOCs have financed their ability to invest overseas in both industrialized and developing countries. That situation is ending as competition enters the local loop and the RBOCs are withdrawing from some foreign investments. Now the FCC will have to wrestle with the problems of "costs" and interconnection. Limited by the desire of the individual U.S. states to control intrastate communications, and without a unified regulatory system, it seems unlikely that the FCC will be able to pressure the WTO into accepting as universal those rules favorable to U.S. companies that it cannot impose within its own domestic market. Hence, for the time being, the U.S. universalist culture within multilateral institutions may diminish in telecommunications, to be replaced by increasing bilateral demands on operators to behave as the FCC wishes or face exclusion from the U.S. market.

In general, the restructuring of world telecommunications reflects the resurgence of the North and particularly the United States. Its domestic and international structure mirrors the increasing disparity between rich and poor. Despite the promise of cheaper technologies, the potential for their use to create greater democracy and equality, and the technological utopias such as the information superhighway—proselytized by the North as of benefit to the South—the reality of liberalization and privatization has been to benefit multinational companies and Northern mercantilist states. The enduring hallmark of the 1990s is the power wielded by multinationals in the drive for world economic integration, of which telecommunications is the vanguard. Multilateral agreements, such as that of the WTO, limit the sovereign rights of states and institutionalize the rights of penetration by the West. Further, the investment agreement in the process of negotiation in the OECD in 1997 promises to exclude national regulation to control multinational companies and to rollback the respect for sovereignty which formed the central plank of postwar international arrangements in the United Nations.[21] Hence, the current U.S. pressure in telecommunications that presages, by logical extension, the replacement of operators within sovereign states by two or three global satellite/cellular operators, subject to weak or nonexistent international regulation, is no more than an indication of a fundamental restructuring of postwar world economic relations set to institutionalize U.S. current competitive advantage, to further empower multinationals and resurrect the colonial political economy of the 1890s.

Notes

1. Charles Hampden-Turner and Fons Trompenaars, *The Seven Cultures of Capitalism* (New York: Doubleday, 1993).
2. Don Cruickshank, "From Regulation to Competition," *CSIS Internatonal Communications Studies program* (Washington: CSIS, 12 February 1997).
3. Eli Noam, "International Telecommunications in Transition" in Robert W. Crandall and Kenneth Flamm (eds.), *Changing the Rules: Technological Change, International Competition and Regulation in Telecommunication* (Washington DC: Brookings Institute, 1989), pp. 257-97.
4. Herbert Schiller, *Mass Communications and American Empire* (New York: Beacon Press, 1969).
5. Jill Hills, *Deregulating Telecoms. Competition and Control in the US, Japan and Britain* (London: Pinter, 1986).
6. G.C. Staple (ed.), *Telegeography* (London: International Institute of Communication, 1993).
7. ITU, *World Telecommunications Development Report 1994* (Geneva: ITU, 1994).
8. Azoulay, Pierre, "The GSM standard: An Impetus for the globalisation of Mobile Communications?" *Communications & Strategies* 21 (1996): pp. 95-134.
9. ITU, *The Missing Link, Report of the Independent Commission for Worldwide Telecommunications Development* (Geneva: ITU, 1984).
10. Jill Hills, "Dependency theory and its relevance today: International institutions in telecommunications and structural power," *Review of International Studies* 20 (1994): 169-186.

11. Commission of the European Communities, *Towards a Dynamic European Economy: On the Development of the Common Market for Telecommunications Services and Equipment,* Green Paper, Com (87) 290 (Brussels: 10 June 1987).

12. Commission of the European Communities, Commission Directive 95/51/EC, *Official Journal of the European Communities* L256/49 (26 October 1995).

13. Bangemann Report, "The High Level Group on the Information Society," *Europe and the Global Information Society. Recommendations to the European Council* (Brussels: CEC, 1994).

14. Cruickshank, "From Regulation to Competition."

15. Ibid.

16. Nicholas Denton, "Phone use grows as more prefer surfing to talking," *Financial Times* (13 March 1997).

17. Nancy Dunne, "US to urge cut in foreign monopolies' phone charges," *Financial Times* (18 December 1996).

18. Jill Hills, "A global industrial policy. US hegemony and GATT. The liberalization of telecommunications," *Review of International Political Economy* 1, no. 2 (1994): 257-280.

19. ITU, "The World Telecommunication Policy Forum Reaches Broad Consensus," *ITU News,* October 1996, pp. 3-7.

20. Nicholas Denton, "Value of telecoms deals double to £81bn," *Financial Times* (6 Jan 1997).

21. George Monbiot, "A charter to let loose the multinationals," *The Guardian* (15 April 1997).

The Privatization of Telecommunication

NICHOLAS BARAN

Much has been made of the great promise of the information age and the information highway. Self-proclaimed visionaries such as Bill Gates and Nicholas Negroponte envision a new golden age: with humanity globally connected, information at everyone's fingertips, and intelligent electronic agents liberating us from the mundane tasks of our daily lives—automatically paying our bills, retrieving electronic newspapers, making our coffee, and so forth.

Unfortunately, this panacea has little to do with the reality of the telecommunications industry today and in the foreseeable future. While much of the technology exists to fulfill Gates's wildest dreams, it runs up against the realities of profit margins and oligopolistic markets. Instead, we are likely to see many promising technologies shelved because they are not profitable, other technologies developed primarily for luxury consumption, and advertising and entertainment dominating the "content" of the information highway. This trend is already taking shape as more and more sites on the World Wide Web are cluttered with advertising banners scrolling across the screen and major Internet service providers are beset with huge financial losses.[1]

A Technological Transformation

It is nevertheless true that the telecommunications industry is at the threshold of a major technological transformation, which will have an enormous impact on our society. The basis of this transformation is the convergence of the digital computer and the analog telephone into a single communications device.

To briefly summarize what this transformation means:

Today, most telecommunications, such as telephone conversations and radio and television broadcasts, are transmitted by means of an *analog signal.* The analog signal is the natural *wave form* of most natural phenomena such as sound and light; for example, the *sine wave,* which gradually moves back and forth between a maximum and minimum value, is an analog wave form. It is, however, much more efficient to transmit these analog phenomena in *digital format,* which is represented by a simple on/off signal—that is, the signal is in one of two states: on or off.

As computers have become more powerful and software more sophisticated, it is now possible to convert virtually all forms of information, from photographs to feature length movies, into digital format. And the beauty of it is that once voice and graphic images are represented in digital format, they can be manipulated on a computer or transmitted on a computer network, just like any other digital data. It is the computer being able to manipulate sound and light that is the basis of the "digital age."

In a rational society, the prospect of the digital age could be very exciting. The recent advancements in digital communications could be used for education, for sharing information all over the world, for the enabling of political participation in remote areas, and for many other socially worthwhile endeavors.

Until its commercialization, the Internet was an example of a potentially positive development emerging from the so-called telecommunications revolution. If developed with international government sponsorship and cooperation, the Internet could indeed become an international communications network, available to people of all nations, rich and poor alike. But it is increasingly unlikely that this scenario will happen. The Internet is in the process of becoming a communications network for the affluent segments of society, supported by advertising and access fees that are unaffordable for a large segment of the population.

The reasons for this gloomy assessment are straightforward. The Internet has been turned over to private enterprise and major capital investments will be needed to support its growth and the demand for improved performance. Internet services providers (ISPs) such as America On Line (AOL), Compuserve, and Netcom, are sustaining huge losses due to cutthroat competition and the need to invest in additional capacity.[2] To finance these investments, the providers of Internet access are turning to advertisers, since most consumers have so far shown an unwillingness to pay higher access fees. In fact, in late 1996 ISPs reluctantly switched to a fee structure of twenty dollars per month with unlimited access, and the consequences have been devastating. It is safe to predict that these low access fees won't last. And aside from the Internet, the telecommunications infrastructure in general is in need of major upgrading that will require huge capital investments to support the high-speed digital services being touted by the telecom companies.

The Commercialization of the Internet

The Internet has evolved from a government-sponsored research network into the de facto information highway. The fact that the Internet exists at all, by the way, is testimony that government-sponsored institutions can sometimes be enormously effective. But for all of the valuable resources it has provided, such as electronic mail and database access, the Internet is heading toward full-scale commercialism. It is likely that within a few years users will have to wade through screens of commercials before they can access those resources. As mentioned earlier, this trend is already well underway. In addition, only users paying expensive fees will have high-speed access to the Internet. Several ISPs are in the process of changing from flat-fee unlimited access to a "pay-as-you-go" fee structure.[3]

It is worth briefly reviewing the Internet's history to understand its transformation into a commercial enterprise. Although the Internet has its origins in Defense Department research done in the late 1960s, it grew primarily out of a network designed to link up the National Science Foundation's (NSF) five supercomputer sites at the University of California at San Diego, Cornell University, University of Illinois at Champaign-Urbana, Carnegie Mellon University in Pittsburgh, and the National Center for Atmospheric Research in Boulder, Colorado. Called NSFnet, the network began operation in 1987 and provided high-speed connections between the supercomputer sites, so that researchers and scientists could access these sites remotely from government agencies and academic institutions. Regional networks were connected to the NSF "backbone" (a backbone can be defined as a continental-scale network carrier providing connectivity to regional networks), as well as to a similar network developed by the National Space Administration (NASA) called the National Science Internet. Thus the Internet grew into a national and ultimately international system of linked networks, allowing global access to electronic mail and databases, as well as other Internet resources such as news groups and, more recently, the World Wide Web.

Until a few years ago, the Internet was largely funded by the NSF, NASA, and other government agencies, and by academic institutions, which pay for access to the Internet. The actual services to operate the Internet were supplied under contract to the NSF by a company called Advanced Network & Services (ANS), which was a services company set up by MCI, IBM, and Merit Networks. This contract was terminated in the spring of 1995 as part of a transition from federal funding to full private commercial operation of the Internet. With the end of the contract with NSFnet, the equity partners (MCI, IBM, and Merit) sold ANS to AOL (essentially a sale of high-speed phone lines and related equipment, or "backbone infrastructure").

The Internet today is almost entirely funded by private enterprises ("network service providers") such as MCI, AT&T, and Bolt, Baranek, and Newman (BBN). These enterprises operate regional "network access points," which in turn sell Internet access to local service providers, private companies, universities, and now to government agencies. The government is essentially just another commercial customer. For example, the National Library of Medicine in Bethesda, Maryland, used to obtain Internet access through the NSFnet backbone, but now purchases connectivity from SURAnet, a regional network owned by BBN. Likewise, universities buy their network access from various service providers: Stanford University purchases network access from BARRnet, another regional network owned by BBN. Meanwhile, the government has started a new experimental research network under the auspices of the NSF called the Very High Speed Backbone Network Service (vBNS), which will continue to connect the supercomputer sites and provide the testbed for new "very high speed" network operations.[4]

Large institutions and corporations generally purchase their Internet access directly from the large regional service providers, paying substantial monthly fees which include twenty-four-hour support, guaranteed service, and other amenities. Smaller businesses and individuals, however, buy their access from local Internet service providers. Many of these providers are "mom and pop" operations that lease a few phone lines and sell access time to their customers. Because demand is increasing at a rapid rate, and the competition is fierce, it is likely that many of these "mom and pop" service providers will go out of business within the next few years. Even with the big ISPs increasing their access fees, the small-time players will be unable to keep up with the demands for new capacity and still make a profit.[5]

The Capacity Problem

As anyone knows who uses the Internet on a regular basis, its capacity is lagging behind the increased demand. Many resources are frequently unavailable. Transmission of graphic images crawls along at a snail's pace, and e-mail is becoming increasingly unreliable. The solution is to expand capacity by adding more high-speed telephone lines and network equipment, which will require huge investments by the telecom companies. This requirement for sizable investments in new capacity will ultimately force out the small-time service providers and increase the cost of Internet services.

The issue of capacity, or "bandwidth," is central to the economics of the Internet and other telecommunications systems, so it is worth considering in more detail.[6] The capacity to deliver electronic information is conceptually similar to the capacity of a pipe to deliver water—the larger the pipe, the greater the flow. Telephone lines can deliver information (whether voice or data) at a maximum rate that depends on the type of cable that is used and the type of information that is being transmitted. Transmission of the human voice requires relatively low capacity or low bandwidth cable, and the twisted pair copper cable found in every home or office is adequate to the task. Twisted pair copper cable is also adequate for fax transmissions and transmission of primarily text-based data files via modem. But twisted pair cable starts to bog down when transmitting graphic images or "multimedia" information consisting of sound and video. This bandwidth limitation is a major obstacle to the growth of the Internet and of technologies such as "video on demand," in which consumers will be able to rent movies across the phone line.[7]

Some technologies have been implemented to increase the bandwidth of twisted pair copper cable. The most popular of these is called Integrated

Services Digital Network (ISDN), which offers speeds more than twice as fast as the highest speed conventional modems available today. While it greatly improves the performance of the Internet, ISDN is still inadequate for full motion video and other multimedia services, and is expensive and complicated to install.[8]

Fiber Optic and Coaxial Cable Are The Solution

The two types of cable that offer the highest bandwidth are fiber optic cable and the coaxial cable used for cable television. Virtually all long-distance lines in the United States and transcontinental lines to Europe and Asia now consist of fiber optic cable. But these lines are the major trunk-lines that handle millions of telephone calls simultaneously, and also comprise the main back-bone lines of the Internet. Only a small percentage of local phone loops, which feed into offices and homes, employ fiber optic cable. These local lines are for the most part still twisted pair copper cable. It has been estimated that to wire most of the United States with fiber optic cable at the local level will cost from $200 to $400 billion and will take from twenty to thirty years to complete.[9]

Coaxial cable for cable television, on the other hand, is already installed in over 60 percent of U.S. homes, and "passes by" close to 90 percent of U.S. homes. This cable is owned by cable television companies such as Tele-Communications, Inc. (TCI) and Viacom. Coaxial cable can easily supply the bandwidth for high speed Internet access, as well as for multimedia and other digital information.

But there's a hitch—coaxial cable as installed today is designed for one-way communication. The current cable system uses *unidirectional analog amplifiers* to boost the signal transmitted from the cable company's distribution point, called the *headend,* out to the homes of its customers. These amplifiers will have to be replaced to accommodate the two-way communication necessary for Internet usage or other "bidirectional" communications, and this is an expensive prospect. In addition, although cable television is almost ubiquitous in residential areas, it has very little penetration in the office and business sector. The cable companies will therefore have to make major investments in new cable installations in office buildings to attract business customers. At this writing, only a few trial bidirectional cable projects are underway and access fees are considerably higher than for conventional Internet access.

The fact that a large coaxial cable infrastructure already exists in the United States gives the cable companies a technical edge over the telephone companies in establishing high-bandwidth network services. However, the cable companies don't have the cash to make the required infrastructure improvements. This lack of cash prompted a great deal of merger activity a couple of years ago between the telephone and cable companies, the most prominent being the proposed TCI-Bell Atlantic merger, which was initially valued at $16 billion, followed by the SBC (formerly Southwestern Bell)/Cox Cable merger valued at close to $5 billion.

These and other "cable/telco" mergers fell through shortly after they were announced. The ostensible reason for the collapse of these mergers was the lowering of cable TV rates by the Federal Communications Commission (FCC). The real reason, however, was that the telephone companies got cold feet. They weren't sure that consumers would be willing to foot the bill for the enormous investments required to build the so-called information highway. These fears have been substantiated by both customer surveys and actual trials of "broadband services" such as video-on-demand (Time Warner in Orlando, Florida, for example). Consumers are unwilling to spend more than about twenty-five dollars per month for information services, roughly what most consumers spend now for basic cable TV.[10]

Consumer resistance to higher fees, coupled with deregulation, make the prospect of major capital investment not only daunting, but extremely complicated. Currently, the regional Bells enjoy monopolies in their service areas. But what happens when several telecom companies all want to provide fiber optic service in the same neighborhood? Who is then responsible for maintaining the infrastructure? Or will we see competing companies digging ditches across the street from each other to lay their own fiber optic cable? A more likely scenario is that the telecom companies will try to maintain monopolies in their service areas by buying out their competitors. The proposed SBC-Pacific Telesis and Bell Atlantic/NYNEX mergers are good examples.

What Happened to Interactive TV?

At the time of the proposed cable/telephone company mergers in early 1994, most analysts and industry experts (including Bill Gates) predicted that interactive television would be the next major technological breakthrough in the telecommunications industry. The concept of interactive TV is also based on the convergence of digital and analog technology; in this case, the convergence of the personal computer and the television.

The idea of interactive TV is to place computing and telecommunications capabilities in a small "set-top box" that would control the television, allowing all sorts of digital information to be displayed on the television and enabling the viewer to respond much like he or she would on a personal computer, using an infrared pointing device or a keyboard (hence the term "interactive TV"). "Video on demand" (renting movies across the phone line) was to be the first service offered on interactive TV, followed by services such as those found on the Internet (electronic mail, electronic journals and libraries, electronic retail services, and so forth).

So far, interactive TV has been a bust, and there are a number of reasons for this. First, interactive TV is a far greater technical challenge than many of its proponents (namely the cable, entertainment, and telephone companies) had ever anticipated. Not only does interactive TV require enormous bandwidth (either fiber optic or several coaxial cable lines directly into the home), but it also requires enormous computing power and digital storage capacity. On top of that, the software required to control an interactive TV system is on a level of complexity similar to that of the air traffic control system, and it has proved to be a daunting task to develop this software.

These technical hurdles, coupled with consumers' reluctance to pay, have become a major source of discouragement to the telecom companies interested in interactive TV. In addition, the booming Internet became an attractive and very convenient alternative. After all, the Internet already exists and it is relatively inexpensive for consumers. The problem is that if the Internet is to evolve to provide the kinds of services envisioned for interactive TV, the same technical hurdles will have to be addressed, again requiring major new investments from the telecom companies.[11] It is ironic that the most recent attempt to combine TV and the Internet, called WebTV, has been a total flop, although the company has been acquired by Microsoft.[12]

Wireless Is Not The Answer

Wireless communication is not a viable solution to the capacity problem. For one thing, there is a finite and very limited amount of radio spectrum available. While there are virtually no physical limits to the expansion of our wired communications systems (we can just keep adding cable), we can't add to the radio and microwave spectrum. And radio frequencies have become a precious commodity. The FCC recently made available some frequency bands for so-called Personal Communications Services (PCS), which are intended to augment cellular telephone service with new features such as news and stock ticker reports being transmitted to hand-held devices. The FCC has been auctioning off licenses to use these frequency bands to companies that intend to offer PCS services, and has been receiving bids totaling close to $10 billion.[13] With such exorbitant entry rates, we can be sure that these PCS services will only be for the well-heeled consumer or business executive. In fact, many of the companies that won the bids for these frequency bands were to come into financial difficulties.

Cellular telephony is fine for voice communications, but offers limited capacity for digital data transmission, which requires much more precision than does the transmission of the human voice. Cellular telephony operates on the principle of cellular base stations "handing off" the signal from one station to the next. (Each base station serves a hexagonal area of approximately eight miles in diameter, which is called a cell—hence the name "cellular.") If you've ever had a conversation with someone on a cellular phone, especially long-distance, you can hear the pauses and "blank spots" as the signal is "handed off" from one cellular base station to another. These blank spots are a minor annoyance in a telephone conversation. They cause big problems, however, when data is being transmitted. Some digital techniques are now used with cellular telephony to allow transmission of data, but the bandwidth is low and the cost is high.[14]

The bottom line is that it makes much more sense to add fiber optic cable than to employ wireless communications to increase capacity. Wireless communications are well-suited for mobile applications, and for radio and television broadcasts (including satellite), and will most likely continue to be used primarily for those purposes.

Market Forces Will Ruin a Good Thing

As I mentioned earlier, the Internet was developed for research purposes, with funding from the federal government. The Internet was a brilliant technical achievement that never would have happened in the free enterprise marketplace. Until its recent privatization, the Internet existed for close to ten years without generating any appreciable profit for anyone; it certainly was not a big moneymaker for ANS, the private consortium that provided the network services. It has been an enormously useful resource for researchers and students, and for government agencies. It has provided links between scientists and researchers all over the world. It has allowed users to locate documents at far-flung libraries worldwide, and to access databases of scientific and medical research. It has also shown enormous potential as a vehicle for people to share information worldwide, as a powerful method to circumvent censorship and suppression of free speech. A good example was the use of the Internet by the people involved in the Chiapas revolt in Mexico to file reports that were suppressed by the Mexican media. Similar communications techniques have been used by the revolutionary movement in Burma.

The Internet has been a model of what can be achieved through the combination of public funding and innovative technology. Today, it is being transformed into an electronic shopping mall and sales catalog. And it is only a matter of time before many of the Internet's most useful attributes disappear in the wake of commercialization.

Similar considerations apply to the telecommunications infrastructure. With the current U.S. move to deregulation and the privatization of telecom companies around the world, it is clear that market forces will determine when and where the telecommunications infrastructure is modernized. The recent World Trade Organization pact to open up international telecommunications markets will only accelerate privatization on a global scale and the domination of the telecommunications behemoths.[15] This move to privatization in telecommunications is akin to turning over the transportation infrastructure (e.g. roads, highways, bridges) to private enterprise and then charging exorbitant tolls to travelers. (In fact, this very thing is beginning to happen with the privately financed construction of several new highways in the United States, which will only be accessible to paying customers.)

With telecommunications becoming a "product" controlled by private enterprise on a global scale, there is little doubt that a huge segment of the world's population will be denied the benefits of high-speed telecommunications. The technology will go where there is money to be made. Bill Gates and his fellow "visionaries" are not altruistic humanitarians. They are capitalists with a vision of ever greater profits, and unfortunately this appears to be the vision that will guide the information highway.

Notes

1. *The Economist,* 8 March 1997, p. 75.
2. Ibid.
3. Ibid.
4. For more background on the Internet, see N. Baran, "The Greatest Show on Earth," *BYTE,* July 1995.
5. N. Baran, "Privatizing Cyberspace," *The New Internationalist,* December 1996.
6. The term "bandwidth" comes from the term "frequency band," which has its roots in radio. In the context of analog radio, the wider the band, the more stations can transmit at the same time. In computer terminology, the wider the band, the more data can be transferred in a given period of time. For a more detailed discussion, see N. Baran, *Inside the Information Highway Revolution* (Coriolis Group Books, 1995).
7. The telecommunications companies have heavily promoted the concept of "broadband services," which basically means the transmission across the phone line of movies and other entertainment requiring high bandwidth (hence the term "broadband").
8. For more on ISDN and other technologies for twisted pair, see A. Reinhardt, "Building the Data Highway," *BYTE,* March 1994.
9. From a study commissioned by Hughes Electronic Corporation, a satellite manufacturer; see *PR Newswire,* 3 May 1994.
10. From a survey commissioned by Hewlett-Packard; see *Wall Street Journal,* 29 November 1994.
11. For more on interactive TV, see Baran, *Inside the Information Highway.*
12. *The Economist,* 8 March 1997, p. 75.
13. *Wall Street Journal,* 1 April 1996.
14. For more on wireless communications, see Baran, *Inside the Information Highway.*
15. "Telecom's Potential Shines in WTO Pact," *Los Angeles Times,* 17 February 1997.

Selling Our Children:

Channel One and the Politics of Education

MICHAEL W. APPLE

This is a time in which we are told that students are simply ignorant of the world around them and are incapable of fulfilling their duties as "citizens and workers." A good school must both be geared to economic needs and teach the right dispositions. Since schools are not doing either of these now, they must be radically "reformed." And those reforms that will work the best, we are again told, are either market-driven or entail the imposition of conservative mandates on values, religion, and "official" knowledge.[1] In this chapter, I want to focus on one of the fastest growing elements of "neoliberal" market-driven reform, one that turns schools and students into sites of competition for profit.

A harbinger of things to come has appeared, accompanying the recent growth of plans for privatization, for corporate control and funding for schools, for industry/school "cooperation." I am referring to a specific kind of "reform," a phenomenon known as Channel One. It is a commercially produced television news program that is now broadcast to thousands of schools in the United States. A description of it is overtly simple—ten minutes of international and national news and two minutes of commercials, originally produced very slickly by Whittle Communications, one of the largest U.S. publishers of material for "captive audiences." It has recently been purchased by K-III, a corporation that is listed in the Fortune 500 as earning $1.3 billion in 1996, and that is controlled by the leveraged buyout firm of Kohlberg, Kravis, Davis, and Roberts.[2] While the description of Channel One is easy, the implications are more profound.

Of course, twelve minutes of "the news" will not transform education. It will not automatically make students into "better informed citizens," able to take their respective places as more enlightened participants in the supposedly pluralistic democracy that is given such rhetorical weight in current discussions about the need for a more knowledgeable (and more disciplined and more competitive) citizenry. Yet, it is what Channel One signifies—the *officially sponsored* opening up of school content to commercial sponsorship and organization—that is the sea change here. In order to understand this, we need to place Channel One in its economic, political, and ideological context.

Taxes and Television

We have entered a period of reaction in education. Our educational institutions are seen as failures. High drop-out rates, a decline in "functional literacy,"[3] a loss of standards and discipline, the failure to teach "real knowledge," poor scores on standardized tests, and more—all of these are charges leveled at schools. And all of these, we are told, have led to declining economic productivity, a loss of international competitiveness, unemployment, poverty, and so on. Return to a "common culture," make schools more efficient, more competitive, more open to private initiative; this will solve our problems.

As I have claimed elsewhere, behind this is an attack on egalitarian norms and values. Rhetorical flourishes aside, the critics argue, in essence, that one of the major causes of "our" declining economy and culture is too much democracy, culturally and politically.[4]

As is all too well-known, the conservative restoration is not only occurring in the United States. In Britain, Australia, and many other nations, similar tendencies are quite visible. The extent of the reaction is captured by the former British secretary of education and science in the Thatcher government, Kenneth Baker, who evaluated nearly a decade of rightist governmental efforts by saying in 1988 that "the age of egalitarianism is over."[5] He was speaking positively, not negatively.

The threat to egalitarian ideas that this represents is never made explicit since it is always couched in the discourse of improving standards and quality in an educational system that is seen as in decline if not in crisis. This is especially the case with Whittle Communications' (and now K-III's) entire package of "reforms," from the founding of Channel One to Whittle's recent proposal to establish a national chain of private schools.

Channel One needs to be seen in the context of this conservative reaction. Its status as a "reform" and its acceptance in many schools can only be fully understood as a partial embodiment of a larger conservative movement that has had a considerable effect, not only on education, but on all aspects of the common good.

One result has been the transformation of our collective sense of the social roles schools are to play. Equalization of the opportunities and outcomes of schooling has increasingly been viewed, not as a public right, but as a tax drain. Public schooling—unless it is defined as meeting the more conservative goals now in ascendancy—is too expensive, economically and ideologically.

In the United States, among the major effects of this changing perception of schooling is that many states have had to make draconian cuts in education because of sharply diminished tax revenues and a loss of public support for schools. This has created a situation in which federal and state aid to local school districts—never totally sufficient in many poor districts—has been less and less able to keep up with mandated programs, such as classes for children with special needs or who speak languages other than English. It has meant that for many schools it will be nearly impossible to comply with, say, health and desegregation programs mandated by the state and federal governments, to say nothing of other needs.

Part of the situation has been caused by the intensely competitive economic conditions faced by business and industry. Their own perceived imperative to cut costs and reduce budgets (often regardless of social consequences) has led many companies to exert considerable pressure on states and local communities to give them sizable tax breaks, thereby cutting off money needed to finance public education. Such tax exemptions are not new by any means. However, in the increasingly competitive situation in which companies find themselves, and in a context governed by capital flight in which states and communities are justifiably fearful that businesses will simply go elsewhere, such breaks have drastically grown.

State, city, and county governments assemble packages that include the elimination or reduction of sales or property taxes or both, exemptions on new equipment, tax breaks for training new employees, and reductions on taxes for school improvements. In some states, the rewards go further. In Florida, for example, companies even get tax breaks for fuel consumption.

This has become a highly politicized area. For example, over the last few years teachers on strike in the state of Washington included a specific demand to eliminate corporate tax breaks in their list of grievances. In Cleveland recently, the school system was facing a $34 million annual deficit. The school district filed a complaint with the courts that maintains that it has been repeatedly damaged by the tax breaks that the city has given to business in the name of economic development.

The issues surrounding such breaks and outright exemptions are made even more powerful when compared to the withering criticism that the business community has leveled at the schools. This is coupled with the fact that business and industry have engaged in highly publicized programs of gift-giving to specific schools and programs. Such gifts may increase the legitimacy of the business community in the eyes of some members of the public. Yet, it is clear that the amount of money involved in these public displays is considerably less than the taxes that would have been paid. The results are often all too visible in the classrooms of America.

For many chronically poor school districts, the fiscal crisis is so severe that textbooks are used until they literally fall apart. Basements, closets, gymnasiums, and any "available" space are used for instruction. Teachers are being laid off, as are counselors and support staff, including school nurses. Art and foreign language programs are being dropped. Extracurricular activities— from athletics to those more socially and academically oriented—are being severely cut back. In some towns and cities, the economic problems are such that it will be impossible for schools to remain open for the full academic year.[6]

The superintendent of schools of one East Coast district put the situation bluntly: "I think it stinks." Facing even more reductions in essential programs, he concluded: "Nobody seems to care. They just say, 'Cut the Budget'." In the words of Harold Reynolds, Jr., at the time the commissioner of the Massachusetts Department of Education, "We really are in a kind of catastrophic situation."[7]

In the context of such a financial crisis—one that is spreading even to more economically advantaged districts—even those school systems that know that corporate gifts almost never equal the amount that is lost in "tax bargaining" will by necessity look for whatever assistance they can get. A contract with Channel One can seem quite attractive here.

The contract calls for schools to receive "free" equipment that will enable them to receive the broadcasts—a satellite dish, a VCR, and what amounts to approximately one television monitor for each classroom. At the same time, schools must guarantee that 90 percent of the pupils will be watching 90 percent of the time. The ten minutes of "news" and two minutes of commercials must be watched every school day for three to five years as part of the contractual agreement. The entire program must be shown; no editing of the advertisements is allowed.[8]

Always controversial, Channel One has a growing list of strong supporters. Thus, Texas has more than 1,000 schools that are committed to Channel One. One California school voted to reinstate Channel One even in the face of a warning by the state education authorities that they would cut off state funding to schools that were integrated into the network.[9]

The combination of "free" equipment and a content that most educators, community members, and the business community believe is important (the "news") makes it difficult to resist. When combined with Channel One's aggressive advertising campaign, which portrayed the program as a crucial ingredient in the transformation of a stagnant and overly bureaucratic educational system that left its students unprepared for the "real world," school officials can be convinced that allowing their students to be something of a "captive audience" is not a bad bargain. The partial success in this strategy can be seen in the fact that, while a number of states have prohibited or limited its use, nearly 10,000 middle schools and high schools have agreed to broadcast Channel One's version of the "news" everyday.[10]

Economic crisis; a sense that public schooling is in serious trouble; a feeling that students are not being taught the knowledge that they need in order to be competitive—all of this creates conditions in which Channel One becomes acceptable. This is reinforced by the increasing success of the right's hegemonic project of radically altering our discourse about education and all things public. It can be seen by some educators, then, not only as a warranted trade-off among equipment, "news," and an audience for commercials, but also as a legitimate reform that shows the way how business and education can cooperate. Indeed, William Rukeyser, executive editor of Channel One in the early 1990s and a former managing editor of *Fortune* and *Money* magazines, characterized Channel One as a "test case for the viability of 'vigorous partnership' between business and education."[11]

Creating the Captive Audience

We shall miss much that is happening here if we keep our focus only on internal educational issues. Rather, we need to keep in the forefront of our analysis a simple fact: Television, such as what we are considering here, is first and foremost a business.[12]

Chris Whittle founded Whittle Communications in 1970. Its primary targets have always been what I have called captive audiences, such as patients in doctors' offices. In a manner that presaged Channel One, Whittle would provide reading material free of charge for patient use if physicians would guarantee that no other magazines would be made available in the waiting area. Similar things were done with wall posters on health related issues, the assumption being that people with "time on their hands" would naturally read anything available, including material on a wall. Of course, advertisements were a key part of all the material.

In 1976, Whittle had revenues of $3 million. By 1989, its revenues topped $152 million at the beginning of the pilot project for Channel One. After its inception, revenues jumped to $210 million by June 1991.[13]

After completing the pilot program for Channel One, Whittle was more than a little optimistic, and deservedly so. Its field representatives aggressively recruited school systems throughout the country. The goal was 1,000 schools by March 1990 and 8,000 schools by 1992. Contracts exceeded that goal considerably by 1991.[14]

Channel One's rapid rise is truly phenomenal. After two years of development, it was launched nationally in March 1990. By June 1991, it had involved 8,700 schools in forty-seven of the fifty states, plus the District of Columbia. It had a viewing audience of 5.4 million students. This was fully one third of the population of thirteen- to eighteen-year-olds in the entire nation.[15] It is now seen by more than 40 percent of students in middle and high schools in the United States, and is increasingly making inroads into schools attended by our poorest youth.[16]

Whittle Communications' and now K-III's recognition of the realities of the fiscal crisis, and how it can be used rhetorically, is clear. Comparing Channel One to other attempts at producing news for classrooms, a spokesperson for Whittle put it succinctly: one word—*equipment*. No one else "provides schools with the equipment to receive and use their programming in the classrooms. [Other] services provide quality programming but it is like having a lot of gasoline and no automobile. Both have to be available to get anywhere."[17]

Yet, this is more complicated than it seems at first glance. The idea of a captive audience is given added meaning in the fact that not only are students sold as commodities to advertisers, but the satellite antennae itself is *fixed* to the Channel One station and, except in a few instances where courts have ruled otherwise, cannot be used to receive other programs. In essence, after the pilot program—which did offer "free hardware"—Whittle's representatives offered only free installation and the use, not the ownership, of a satellite dish and a number of television monitors.[18] The equipment itself would be lost if the contract was not continued.

Employing the discourse of the fiscal crisis as a rhetoric of justification has proven to be very effective, even given the fact that the "gift" of equipment is not quite as it seems. Yet, this discursive strategy doesn't fully encompass how Channel One works ideologically on the fears of many groups of people.

In order to accomplish its economic goals, Channel One became even more subtle in its attempts to link its concerns to the ideological tensions and conflicts being produced in the current "educational crisis." Channel One's advertisements capitalized on a particular construction of the literacy crisis. Students simply do not know enough about the world around them to participate effectively in a democratic society. Thus, one advertisement gives the example of a student who thought that Jesse Jackson was a baseball player and that silicon chips were a type of snack food.[19]

Channel One continually plays on this feeling that students are horribly misinformed about the world. In other promotional material, Channel One is seen as a workable solution to the problems generated by the fact that many secondary schools students identified "the District of Columbia as a Central American country and Chernobyl as Cher's full name."[20] At the same time, then, both business and education would form a partnership "in which each party receives direct and immediate benefits."[21]

This strategy of combining the overt urge to provide educational assistance with the aggressive search for profit has not been lost on the business community. Advertising agencies have also been quick to recognize the linkage between "ignorance of the world" and product advantage. A number of advertising directors have endorsed Channel One as a "media vehicle"; one called it "a very interesting medium for reaching an audience that's hard to reach." Said another: "It's an age when [students have] got to take tests on American and world geography and have no idea not only what the capital of their state is, or who their senators are, but think that Calcutta is a team on the National Football League. If this helps teach, and get facts across in an interesting and meaningful way, I don't see why educators wouldn't endorse it." With all this said, however, the primary reason advertisers have looked so positively on Channel One is stated rather starkly by one advertising executive: "Channel One provides an excellent targeting opportunity."[22]

That this is a *profitable* strategy is documented by the fact that a thirty-second commercial spot on Channel One was selling for approximately $120,000 in mid-1991, and is now as high as $200,000.[23] This should rise as more schools accept the program. To place this in context, it is a figure that is at least double the top-rated prime time news program. That this is a profitable *strategy* is evident in Whittle's own words. "Underneath everything we do . . . is the concept of targeted, high-impact, proprietary media systems. . . . Home-based media has dramatically declined as an environment for sending advertising messages. Place-based helps you target."[24]

Surrounding this, though, is still the public justification of providing content and material to schools who can ill-afford it. Thus, Channel One points out that expenditures for "defense" are ten times larger than those spent on education, at the very same time that in many states the amount of money spent on textbooks annually is as low as twenty dollars per student. As one spokesperson put it, "Somebody has to pay the bill for education, and commercials are the most direct way to pay."[25]

Notice what is happening here. At the same time that capital is involved in intense struggles to reduce the amount of taxes it pays and is engaged in concerted political, economic, and ideological attacks on schools, Channel One and its supporters are able to sell their own package of reforms by pointing out that business—through payments for commercials—will be paying for an enhanced education in citizenship for American students. The contradictions here are remarkable.

In the process, not only are schools increasingly incorporated into the market governed by the "laws" of supply and demand and by the "ethic" of capital accumulation, but students themselves become commodities. They too are bought and sold as "targets of marketing opportunity" to large corporations. Of course, schools have always been subject to pressure—often intense—by economically powerful groups. At the level of curriculum, as well, conglomerate publishers of textbooks have always seen schools and their pupils as sites for the generation of profit.[26] Yet there is an immense qualitative difference between wanting the educational system to do a better job at the "production of human capital" or at buying textbooks and material for classroom use, and the actual selling of students as potential consumers.

Inside Schools

While what actually counts as news on Channel One and in the media in general is a crucial issue (and the conservative nature of these choices has been discussed in considerably more detail elsewhere),[27] we need to remember that Channel One is of course *aimed* at someone—students. And students are not passive in the face of either Channel One as a whole, or its construction of important events and the "accepted" interpretation of them.

In many instances, the news was unimportant. Students and teachers *used* Channel One for different purposes. In my own research, teachers often pointed to the benefits of Channel One for them at the same time as they described how students used it.[28] As one teacher from Texas put it, "The best thing about it is the VCR. The kids and I basically ignore the news. But we can use the VCR in a lot of other areas." The idea of schools *using* Channel One to get what they can't usually afford documents the strategic moves going on from below, and this is important. However, and crucially, this same teacher went on to comment: "It was the commercials that got to the kids. My seventh and eighth grade students would try to guess which commercials would be on and would sing along with the jingles."

Here we need to understand what joy students get from commercials in the classroom, as opposed to the normal routine of school life. Without getting too postmodern, there is a complicated politics of pleasure at work here. Commercials provide an opportunity for "play," for collective enjoyment. The commercials are sometimes even parodied by the students in a manner not unlike Bakhtin's discussion of how carnival is employed to subvert authority.[29]

Let us not fall too easily into romanticism here. This possible subversion is fully contradictory, of course. The students *pay attention* to commercials. For all the fun they make of the ads, students are still being addressed as a consumer, positioned as a purchaser. While postmodern theory asks us to pay particular attention to the politics of consumption as a site of possible emancipatory actions, we still need to remember that here the students cannot collectively employ such subversions in any lasting collective ways.

Thus, we need to be very careful about being utopian in regarding what can go on in schools with Channel One. The program is seen by students and teachers inside classrooms, and there is no small amount of research on schools that documents how powerful the daily routines and pressures on students and teachers actually are. The structures of classroom life as well as the political economy of teachers' time and labor may make it very difficult for either teachers or students to engage in a *disciplined* deconstruction of Channel One, that would lead to a more organized critical sense of the politics of the news or of the carnivalesque of commercials.

Indeed, especially for teachers, this may be more difficult given the *intensification* of their work.[30] Teachers' work is becoming considerably more time-consuming. Almost never is anything dropped from the curriculum. Instead, time and again, more is added. And given the steady growth of accountability measures and tests, the amount of paperwork for which teachers are responsible is often overwhelming. It is more than a little romantic to assume that a large number of teachers will be able to spend already scarce time with students on deconstructing the news or "playing" with the commercials.

Thus, as teachers' work becomes increasingly intensified, even when teachers want to, there may be almost no time to counteract Channel One. This has to do not only with what time pressures will be like in classrooms, though that will be of considerable moment. We also need to focus on the lack of time outside the classroom as well. As I argued in *Teachers and Texts*,[31] many teachers have very little time even to simply keep up with their respective fields, more and more having to rely on outside "experts" and prepackaged curricular material and standardized texts, given the immense pressures placed on them to do and teach *more* in their classrooms.

This pressure-cooker atmosphere spills over into one's time at home as well. As has been well-documented,[32] the amount of paperwork to be done by teachers now has often reached such extreme levels that many teachers come in early in the morning and stay late after school, while facing up to two more hours at home each night, simply to keep up with the daily record-keeping, grading, and so on. This situation has been exacerbated considerably by the current accountability movement, where one gets the impression that administrators, legislators, and economically powerful groups have tacitly said that, in classrooms, if it moves it must be measured.

In such an intensified situation—where there is always more to do and less time to do it, for students as well as teachers—it is unrealistic in the extreme to assume that most teachers will have the time and resources to expand on and/or reconstruct what Channel One has determined is "the news." Whose "news," guided by what norms and values, taking what vision of society for granted, are questions of immense interest here. Commercials act as a "relief" in this situation, even while offering the theoretical possibility of a more politically interesting discussion.[33]

However, we still do need to remember that both students and teachers will not be passive. They will not simply internalize "the message sent." The lack of focus by students on the news itself, the fact that many students may read Channel One quite critically, the parodying of the commercials by some students—these things should make us sensitive to the ways in which Channel One can have complicated effects. All of this *does* offer possibilities for socially critical and committed teachers. But, once again, being sensitive and being naive about how students are positioned as consumers and sold as commodities, about whose perspectives *are* being presented, are not the same thing. We still need to face up to what is happening as honestly as possible.

Of course, there are other ways to contest Channel One aside from inside the classroom. This has been recognized by students themselves. Among the most interesting groups formed to challenge Channel One is UNPLUG, a youth-led organization that was founded in 1993 to fight commercialism in schools.[34] It has been a prime mover in the attempt to keep Channel One from entering into schools, to remove it from schools, and to employ it as a mobilizing device against the commercialization of education. The fact that the organization is youth-led shows that students and their supporters can be important sources of counterhegemonic activity in education.

Conclusion

Channel One is indicative of some of the ways larger economic, ideological, and cultural pressures from above and below create a context in which neoliberal and neoconservative movements tend to dominate education. It should not be seen simply as an imposition. Educational policy and practice are now and have always been the results of compromises at many levels with dominant groups attempting to shift the terms of the compromise onto their own terrain.[35] The example of Channel One demonstrates how a depressed economy, the discourse of crisis, and the concrete needs of schools create a climate that is conducive for the creation of students as a captive audience. A business/school partnership is formed in which business gets profits and legitimacy while schools get equipment and students get to be "informed citizens."

However, and this is absolutely crucial, the Channel One phenomenon also signifies something well beyond what happens to students and teachers in classrooms. It is a paradigm case of the social transformation of our ideas about public and private, and about schooling itself.

It is not just at the level of social goals or curriculum and teaching that the "industrialization" of education has proceeded. Channel One stands at the intersection of other tendencies as well. The right has attempted to turn our perception of schooling away from the idea of a common ground in which democracy is hammered out—an intensely *political* idea involving interactive notions of citizenship in a polity. Instead, the common set of democratic political commitments (no matter how weak) is replaced by the idea of a competitive marketplace. The citizen as a political being with reciprocal rights and duties is replaced by the self as *consumer*. Schooling (and students) becomes a "retail product." Freedom in a democracy is no longer defined as participating in building the common good, but as living in an unfettered commercial market, in which the educational system must now be integrated into that market's mechanisms.[36]

Elsewhere, I have discussed the inherent weaknesses of these consumerist proposals, such as voucher and choice plans.[37] The important point is to see the ideological reconstruction that is going on, to understand that in the process of making the school (or in the case of Channel One, the students as a "captive audience") into a product to be bought and sold, we are radically altering our definitions of what it means to participate in our institutions.

Participation has been reduced to the commercialization of all important public social interaction. The unattached individual, one whose only rights and duties are determined by the marketplace, becomes ascendant. While we don't want to be overly economistic in our analyses, the ideological imprint of our economy is hard to miss here. Perhaps the strongest example and symbol of this is Channel One.[38]

For the right, this has meant convincing the citizenry that what is public is bad and what is private is good. Hugh Stetton evokes the tenor of these claims when he says that:

> The commonest trick is this: of people's individual spending, mention *only the prices they pay*. When they buy a private car and a public road to drive it on, present the car as a benefit and the road as a tax or a cost. Tell how the private sector is the productive sector which gives us food, clothing, houses, cars, holidays and all good things, while the public sector gives us nothing but red tape and tax demands.[39]

While the convictions of a majority of the American people may not have been totally swayed by such conservative ideological tendencies, it is clear that the processes of redefinition are part of the larger strategies involved in the conservative restoration. Recent polls have shown movement toward acceptance of some of the positions represented by the right, by groups within the larger society.

Beyond ideology, the rapid growth of Channel One indicates that the internal dynamics of curriculum and teaching inside our classrooms—and our very children themselves—are now subject to major transformations. Like all "citizens," students will now be known as consumers. To go further, our children will now be bought and sold, consumed, as well. In everyday life, there is good news and bad news and news in between. Channel One is bad news.

Notes

1. See Michael W. Apple, *Cultural Politics and Education* (New York: Teachers College Press, 1996) and *Official Knowledge* (New York: Routledge, 1993).
2. Alex Molnar, *Giving Kids the Business* (Boulder: Westview, 1996), p. 74.
3. Definitions of functional literacy are not neutral and change over time. See Carl Kaestle, Helen Damon-Moore, Lawrence C. Stedman, Katherine Tinsley, and William Vance Trollinger, Jr., *Literacy in the United States* (New Haven: Yale University Press, 1991).
4. For further discussion of this, see Michael W. Apple, *Education and Power*, second edition (New York: Routledge, 1995), especially Chapter 6.

5. Madeleine Arnot, "Schooling for Social Justice," unpublished paper given at the l2th National Conference of the New Zealand Association for Research in Education, Auckland, New Zealand, 1990, p. 2.

6. Jonathan Kozol, *Savage Inequalities* (New York: Crown, 1991).

7. William Celis, "School Districts Reeling in Weakened Economy," *New York Times,* 5 June 1991, p. B10.

8. Alex Molnar, *Giving Schools the Business* (Boulder: Westview, 1996), p. 55.

9. For more on the California controversy, see ibid.

10. Larry Hoffman, "The Meanings of Channel One," unpublished paper presented at the American Educational Research Association Annual Meeting, Chicago, April 1991, p. 31. These figures are subject to change given the rapid growth of Channel One.

11. Ibid., p. 4.

12. Quoted in ibid., p. 32.

13. Ann Marie Barry, "Channel One: Controversial Partnership of Business and Education," unpublished paper, Department of Communications and Theater, Boston College, 1991.

14. Ibid., p. 1.

15. Ibid.

16. Molnar. *Giving Kids the Business,* p. 72.

17. Barry, p. 4.

18. Ibid., p. 2.

19. Ibid., pp. 9-10.

20. Ibid., p. 5.

21. Ibid., p. 18.

22. Ibid., p. 17.

23. Molnar, *Giving Kids the Business,* p. 66.

24. Barry, "Channel One," p. 25.

25. Ibid., p. 23.

26. See Apple, *Official Knowledge* and *Teachers and Texts: A Political Economy of Class and Gender in Education* (New York: Routledge, 1988).

27. Apple, *Official Knowledge.*

28. See ibid., pp. 93-117.

29. Peter Stallybrass and Allon White, *The Politics and Poetics of Transgression* (Ithaca: Cornell University Press, 1986).

30. Apple, *Teachers and Texts* and *Official Knowledge.*

31. Apple, *Teachers and Texts,* Chapter 2.

32. Andrew Gitlin, "School Structure and Teachers' Work," in Apple and Weis (eds.), *Ideology and Practice in Schooling* (Philadelphia: Temple University Press, 1983), pp. 193-212.

33. Thus, in many ways, the students' collective joy in playing with the commercials is equivalent to the machinists' creation of "homers," pieces of informal art that they make from scraps of metal left over when their quota of production is completed. Such "homers" are often aesthetically and personally interesting, but they do not interfere

with management's control of the content and process of the labor process. For further discussion of this, see Apple, *Education and Power.*

34. Molnar, *Giving Kids the Business,* p. 72.
35. For more on this, see Apple, *Cultural Politics and Education* and *Education and Power.*
36. Ibid.
37. Ibid.
38. It is important to note, however, that capital is not united in its support of Channel One and this may give us some reason for optimism. There is a split in the business community on this proposal, one brought on both by a fear of an expanding sphere of competition and a dislike for what might happen to students. Thus, the president of McDonald's in the United States, in arguing against programs such as Channel One, asks, "Do we want the classroom to become the new battleground for our companies? . . . The right thing to do is to give schools the audio-visual equipment for education, not for competitive advantage." See Barry, "Channel One," p.16.
39. Quoted in David Horne, *The Public Culture* (Dover, NH: Pluto Press, 1986).

Work, New Technology, and Capitalism

PETER MEIKSINS

The spread of computers and electronic means of communication has clearly transformed contemporary workplaces. Computers now sit on the desks of virtually all office-based workers, linking them to one another through local area networks (LANs), electronic mail, and complex information systems. Employees whose jobs involve significant amounts of travel are increasingly armed with an electronic arsenal of laptops, hand-held computers, pagers, and cellular phones. Programmable machinery, computer-aided design, computer-based inventory systems, and other innovations have reshaped industrial processes. And, arguably, the separation of work and residence that has characterized industrialized societies is being undermined by the emergence of electronically mediated home work.

Reaction to these innovations has been sharply divided between those who believe that they represent a radical transformation of the capitalist order and those who believe that they are just more of the same. Some take an optimistic view of the new technology, stressing its ability to empower workers by providing them with information and arguing that complex technologies require better-educated, more autonomous workers.[1] Futurists such as Alvin

Toffler predict the replacement of bureaucratic, centralized workplaces by home-based work in what he terms "the electronic cottage."[2] Some progressives share these visions of a transformed capitalism, arguing that we have entered an age of "flexible specialization" in which new technologies support loose networks of autonomous producers and create a workplace populated by autonomous, skilled workers.[3]

Most progressives, however, take a darker view of the new technology, emphasizing its capitalist character and its tendency to extend and deepen the harsh consequences of capitalist relations of production. They point to the use of computerized technology and networks to extend employer control over workers, even over long distances, and to create automatic systems that can replace the judgement and discretion of expert employees.[4] The reemergence of home work in the age of computers represents to these critics not the advent of decentered, autonomous work, but the growth of contingent, insecure employment, the cheapening of production, and the intensification of work.[5] It also reproduces and reinforces traditional patterns of gender subordination under capitalism, as women workers are obliged to take low-wage, insecure jobs that simultaneously perpetuate their status as the sole providers of (unpaid) child care and domestic labor.[6]

As is generally the case in such a polarized debate, it is possible to construct a strong argument that the truth lies somewhere in between. As will become clear below, both of these views of new technology are correct, for each points to a partial reality. However, simply saying that both views are "too extreme" is insufficient. For as is also often the case in polarized debates, the truth lies somewhere else. In focusing on the question of whether computers and electronic communication enhance or degrade work, we may have missed the point about these new technologies. The real lesson of contemporary technological change, I will argue, is that it reveals the conservative character of capitalism, its tendency to frustrate progressive social change. In Marxist terms, it reveals both the contradiction between the forces and relations of production and the prefiguring within capitalism of a new social order that cannot be realized without transcending capitalism.

New Technology and Networks of Firms

Coordinating the activities of disparate producers and finding effective ways of making their products available to consumers is one of the abiding problems of economic organization. This problem obviously becomes more difficult as economies grow in size and complexity. In advanced capitalist societies, it has been dealt with through large, centrally controlled economic units—corporations—whose apparently irreversible growth has marked the economic history of the twentieth century. Whether it was because they sought to eliminate or control competition, secure reliable sources of raw materials, increase market share, reduce their reliance on single product lines, control the pace of technological change, or assure commercial outlets for their products and services, capitalist enterprises have grown relentlessly—creating oligopolies or even monopolies, integrating vertically, and buying up unrelated enterprises. Such corporations substitute the "visible hand" of the organization for the invisible hand of the market, coordinating producers and consumers through the creation of enormous centers of economic power whose political, environmental, and social consequences have long been the object of radical critique.[7] Among other things, these economic giants have been criticized as the source of intrusive control over people's lives, both at work and outside of it, and as a homogenizing force which tends to eliminate individual liberty, spontaneity, creativity, and freedom of choice.

A parallel set of problems affected the countries of "actually existing socialism." In their efforts to eliminate petty-bourgeois enterprise and to accelerate the pace of economic growth, these societies also spawned massive economic and political units. Bureaucratic administrative structures and complex economic planning became the central mechanisms for the coordination of economic activity within and between these giant organizations. One of the most enduring criticisms of the erstwhile Soviet bloc focused on precisely this aspect of its social development; the giant enterprises and state bureaucracies that dominated its social landscape were generally regarded as inimical to freedom and creativity and were frequently counterposed to the alleged diversity and individual freedom characteristic of the West. While the latter is clearly mythical, this in no way alters the fact that the Soviet Union and its allies were grey, bureaucratic, and overly centralized.

Both capitalist and socialist versions of giant enterprise have always been based on the assumption that centralized control of economic activity is desirable and necessary in order to ensure that otherwise egoistic individuals and/or enterprises coordinate their activities behind goals imposed from above and pursue these goals in a reasonably predictable way. Yet this assumption has always been partially contradicted by the realities of economic life. Within capitalist enterprises, top managers learned that it was impossible to coordinate complex hierarchies using simple bureaucratic procedures; instead, they were forced to experiment with what one business historian has referred to as "decentralized centralization," allowing managers at various levels of the corporate hierarchy a degree of autonomy.[8] Similarly, the countries of the former Soviet bloc were led to experiment with various kinds of market mechanisms as they searched for an antidote to the problems of the highly centralized planned economy.

One of the potential consequences of the new technologies is to create a technological basis for alternative ways of organizing economic activity, for pushing further some of the embryonic efforts to decentralize economic activity mentioned above. Since these technologies facilitate rapid communication over long distances, it now is possible for widely separated enterprises to coordinate their activities. Moreover, since they also are able to provide individuals and/or enterprises with sophisticated, up-to-date information about markets, the behavior of other actors within the technological network, and other relevant matters, those individuals and/or enterprises no longer need to be confined within rigid, prescriptive plans and procedures set well in advance. Instead, with an understanding of what is expected of them, they can react autonomously and creatively to the information provided through the technological link.

There is already some evidence that these possibilities are being explored, although in capitalist ways, which largely contradict their potential. For example the much-publicized reengineering of capitalist enterprises has encouraged the externalization of activities once performed in-house. Companies now rely more and more on networks, consultants, business service providers, and suppliers; vertical integration is no longer regarded as, in itself, the best option for the coordination of economic activity. As companies have moved in this direction, however, they have had to learn to coordinate the activities of growing numbers of often physically distant providers over whom they lack direct, bureaucratic control. While this problem involves more than simply technology, it is clear that new technologies have been very important to the solution of these problems, as they allow for the development of complex "just-in-time" processes that require split-second timing. They also facilitate quick, effective communication among cooperating enterprises, and allow for work to take place offsite and still be linked to the central activity it supports. Such developments have encouraged speculation about the emergence of network firms, i.e., the replacement of giant, bureaucratic corporations by loose associations of cooperating enterprises.[9]

Some fragmentary evidence exists of real cooperative relationships based on these developments. For example, Annalee Saxenian argues that in the Silicon Valley, traditional corporate boundaries have broken down at least in part, allowing for cooperative relationships among companies and their suppliers, and for communication and information-sharing among companies that actually compete with one another.[10] Similarly, some observers contend that the relationships among companies and their suppliers in Japan involve substantial cooperation, reciprocity, and sharing of risk, aided by electronically mediated information exchange.[11] Yet while one can point to instances of such cooperation, most of the evidence on networks, industrial regions, and inter-firm cooperation suggests a very different reality. Bennett Harrison's recent synthesis, *Lean and Mean,* argues persuasively that most examples of interfirm cooperation turn out, upon examination, to be illusory or, at least, to involve relations of domination and subordination among firms. The much-vaunted industrial districts, where cooperative networks of firms are supposedly most developed, turn out to be vulnerable to the emergence of dominant firms or to intrusion by giant corporations from outside. Rarely are relations between suppliers and their customers as reciprocal as they are characteristically represented in the Japanese case; instead suppliers tend to be subordinate to the larger companies they supply. Overall, Harrison finds that the contemporary economy has been marked by decentralization, but that economic power remains highly concentrated.[12] The capitalist character of economic organization militates against true cooperation and reciprocity, encouraging instead the continued concentration of economic power in a few hands and the imposition of control from the center.

A similar phenomenon may be observed in the case of franchising. In many ways, franchising suggests a solution to the problem of how to combine a degree of centralized control and planning with a level of individual enterprise autonomy. The central franchising agency could serve as coordinator, receiving information and commentary from individual franchises, which now can be transmitted and processed extremely rapidly as a result of new technologies. Individual franchises, however, could remain substantially autonomous, engaging in an electronically mediated dialogue with the central authority and with other franchises, and responding creatively to feedback and information received from both sources. Thus, a kind of centrally coordinated noncoercive network might replace the bureaucratic controls characteristic of traditional enterprises in both the capitalist and socialist worlds. Yet as virtually all analyses have shown, franchising is rarely if ever about balancing autonomy and central control. Instead, the emphasis within franchise arrangements has always been on decentralizing risk and centralizing control; both legal arrangements and new technologies are used to eliminate local autonomy and to maximize the degree of control from the center.[13] Franchises have been the very opposite of what they might be, to the point that it almost seems absurd to speculate in this way.

Informating Technology?

A second example of the contradiction between the possibilities of the new information and communication technology and capitalist relations of production may be seen in the use of information systems within capitalist enterprises. Many of the new technologies make possible the dissemination of sophisticated information to individuals throughout organizations; this information could become the basis for enhanced decision-making at all levels. As one observer has put it, new technologies can be used to "informate" rather than to automate, placing human discretion back at the center of economic activity.[14] However, the reality is that corporations resolutely resist this approach and attempt to use new technologies to centralize authority even further.

As has been well documented, sophisticated computer-based technology has affected the job of machinists in profound ways. Computerized numerical control (CNC) machinery effectively links machine tools to computers and builds in sophisticated feedback loops so that the computer can adjust to changing conditions while operations are going on. In effect, this technology allows machinists' skill and experience to be programmed, threatening their eventual elimination. At the same time, CNC's effects are not unambiguously negative. Computers need to be programmed, and the possibility exists that machinists could be retrained as programmers rather than be eliminated. More importantly, CNC devices can be installed so that they allow for direct intervention by workers on the shop floor. In this way, machinists are not eliminated from the process; on the contrary, they are given a degree of control over increasingly sophisticated machinery, which allows them to do work which they would have been unable to do before. Indeed, some studies of CNC indicate that some machinists see the ability of new technology to work to finer tolerances as a tangible benefit of technological change.

Under capitalist conditions, however, it is the dark side of CNC that tends to be emphasized. Employers define the new technology as a way of replacing expensive, recalcitrant skilled workers, and are reluctant to allow them to intervene directly in its use. At best, machinists are retained only as a safeguard against inevitable failures and breakdowns of any complex technology. Similarly, employers are generally reluctant to retrain machinists as programmers, despite the obvious advantage of making use of their expertise, because they are more interested in lowering the cost of labor and in replacing unionized machinists with programmers, who typically are not unionized.[15]

In a different context, new information systems in banking illustrate a very similar process. The installation of sophisticated information systems allows banks to generate, process, and circulate information about customers, financial markets, and other matters almost instantaneously. Because these data are generated automatically, and because they are on-line, they can, in principle, be accessed by any bank employee with a networked computer terminal. The "informating" implications of this technology are quite clear; but how has the technology, in fact, been used?

Studies of contemporary banking indicate that the technology has been defined largely as a device for replacing labor, in this case, middle management labor. Middle managers, who once generated much of the data that is now processed automatically, and who supervised lower-level tellers and bank workers, are being replaced as the computers do their work for them and as some of the work they once did is delegated, in highly formatted ways, to lower-level workers linked to computer terminals. The distinction between bank managers' work and that of tellers is increasingly blurred: tellers are slowly replaced by on-line banking systems such as ATMs, and the information systems are used to allow for centralized control over those tellers who remain.[16] Studies of contemporary office automation find a similar process of replacing middle-level managers and professionals.[17] As Shoshana Zuboff found in her original discussion of "informating" technology, managers have great difficulty accepting technological change unless it is defined as a way of replacing labor and reducing labor costs.

Thus, capitalist relations of production constitute technology as a way of controlling and replacing labor, and impede the possibility that technology might democratize the workplace. Yet, even under capitalist conditions, the contradictions of this use of the new technology begin to become apparent. In their zeal to create information systems that restrict employee behavior and control their actions, designers and managers may actually disable the organization; by failing to incorporate formal organizational practices into the design, they may prevent employees from doing their jobs. The result is that they may be forced to disable the very systems and turn them, at least in part, to their own ends.[18] In the case of banking, the contradictions are even more obvious. Systems are installed with the explicit purpose of reducing teller discretion, replacing middle management, and increasing centralized control over information flow and the behavior of employees. Yet at the same time, under pressure from external markets to extend the range of banking services available to customers, banks are forced to "upgrade" tellers; the new technology is used to provide tellers with information and abilities that they can use to sell a wide variety of banking services and products to customers. Banks are clearly uncomfortable with this contradiction, and do whatever they can do to limit and "program" away teller discretion. Nevertheless, the underlying contradiction does not disappear and the possibilities of the new technology cannot be entirely suppressed.

Home Work

Finally, we come to electronically mediated home work, which has become the focus of much contemporary comment on the effects of new communication and information-processing technology. Much of the speculation about how new technologies are revolutionizing the work/home distinction may be dismissed as pure fantasy or wishful thinking. Such a radical transformation of fundamental social relations is simply not compatible with capitalist relations of production. However, careful examination of the realities of electronically mediated home work under capitalism reveals how the new technologies might, under different circumstances, facilitate such a transformation. Indeed, it is already emerging, in embryonic form, in the experiences of certain kinds of contemporary home workers.

It is abundantly clear that the new information and communication technology does make possible a significant shift of work away from centralized workplaces. In particular, the ability of individuals to log on to computerized information systems and networks from remote locations eliminates many of the traditional obstacles to working offsite. Most jobs require access to information and a degree of communication among individuals. New technologies have substantially reduced the degree to which these are dependent upon spatial proximity. Some limits on real work may remain, making speculation about the demise of all central workplaces unrealistic. For example, there is considerable evidence that certain kinds of team work, especially that involving brainstorming, depend on direct, face-to-face interaction.[19] It is also unclear that everyone would want to work offsite all the time, even if such work were organized in desirable ways; some individuals clearly prefer to separate work and residence, and find the experience of working at home to be isolating. Nevertheless, the potential for a considerably more decentralized workplace exists, in large part because of the development of new communication and information technologies.

The existing research on home work indicates that it is a diverse phenomenon, including everything from highly exploited low-wage workers to well-paid professional telecommuters. Few generalizations about such a diverse group of workers are possible. However, if we consider the experiences of one segment of the emerging group of electronically mediated home workers, the potentially transformative implications of home-based work become apparent. The fact that their experience is not typical indicates the degree to which capitalism impedes the development of potentially desirable new work arrangements that use new technologies in creative ways.

As indicated above, one segment of the new electronically mediated, home-based workforce consists of well-paid telecommuters. Cultural workers, technical professionals (such as engineers or computer professionals), business consultants, and others are able to perform much of their work at home while retaining many of the most desirable elements of their jobs. As Phizacklea and Wolkowitz note in their study of home work, such workers are able to avoid choosing between work and a career; instead, they are able to combine gratifying work, high incomes, and high levels of autonomy with the personal satisfaction of being able to avoid travel and spend more time with their families. These home workers may pay a price in the form of delayed or even reduced career opportunities. But one can argue that this is a choice they have made freely and that the cost is relatively low, inasmuch as they still have desirable jobs and have enhanced other aspects of their day-to-day lives.[20] They are in the unusual position of having been able to negotiate flexible work arrangements of a kind that significant numbers of employees apparently would like but are unable to obtain because of the rigidity of most employment relationships.[21]

While the experiences of these home workers indicate the potential of new technologies to support desirable, alternative work arrangements, the experiences of most workers suggests that these are highly unlikely to be realized under capitalism. To begin with, the experience of these relatively privileged home workers is not typical; most electronically mediated home work is of a very different, far less desirable character. Most employers define home work as something they allow if it is cheaper than on-site work. Given this motivation, it should not surprise us that large numbers of home workers are poorly paid clerical and manual workers who perform routine labor. Such workers are particularly likely, as well, to have insecure and/or part-time jobs that offer few or no benefits and are subject to obtrusive, sometimes electronic supervision. Under capitalism, the imperative to reduce labor costs trumps all other determinants of the organization of work, making the worker who does billing for an insurance company, not the highly paid professional, the paradigmatic home-based worker.

Moreover, it is striking that most employers resist the extension of home-based work. In general, they are reluctant to allow it in high-skill, high-pay jobs; unless they are under real pressure, such as the need to recruit and retrain individuals with scarce skills, employers tend to define this kind of work as inappropriate for remote work. Instead, they continue to organize these jobs on the assumption that they must be performed on-site and demand the absolute, undivided attention of the employee. Such employment, in other words, continues to require long hours and demonstrations of employee loyalty and commitment. The true measure of that loyalty and commitment continues to be hours spent at work, on site.

At the root of this reluctance to extend opportunites for desirable forms of home work are employer concerns about control.[22] Employers resist off-site work because they are uncomfortable with the idea that they cannot physically observe the work being performed. This is a particularly formidable obstacle for more desirable forms of work; because of their inability to oversee such work in rigid, obtrusive ways, employers have traditionally relied on unobtrusive forms of control, including the construction of project teams (within which employees supervise one another), tests of loyalty (involving extreme time demands), and meetings (in which both formal and informal pressures can be applied). They recognize that allowing off-site work would require them to develop new ways of supervising professional workers. In the absence of effective economic pressures to increase the amount of home work, they prefer to rely on traditional methods for organizing such work, which allow them to use the physical location of the worker as part of a system of control. Employers continue to insist on being able to see professional and other privileged workers, despite the fact that the small numbers of home workers in these fields show no indication of being any less productive than their on-site counterparts. Home work is thus confined for the most part to forms of routine work, in which the employer can determine for the worker how work is to performed, and in which mechanisms such as piece work can be used to "motivate" employees. Capitalist impulses to reduce costs and maintain control over employees militate against other possible arrangements.

Finally it should be added that employer reluctance to allow home work is particularly acute in the case of men. When female workers ask for flexible work arrangements such as home work, employers can reconcile these demands with traditional definitions of gender. The assumption that it is women who will be primarily responsible for child care and domestic labor is used to justify seeing home work as "appropriate" for women. In contrast, a man who asks for home work or other unconventional work arrangements is challenging traditional assumptions about gender. The usual justification for home work, i.e., the desire or need to be at home to perform child care, is not available to male workers, even if they were inclined to use it, because employers generally do not see this as legitimate in the case of men.

Moreover, few men are inclined to ask for home work for these reasons. Research on home workers indicates clearly that men are far less likely than women to indicate child care as the primary reason for working at home. Instead, they are likely to mention other advantages, such as autonomy and reduced commuting time. Given the traditional gender division of labor, men perform less domestic labor and are far less likely than are women to feel compelled to rearrange their work to accommodate domestic responsibilities.

As a result, home work is profoundly marked by gender. Most home workers are women and most employers define home work as more appropriate for women than for men. This imposes further limits on the possibilities for extending home work under contemporary capitalism. If home work is only for women with small children, most men will not seek it and will not obtain it even if they do. Moreover, as home work comes to be defined as something for only a specific group of female employees, many women will not seek it either, seeing it, probably correctly, as a kind of "mommy track" employment which at best represents a temporary respite from traditional forms of work, and at worst will have long-lasting negative consequences for job security and careers.

Conclusion

I have argued in this brief review that the most important lesson to be learned from our experience with contemporary electronic and information technology concerns what it tells us about capitalism. These technologies are being used in both positive and negative ways in contemporary workplaces. However, what is most significant is the extent to which employers resist the possibilities for using them in positive ways, even when they are faced with real pressure to do so. In reality, the existence of positive applications of the new technology is testimony to the ability of individuals to resist the normal tendencies of capitalist relations of production, as well as to the contradictory character of capitalism which tends to create impulses for change which it cannot fully accomodate.

Some observers would have us believe that choices about technology and its uses are simply a matter of culture. Zuboff, for example, tends to suggest that realizing the informating potential of new technology is simply a matter of overcoming managerial resistance, defined in largely cultural terms as habit and ideology. Others counterpose the allegedly more enlightened Japanese approach to new technology to the conservative, punitive approach adopted by U.S. companies. There can be no denying the fact that culture, in these senses, is a factor shaping the way technologies are being applied. But it also must be remembered that managerial attitudes do not take shape in a vacuum and that national differences do not eliminate the underlying character of capitalism. The most remarkable thing about the emerging communication and information technologies has been the degree to which, in all countries and companies, there has been resistance to its full development. In this sense, the new technologies are not, as some have suggested, the underpinning of a new "disorganized capitalism," qualitatively different from the one that preceded it.[23] Instead they reveal the extent to which capitalism is organized as it has always been, as a mode of production based on exploitation and control of labor, a fact which makes it unlikely that the potential of the new technology to facilitate the reorganization of work will be realized.

Notes

1. Shoshana Zuboff, *In the Age of the Smart Machine* (New York: Basic Books, 1988); Larry Hirschhorn, *Beyond Mechanization* (Cambridge, MA: MIT Press, 1984).
2. Alvin Toffler, *The Third Wave* (New York: Morrow, 1980).
3. Michael Piore and Charles Sabel, *The Second Industrial Drive* (New York: Basic Books, 1984).
4. Barbara Garson, *The Electronic Sweatshop* (New York: Simon & Schuster, 1988).
5. Eileen Boris, *Home to Work* (New York: Cambridge University Press, 1994), especially Chapter 10.
6. Annie Phizacklea and Carol Wolkowitz, *Homeworking Women* (London: Sage Publications, 1995).
7. Alfred Chandler, *The Visible Hand* (Cambridge, MA: Harvard University Press, 1980).
8. Ibid.
9. Water Powell, "Neither Market nor Hierarchy: Network Firms Organization," in Barry M. Staw and Larry L. Cummings (eds.), *Research in Organizational Behavior*, (Greenwich, CT: 1990), pp. 295-336.
10. Annalee Saxenian, *Regional Advantage* (Cambridge, MA: Harvard University Press, 1994).
11. For example, see Ronald Dore, *Flexible Rigidities: Industrial Policy and Structural Adjustment in Japanese Economy, 1970-1980* (London: Athlone Press, 1986).
12. Bennett Harrison, *Lean and Mean: The Changing Landscape of Corporate Power in the Age of Flexibility* (New York: Basic Books, 1994).
13. For a useful discussion of franchising, see Alan Felstead, *The Corporate Paradox: Power and Control in the Business Franchise* (London: Routledge, 1995).
14. Zuboff, *In the Age of the Smart Machine.*
15. For discussions of CNC, see David Noble, *Forces of Production* (New York: Oxford University Press, 1984); Bryn Jones, "Destruction or Redistribution of Engineering Skills? The Case of Numerical Control," in Stephen Wood (ed.), *The Degradation of Work?* (London: Hutchinson, 1982), pp. 179-200; Leslie Nulty, "Case Studies of IAM Local Experiences with the Introduction of New Technologies," in Donald Kennedy, Charles Craypo, and Mary Lehman (eds.), *Labor and Technology: Union Response to Changing Environments* (Pennsylvania State University Department of Labor Studies, 1982), pp. 115-30.

16. See Vicki Smith, _Managing in the Corporate Interest: Control and Resistance in an American Bank_ (Berkeley: University of California Press, 1990); Harold Salzman and Stephen Rosenthal, _Software By Design_ (New York: Oxford University Press, 1993).
17. See Barbara Baran, "Office Automation and Women's Work: The Technological Transformation of the Insurance Industry," in Manuel Castells (ed.), _High Technology, Space and Society_ (Beverly Hills, CA: Sage Publications, 1985), pp. 143-71.
18. See Salzman and Rosenthal, _Software by Design_.
19. See Peter Meiksins and Peter Whalley, "Technical Workers and Reduced Work: Limits and Possibilities," paper presented to the American Sociological Association meetings, Washington, DC, 1995, for an assessment of some of the technical limits on off-site work.
20. Phizacklea and Wolkowitz, _Homeworking Women_, pp. 112-16.
21. See Lotte Bailyn, _Breaking the Mold: Women, Men and Time in the New Corporate World_ (New York: Free Press, 1993), for a somewhat utopian discussion of this issue.
22. The arguments in this section are developed more fully, with particular reference to the case of part-time professionals, in Peter Meiksins and Peter Whalley, "Expertise at Arm's Length: Controlling Technical Workers in the New Workplace," paper presented to the 14th Annual International Labor Process Conference, Birmingham, UK, March 1996.
23. See Scott Lash and John Urry, _Economies of Signs and Space_ (London: Sage Publications, 1994).

Fighting Neoliberalism in Canadian Telecommunications

ELAINE BERNARD and SID SHNIAD

In today's brave new globalized world, corporations and governments are turning back the clock, dismantling programs, services, and regulations that society has taken for granted for more than fifty years. Nowhere is the destructive collusion more dramatic than in the field of telecommunications.

As has been the case in so many other areas, the neoliberal program in telecommunications has been promoted as beneficial to all segments of society. But the reality has been dramatically different. Antisocial developments in telecommunications foreshadow what may be in store in other sectors if capital is allowed to set its own agenda.

Consider changes in labor-management relations in the socially regulated telephone sector. For fifty years prior to the AT&T divestiture in 1984, North American telecom unions practiced what could be described as "bread and butter" unionism. While telephone workers struck occasionally over wages and benefits, they rarely challenged management's right to manage the industry as it saw fit. This conservative approach to unionism yielded positive results for telephone workers: phone companies paid decent wages and provided stable employment to their unionized employees. Management had good reason to practice this benevolent paternalism, since telephone workers had significant bargaining power in their relationship with management. Because the technology at the heart of the telephone system was far from dependable, it was prone to problems which had to be addressed immediately. Transmission or switching failure could easily disrupt service to a significant number of customers; telephone companies needed large numbers of specially trained and skilled workers to keep their systems functioning smoothly.

At the same time, the skills needed to keep these systems operating tended to be specific to the telephone industry and acquired through on-the-job experience, rather than through outside technical training. In most cases, even the work related to billing activity and interaction with customers was unique to the telephone industry, and therefore of limited use elsewhere. So the fact that these workers and their skills could not be readily replaced served to increase the workforce's bargaining power while the limited applicability of their skills served to tie them to the company that employed them.

Under the regulated monopoly arrangement, the absence of competition gave phone companies flexibility over the pricing of their services and enabled them to carry out long-term planning. These factors, coupled with the steady incremental increase in productivity which characterized the industry, allowed management to accommodate workers' demands for regular wage increases. Because government regulation included the monitoring of phone companies' service quality, management had a bottom-line interest in providing high quality service as well as maintaining the workforce necessary to provide it. In short, a variety of factors contributed to a relationship of reciprocal dependency, creating an implicit social compact in the industry.

The symbiotic relationship that existed between phone companies and their workers was reflected in the fact that telecom unions often sided with employers at regulatory hearings. They felt that their members' wages and job security depended on the companies' prosperity and therefore acquiesced to management's attempts to pass on cost increases to consumers. In this environment, phone unions rarely worked with consumer groups. Consumer activists who participated in regulatory proceedings consequently tended to see telecom unions as being in bed with their employers.

The Scourge of Deregulation

Economic deregulation, which originated in the late 1970s in the transportation industry and spread to communications in the 1980s, constituted an attempt by big capital to end government interference in the market. Big business was keenly aware that governments' regulatory pursuit of social goals raised its telecommunications costs.

Under the social regulation that governed the telecommunications industry, long-distance voice services—mostly used by large companies—were priced above cost. A significant portion of the resulting revenue was used to defer the cost of providing local service, thereby benefiting the general public. This arrangement, known in the industry as cross-subsidization, was the basis for the spread of universally available, affordable telephone service throughout the United States and Canada.

While phone companies were never thrilled with this regulatory arrangement, they were willing to tolerate it because regulation gave them a monopoly over the lucrative portion of the business, guaranteeing them an enviable rate of return. At the same time, however, the existence of government regulation and the resulting structure of socially determined telephone rates was a major irritant to phone companies' corporate customers.

Adamant in their desire to reduce their communications costs and reshape the industry to meet their needs, large business users mounted the campaign that resulted in the deregulation of the phone system. In a forerunner of the process that has since come to be known as globalization, the corporate sector in the United States, Britain, and Japan mounted unprecedented campaigns to force their respective governments to abandon social oversight of the telecommunications industry, and to allow competition in the highly profitable long distance part of the business, in order to reduce their communications costs and to reshape the industry to more closely address their organizational needs.

Thanks to the success of these corporate efforts, the regime of social regulation which prevailed in telecommunications for the first seventy-five years of the century was dismantled. The ensuing deregulation and competition have generated lower communications costs for large corporate users and individuals at the high end of the income pyramid. Contrary to the disingenuous promises made by the promoters of competition when the issue was still in dispute, however, the resulting changes did not benefit ordinary telephone users, since the vast majority of phone users have seen the rates charged for plain old telephone service skyrocket.

At the same time, deregulation has allowed phone companies to neglect service quality. As a result, they have laid off tens of thousands of telephone workers, thereby reducing their costs and increasing their profits dramatically. This traumatic downsizing process marked a fundamental departure from the symbiotic labor-management relationship that had characterized the socially regulated communications industry.

In the turmoil that followed in the wake of the 1984 divestiture of AT&T, phone workers were some of the big losers. According to Jeffrey Keefe and Karen Boroff, "On the eve of divestiture [in 1984], AT&T was the world's largest private employer with over one million employees. . . . Since divestiture AT&T has eliminated some 140,000 bargaining unit jobs, while it has established and purchased major non-union subsidiaries. . . . Since October 1993, major corporate restructuring accelerated. . . . U.S. West announced the elimination of 9,400 jobs. . . . Bell South said it was eliminating 10,800 jobs. . . . GTE announced the elimination of 17,000 jobs. . . . Pacific Telesis said it would downsize by 10,000 jobs at Pacific Bell. . . . AT&T declared it would eliminate another 15,000 jobs on top of already scheduled force reductions of 6,000 operator and call servicing positions and 7,500 jobs at Global Information Solutions, formerly NCR. . . . Ameritech said it would reduce its workforce by 6,000. . . . NYNEX . . . scaled back its plans to eliminate 22,500 jobs to 16,800 positions. . . . From the standpoint of labor-management relations, this massive industrial restructuring is in jeopardy of severing the traditional link between high productivity growth through rapid technological change and rising employee incomes with employment security."

Consumers have also suffered as a result of these developments. Because of the direct relationship between the level of employment in the industry and the quality of service that companies deliver to their customers, service quality has been undermined as companies have downsized their work forces. For example, the New York Public Service Commission, which oversees NYNEX (since merged into Bell Atlantic), recently slapped the company with a $50 million fine after finding that the company's quality of service had been substandard. The commission then threatened to double the size of the fine because of the magnitude of the problem and NYNEX's continuing unwilling-ness to address it.

Phone Deregulation Comes to Canada

Unions, consumers, and antipoverty organizations familiar with the ef-fects that phone deregulation had had on the industry in the United States were determined to prevent its importation into Canada. In addition, the telephone companies in the three prairie provinces of Alberta, Saskatchewan, and Man-itoba had been government-owned and operated since the early years of the century. For nearly ten years, the combined opposition of the popular sector and the prairie provinces kept telephone competition and deregulation out of Canada. In the spring of 1990, however, things changed dramatically when the Unitel company announced that it would seek regulatory permission to com-pete in Canada's long distance market.

Unitel enjoyed strong support from the Canadian corporate estab-lishment, which wanted the lower long-distance rates that deregulation and competition would bring. Backed by enormous financial resources, strong allies in the corporate sector, and Canada's corporate-dominated Conservative federal government, Unitel's campaign to introduce long-distance competi-tion proved unstoppable. In June 1992, the Canadian Radio-television and Telecommunications Commission (CRTC), the regulatory body responsible for overseeing Canadian phone service, gave the company permission to compete in Canada's long-distance telephone business.

As in the United States, the introduction of competition and deregulation has meant that residential customers as well as people living in rural areas and small towns across Canada face significantly higher costs for their basic service. It has put many at risk of being left without access to basic telecommunications services. And Canadian telephone workers, like their American counterparts, have borne the brunt of the resulting change as thousands of employees have been shed from the workforce while telephone companies restructured their operations to meet the needs of large corporate customers in major urban centers.

As Canadian phone companies have mounted their downsizing initiatives, service quality problems have surfaced, and the CRTC has warned several phone companies that their quality-of-service indicators are substantially below standard.

Which Way to the Future?

Left to their own devices, privately owned, market-driven telephone companies would never have made a priority of providing service to high-cost, low-revenue customers. This fact provided the underlying rationale for regulating private monopolies in the first place. As we move into the information age, the obligation to provide access to affordable service acquires a greater importance than ever. In the new competitive environment, however, representatives of the telephone and cable industries seem to believe that they have no responsibility to address the telecommunications needs of the poor or those who live in sparsely populated areas. Their bottom-line position is that companies functioning in a competitive environment have no social obligations.

Without government intervention, the poor as well as residents of rural and remote areas could be left to fend for themselves in the deregulated environment of advanced telecommunications. In the United States since the AT&T divestiture, this has meant a sharp increase in local rates and the outright abandonment of service obligations in many rural areas, with some telephone companies going so far as to abandon rural exchanges, selling outmoded facilities to rural customers for a nominal price. This "subscriber dumping" by companies like GTE and Ameritech signals that they have no interest in providing universal, affordable access to the information highway.

Left to their own devices, rural residents and people on low incomes will not have the funds necessary to build the infrastructure they need to access the information highway. As a result of corporate abandonment of these exchanges and markets, entire communities and social strata could be left with an inferior grade of information facilities and services.

In this deregulated environment, phone workers and consumers are coming to the realization that they have a great deal in common. The connection between workers' needs for stable jobs with decent pay and consumers' need for universal, affordable access to high-quality communications services is clear. This realization and the joint efforts that it fosters provide the key to developing labor-based alternatives to profit-driven industrial restructuring.

Governments and employers understand the powerful potential of a coalition between telecommunications workers and consumers. A May 1985 briefing document on telecommunications policy, written by government bureaucrats for Canada's federal cabinet, warned of the danger of the formation of a "common front" among "consumers, small and medium-size business, unions, anti-poverty groups, and seniors" united in the pursuit of universal, affordable telecommunications service. Recognizing the potential strength of a producer/consumer coalition in this field, the document's authors stressed the need for the government to prevent the formation of this common front.

Finding Common Ground

The idea that unionized workers have an interest in working jointly with members of their communities to confront corporate forces has gained acceptance in recent years. But some unions embraced this perspective long before the onset of neoliberalism. For more than twenty-five years, the Telecommunications Workers Union of British Columbia (TWU) has worked to find common ground with community and consumer groups on issues related to access, service quality, and affordability.

The TWU mounted its first public campaign in the early 1970s, when it opposed the opening of Canada's first self-service Phone Mart. The union recognized at that time that self-service facilities meant a decline in service for the public and a loss of jobs for workers. Although the effort to prevent the opening of Phone Marts proved ultimately unsuccessful, the campaign legitimized the view within the union that it had an interest in contesting management's failure to provide customers with quality service. After the Phone Mart campaign, the TWU continued to work with consumer groups and other organizations on the issue of service quality.

In the fall of 1980, the union took the historic step of intervening in the CRTC hearings to oppose a BC Telephone Company demand for a rate increase. In the course of the hearings, the longest in the CRTC's history, union members served as expert witnesses, offering the public an insider's view on telephone company operations. Providing devastating insight into management's distorted priorities, the union explained why customers' service quality was inferior and argued that any rate increase should be made contingent on an improvement in the service the company provided to the public.

By aligning themselves with consumer and community groups in opposition to the company's requested rate increase, these telephone workers won enormous credibility in the eyes of the general public. The CRTC intervention also helped consolidate the union's awareness of the power of joint action with consumers. The TWU had taken the offensive, publicly challenging management's regressive plans for the future—a position it has not relinquished since.

The favorable press coverage and public support the union received for its intervention at the CRTC hearings proved invaluable. Less than three months later, when it appeared that the company was about to lock out its unionized employees, the TWU seized the initiative. It locked out management.

For five days union members occupied telephone exchanges across the province. By the time the courts ordered the union to vacate the exchanges, its peaceful, disciplined, and militant action, coupled with a high-profile internal campaign to prevent damage to phone facilities, generated tremendous public support. As a result of this effort, the union was able to prevent the victimization of union members and leaders for actions taken during the occupation of the exchanges and during the subsequent all-out strike.

By going out of its way to engage the public, the TWU was experimenting with a new approach to unionism. It was moving beyond narrow, bread-and-butter business unionism. But the embrace of this new approach was not based on abstract philosophical commitments to concepts like class or socialism. Rather, it was on the basis of the recognition that narrowly self-interested tactics and strategies could no longer deliver for its members.

The new relationship with consumer and community groups helped the TWU move beyond a reactive stance and allowed it to assume a pro-active position that shaped its relationship with management. Its outreach to the public in the early 1980s prefigured the strategy the union adopted throughout the rest of the decade. As TWU members found themselves confronting fundamental issues related to the future of their industry, they came to recognize the need for linking up with residents of local communities, environmentalists, women's organizations, and other social advocacy groups. Working together in this manner, they transformed what might otherwise have been a series of isolated labor-management conflicts into broader social debates. In the process they began to formulate a socially based strategy for the industry.

A Social Road Map for the Information Highway

The information highway and the telecommunications industry have been promoted as keys to a bountiful future. Few subjects have received as much hype from government and business. Although the public hears nothing but positive public relations messages about the wonders of the information highway, telecommunications workers—the folks at the front line in this sector—have experienced a great deal of negative change. Some say they face the prospect of becoming roadkill on the information highway.

The impact of competition-driven restructuring on telephone workers has been devastating. Their jobs have been broken into a series of routinized, monitored, intensified, and deskilled tasks. Highly skilled troubleshooting has been transformed into work that can be done by newly hired clerical workers using personal computers. Operators' work, which once required knowledge of call routing as well complex time and charge schedules, has been broken into a series of tiny tasks and subjected to unimaginable speedup. Telephone workers, whose wages and working conditions were once the envy of the rest of the work force, have experienced a declining standard of living, increased stress on the job, and an unprecedented level of insecurity about their employment future.

Popular hype about the information highway not only ignores the negative effects of these changes on the industry's workforce. It also overlooks corporate plans to abandon entire classes of customers. Aware of industry plans for workers and the rest of society, the TWU came to the realization that it had to create an alternate strategy for the information highway, one that addressed a range of social issues.

In 1994, the union conducted a study, "Socio-Economic Implications of an Information Highway in British Columbia," with funding provided by the Science Council of British Columbia, a provincial government agency. The study examined a range of topics, including employment trends in the industry and the steps that had to be taken to ensure that people in all walks of life will have access to the services provided using this new technology. In the end, the study came up with a series of recommendations designed to ensure that access to the information highway in British Columbia would be universal and affordable and that it would be constructed to address the province's social needs.

Contrary to the contention that governments are powerless in the globalized environment, the TWU's Science Council strategy calls upon governments to play a strong role in regulating the behavior of the telecommunications industry. Prominent among the recommendations contained in the report was the suggestion that governments use their formidable purchasing power to ensure that telecommunications companies provide information highway services on a universal, affordable basis. Given that governments are telephone companies' largest customers, their demands—including requirements to meet social criteria—cannot be ignored.

The TWU study points out that governments can use the leverage generated by their purchasing power to ensure that the construction of the information highway incorporates criteria related to physical and financial availability. The fact that telecommunications is now competitive gives governments enormous leverage over incumbent telecommunications companies. The Science Council study argued that pro-active purchasing by governments could be a major element in an overall strategy to ensure that companies address the problem of providing service to costly rural areas and to low-revenue customers.

The Science Council study offered a comprehensive program to ensure that universal, affordable access becomes a reality. The program argued for:

• The inclusion of conditions in broadcasting licenses, telecommunications tariffs, and government procurement contracts requiring the provision of service to designated geographic areas and classes of customers.

• The requirement that sharing of facilities by service providers in rural and remote communities be compulsory.

• That physical access to the information highway be provided on a rolled-out basis. In situations where the cost of providing information highway services to each household is prohibitive, access to these services could be phased in, with institutions and community centers being hooked up first and households being attached over time.

• That the social sector should be allowed to participate in the definition of universal service and to update this definition on an ongoing basis in order to keep pace with changes taking place in the industry.

• That an advisory committee consisting of a range of various public interest groups be established to provide government with continuous feedback on the needs of society vis-a-vis developments in the industry.

• That formal public consultations be held between government and industry, focusing on both economic and social concerns.

Major portions of this strategy have already been put in place in the province of British Columbia.

Counteracting Deregulation and Corporate Strategies

On September 16, 1994, Canada's federal regulator handed down Telecom Decision 1994-19, the Review of Regulatory Framework. This decision stipulated that as of January 1, 1995, phone companies' competitive services would no longer be subject to rate-of-return regulation. Traditionally, the CRTC set an allowable rate of return for the phone companies it regulated.

For example, if a company had $2 billion in assets and its allowable rate of return on equity was 10 percent, it was entitled to earn $200 million in profits in a given year. In this example, if the company earned more than $200 million profit, it exceeded its allowable rate of return and could have been forced to return the excess profits to subscribers.

In Decision 1994-19, however, the regulator announced that it was switching from rate-of-return regulation to a system of price caps, effective January 1, 1998. As of that date, instead of regulating phone companies' profits, the regulator would switch to monitoring the amount that phone companies raised their prices.

The decision caused the TWU great concern. Under rate-of-return regulation, phone companies had no incentive to reduce their costs by targeting their work forces. Any resulting increase in profits would only cause them to exceed their allowable rate of return. But under price-cap regulation, companies would be free to increase their profits by cutting their costs, giving them a major financial incentive to slash their work forces.

Adding to the union's worries about regulatory change, Canada's phone companies began to adopt major portions of the strategy pioneered by Ameritech, one of the Regional Bell Operating Companies created as a result of the AT&T divestiture of 1984. The TWU knew that if these companies were free to follow Ameritech's plan, the consequences for union members as well as the general public would be very negative.

Under its blueprint for gaining market share in a deregulated environment, Ameritech de-averaged rates and introduced Local Measured Service. As a result, rates charged to customers living in thinly populated and remote areas skyrocketed. At the same time, the company promoted "incentive-based" regulation which encouraged phone companies to increase their profits by reducing their costs—particularly by cutting staff. (The system of price caps adopted by the CRTC as part of Decision 1994-19, described above, is a form of incentive-based regulation.)

Ameritech focused on meeting the needs of a "new market segment," described as "the communications intensive household," which represents the top 20 percent of the consumer base and which generates 70 percent of toll usage. The company targeted this market with promotions of second lines, voice mailboxes, and other central office features. At the same time, under the new industry priorities established by the Ameritech strategy, the needs of the remaining 80 percent of the customer base were ignored. The TWU knew that if Canada's phone companies were allowed to adopt this strategy, the impact on Canadian phone workers and consumers would be disastrous.

To prevent Canada's phone companies from deploying the Ameritech strategy, the TWU initiated a multi-pronged strategy. As noted above, the union solicited a grant from the Science Council of British Columbia to conduct its own research on the information highway. Based on the results of this research effort, it worked with the government of British Columbia to establish the BC Electronic Highway Accord, which created an Advisory Council representing unions, companies, and public interest groups to ensure that the industry responds to the needs of all British Columbians. Under the terms of the accord, the provincial government has used its formidable purchasing power to pressure BC Tel to upgrade service in outlying areas, contrary to what the company intended to do under the Ameritech plan.

The TWU also played a major part in creating the National Alliance of Communications Unions (NACU), which included labor organizations from across Canada. The purpose of the NACU was to share information and come up with common strategic responses to counteract what the Canadian companies were planning.

In response to the CRTC's announcement that it would hold hearings to flesh out its pending move to a regulatory regime based on price caps, the TWU prevailed upon the other members of the Alliance to mount a joint intervention. As its expert witness, the Alliance brought in Barbara Alexander, a consumer advocate who had devised means to oversee phone company operations when she was a member of Maine's Public Utilities Commission. Alexander provided the regulator with details of an approach which could prevent Canada's telephone companies from emulating the destructive behavior of their American counterparts, who have used the opportunity provided by the shift to price-cap regulation to increase their profits by dumping tens of thousands of telephone workers and degrading service quality.

To complement its work with governments and regulators, the TWU was active in the creation of both the BC Coalition for Information Access and the Alliance for a Connected Canada, coalitions which bring together unions, consumers, public interest groups, anti-poverty organizations, and other activists to promote universal, affordable access to the information highway and the jobs that go with building, maintaining, and running it.

None of this prevented BC Tel management from emulating their American counterparts' efforts to shrink the size of their work forces. But when the company announced plans to downsize and close rural offices, the TWU responded by sending delegations to municipal councils in the affected towns, explaining why the company's actions were unnecessary and how they were damaging the communities involved. In a related response to management's attempt to downgrade service quality, the union established its own internal, rank-and-file-based Quality of Service Committee which monitored developments at BC Tel and put pressure on the company when it tried to cut back on staffing and service.

Finally, when collective bargaining was in progress, the TWU appealed to members to limit the amount of overtime they worked so that BC Tel could not use overtime to compensate for the understaffing that had been caused by its downsizing efforts. Thanks to solid rank-and-file support, this program generated enormous pressure on the company.

All of these factors came together at the end of 1996 to help the union's bargaining committee negotiate one of the best contracts that the TWU had ever signed. In addition to significant wage and pension increases, the contract included language expanding the TWU's jurisdiction to include the high-end work of the future. And it increases pressure on the company in the areas of both pay and employment equity.

The experience of the TWU provides clear evidence that workers and consumers have a practical common interest in pursuing strategic alternatives to neoliberal globalization, alternatives which address a range of social priorities. This experience shows that even in this era of rampaging capital, it is possible for labor to move from the defensive to the offensive by practicing social unionism and forging solid links with its social allies. In today's world, characterized as it is by capital's wide-ranging attacks on all segments of society, no other approach is adequate to the task.

Propaganda
and Control
of the Public Mind

NOAM CHOMSKY

The following comments were excerpted from a talk given at the Harvard University Trade Union Program, Cambridge, Massachusetts, on February 7, 1997, for a national broadcast produced by David Barsamian for Alternative Radio. The complete talk is available on two cassettes. A free catalog of taped programs with Chomsky, Robert McChesney, and many other progressive voices, is available by written request to Alternative Radio, P.O. Box 551, Boulder CO 80306, or by phone to 800-444-1977.

The war against working people should be understood to be a real war. It's not a new war, it's an old one. Furthermore, it's a perfectly conscious war everywhere, but specifically in the U.S., a very free country, but one which happens to have a highly class-conscious business class—so you have a lot of information about it. They talk; you have their records. They have long seen themselves as fighting a bitter class war, except they don't want anybody else to know about it.

Occasionally someone else gets the news. A rather famous case is Doug Fraser, about twenty years ago—1978, I think—when he pulled out of the

Labor Management Council and condemned business leaders for having decided to fight a one-sided class war against working people, the poor, the unemployed, minorities, even members of the middle class, and for having torn up the fragile social compact that had been achieved during a period of growth and prosperity—which in fact (although he didn't say this) had been achieved primarily through very militant struggle under harsh conditions back in the 1930s.

The only thing wrong with his statement is that it was way too late. That war that he's talking about was initiated, and very openly, as soon as the fragile social compact was established back in the 1930s. You don't have to go to secret records to find out about it. Nor do you have to have been at the wrong end of the clubs when the strikes were broken up in the late 1930s to know about it. It was completely public. The reason it's not well known is because neither the educational system nor scholarship, like Harvard, pay any attention to it. It's not a topic that's studied.

There's no doubt that one of the major issues of twentieth century U.S. history is corporate propaganda. It's a huge industry. It extends over, obviously, the commercial media, but includes the whole range of systems that reach the public: the entertainment industry, television, a good bit of what appears in schools, a lot of what appears straight out in the newspapers, and so on. A huge amount of that comes straight out of the public relations industry, which was established in this country early in this century, and developed mainly from the 1920s on. It's now spreading over the rest of the world, but it's primarily here.

Its goal from the beginning, perfectly openly and consciously, was to "control the public mind," as they put it. The public mind was seen as the greatest threat to corporations, from early in the century. Business power was strong. As it's a very free country (by comparative standards), it's hard, not impossible, to call upon state violence to crush people's efforts to achieve freedom, rights, and justice. Therefore it was recognized early on that it's going to be necessary to control people's minds. I should say that's not a new insight. You can read it in David Hume in the Enlightenment, where it was already recognized. Go back to the early stirrings of democratic revolution in England in the seventeenth century: already there was concern that we're not going to be able to control people by force, and we therefore have to control them by other means—controlling what they think, what they feel, their attitudes toward one another. All sorts of mechanisms of control are going to have to be devised which will replace the efficient use of force and violence. That use was available to a much greater extent earlier on, and has been, fortunately, declining—although not uniformly—through the years.

You don't have to move very far from the Cambridge elite to learn about it. The leading figure of the public relations industry is a highly regarded Cambridge liberal, a Roosevelt-Kennedy liberal who died recently: Edward Bernays. He wrote the standard manual of the public relations industry back in the 1920s, which is very much worth reading. I'm not talking about the right wing here. This is way over at the left-liberal end of American politics. His book is *Propaganda*.

(I should mention that terminology changed during the Second World War. Prior to World War II, the term "propaganda" was used, quite openly and freely, for controlling the public mind. It got bad connotations during the Second World War because of Hitler, so the term was dropped. Now there are other terms used. But if you read the literature in the social sciences and the public relations industry back into the 1920s and 1930s, they describe what they're doing as *propaganda*.)

Bernays's *Propaganda* is a manual for the rising public relations industry. He opens by pointing out that the conscious manipulation of the organized habits and opinions of the masses is the central feature of a democratic society. It's the "essence of democracy," as he later pointed out. He said: we have the means to carry this out, the means to regiment people's minds as efficiently as armies regiment their bodies. And we must do this. First of all, it's the essential feature of democracy. But also (as a footnote) it's the way to maintain power structures, and authority structures, and wealth, and so on, roughly the way it is. . . .

What's called *the industrial capitalist system* today is one in which private power overwhelms government by its combinations and is bribed by its largesse. That's a pretty good description of 1997. With all the changes that have taken place since 1792, there's a good deal of stability to all this, including the commitment to the principle enunciated by James Madison that the primary goal of government is to protect the minority of the opulent from the majority. . . . The increasingly, overwhelmingly significant idea, particularly among liberals (like, say, Bernays), is that it is necessary to control people's minds because they're too much of a danger.

Take a look at, say, the *Encyclopedia of Social Sciences*, a big encyclopedia from 1933, still pre-Second World War. There actually is an entry on propaganda. Remember, "propaganda" was a useable term then. The entry is written by a very distinguished liberal political scientist, Harold Lasswell, one of the founders of modern political science and communications. He says (these are paraphrases, but they're pretty close to quotes): We must not succumb to democratic dogmatisms about people being the best judges of their own interests; they are not. "We're" the best judges of "their" interests, we smart guys. And "we" must therefore ensure that those idiots out there don't get into trouble by actually using their theoretical right to vote to interfere where they don't belong, like in the public arena. So "we've" got to keep them out of the public arena somehow and make sure that it's just us smart guys who are in there. It's for their good, of course: you don't let your three-year-old grandchild run across the street. She may want to run across the street, but it would be improper to let her have that choice. The same is true about the masses. They have to be controlled at the workplace, they have to be kept out of the political arena, and they're not going to understand the need to protect the opulent minority against the majority. They're going to have all these strange leveling impulses and will do all kinds of things that will mess the world up in all sorts of horrible ways.

So for their benefit "we" have to regiment their minds the way an army regiments their bodies, and ensure that they're under control—make it very clear that they don't participate in workplace management, and certainly not in the political arena. They're to be outside somewhere.

The dedication with which this task has been pursued is pretty awesome. Right after the fall of the house of labor in the 1920s, when American labor really was smashed, people were privatized and they tried to accommodate individually to "a most undemocratic America" (as David Montgomery and others have pointed out). That was a time when there was great awe about the end of history and the utopia of the masters: "It's all over. Us good guys have won. Everybody else is at our feet." Kind of like some of the stuff you read today. . . .

A few years later the whole thing collapsed, and there was militant working class struggle and other popular activism. There had to be an accommodation of some kind to these unwashed masses who were getting out of line with sit-down strikes. There was this fragile social compact that Doug Fraser referred to, meaning labor laws and the limited social system. It was *established*. It wasn't a gift. It was won through struggle. (In fact, American workers in the 1930s began to get the rights that had been standard long before, even in much more brutal societies; read the right-wing British press over the early part of this century—they can't believe how bad American workers were treated.) . . .

But by the 1930s the United States was brought into the mainstream of industrial society in these matters—to a limited extent. That caused hysteria among the masters by 1936 or 1937. (Again, these are things which in a really free society everybody would study in elementary school, because they're important to give the real framework of the society.) In the business press, they were talking about the hazard facing industrialists and the rising political power of the masses, and how "we must do something to save ourselves or our way of life will be gone. We don't have a lot of time to do it." They started right away.

By the late 1930s a big anti-labor campaign had been built up with new techniques. There was still use of force, but it was understood that this was not going to work the way it had. So there was a shift to more propaganda. The main idea was called the "Mohawk Valley formula," designed by a lot of public relations hotshots around 1936 or 1937, during some of the steel strikes, to have what they called *scientific methods of strikebreaking:* We don't just come in with clubs and shoot people and smash their heads. We do it the scientific way, because the old way didn't work any more.

The scientific methods of strikebreaking were in fact drawn from public relations ideas of the kind that I talked about. The main idea was to mobilize the community against the strikers and the union activists, to present a picture which is by now so standard you can hardly turn on the tube without seeing it. It's just poured out in streams ever since then.

The basic idea is to present a picture of the world that looks kind of like this: There's "us," a big happy family in the community. The honest workman going off every morning with his lunch box, his loyal wife making the meals and taking care of the kids, the hardworking executive who's toiling day and night in the interests of his workers and the community, the friendly banker running around looking for people to lend money to. That's us. We're all in harmony. Harmony was a big word. We're all together. It's "Americanism."

You might take a look at that word "Americanism," an unusual term. It's the kind of term that you only find in totalitarian societies, as far as I know. So in the Soviet Union, "anti-Sovietism" was considered the gravest of all crimes. And the Brazilian generals had a concept like that, "anti-Brazilian." But try publishing a book on, say, "anti-Italianism" and see what happens in the streets of Rome and Milan. People won't even bother laughing. It's a ludicrous idea. The idea of "Italianism" or "Norwayism" would be the object of ridicule in societies that have some kind of residue of democratic culture—inside people's heads, I don't mean in the formal system. But in totalitarian societies it is used, and as far as I know the U.S. is the only free society that has such a concept. "Americanism" and "anti-Americanism" and "un-Americanism" are concepts which go along with harmony and getting rid of "those outsiders."

Another part is simply to induce hatred and fear among people. It's a diverse society—if you go to Europe, most places are pretty uniform—so it's easy for propagandists to get people to hate the guy next door because he looks a little different. Huge campaigns go on to instigate divisions among people. But these are very natural techniques of social control.

Going back to the Mohawk Valley formula, the idea was to move into a community where there's a strike going on, flood it with propaganda, take over the media, the churches, the schools; pour in this propaganda about harmony and those bad guys out there who are trying to disrupt our harmonious lives. Like that union organizer—he's probably a communist or an anarchist anyway, and probably un-American. He's trying to destroy all these wonderful things we have. We've got to band together and kick him out. We have to defend our way of life against this.

A lot of religion gets thrown in. Remember that the United States is an extremely fundamentalist country. You look at comparative statistics: usually religious fundamentalism declines as industrialization goes up. It's a very close correlation. The U.S. is off the chart. It ranks with devastated peasant societies. It's probably more fundamentalist than Iran. Why this is so is a complicated question. But one factor is that it was certainly consciously fomented by business leaders, way back in the nineteenth century. John D. Rockefeller's favorite evangelist, who he poured a lot of money into, was a guy who said that people ought to have more enlightened ideas than labor agitation. The "more enlightened ideas" are: go to church, listen to orders, do what they tell you, and shut up.

It's a really interesting case, because Mohawk Valley was the model that was later used for strikebreaking and destruction of the labor movement in the postwar period. Incidentally, I don't know of any literature on this, do you? These are untouchable topics. You can almost say that anything that's important—that's going to matter for people's lives—is off the agenda. And it sort of makes sense. You don't want people to know about it. You don't want people to know the wrong kind of thing. It's not a conspiracy, it's just common sense: If you have a certain degree of power and authority and privilege, you just don't want people to know things that might be harmful to them. They're really like children. We're the ones who have to make the decisions for them.

Enormous amounts of money and effort go into this. . . . It's another technique of trying to create the marginalization of people, removing people from the actual social and political struggles that might make their lives better, and to keep them from working with one another by dividing them up in all sorts of ways. . . .

A couple of days ago, I put myself through the pain of reading the *New York Times* every day for some masochistic reason which I won't try to explain. But they've got a big chief correspondent, sort of the main thinker, a guy named Thomas Friedman, who had an article three or four days ago, a big think piece, in which he said: The Cold War's over, so the breakdown isn't hawks and doves any more. . . . [The new break] is between integrationists and anti-integrationists [according to Friedman]. That means people who are in favor of more globalization and what they call free trade (which isn't free trade), and people who want to slow it down or end it. That's one break. The other is between people who are in favor of a safety net, and those who think that everybody ought to "be on your own" and "get what you can." . . .

[Newt Gingrich] is put in the corner that says "integrationist" and devil take the hindmost, everybody for themselves. It's testable that that's Gingrich's position. For example, on the question of whether Gingrich is an integrationist, in favor of free trade, we can ask how he reacted when the Reagan administration instituted the greatest wave of protectionism since the 1930s. That's just straight protectionism, alongside of a huge increase in public subsidies to private power, to industry—along with the biggest nationalization in American history, the takeover of Continental Illinois Bank. That's all radically anti-integrationist. How did Newt Gingrich react? We can ask that question. The answer is, he thought it was great.

What about the safety net story? Gingrich is in favor of people being out there on their own, rugged entrepreneurs. You can check that, too. He represents Cobb County, Georgia, and he happens to hold the national championship in bringing federal subsidies to his rich constituents. To be precise, among suburban counties in the U.S., Cobb County ranks third in federal subsidies, right after Arlington, Virginia, which is part of the federal government—so they get a lot of federal subsidies; the Pentagon's there—and Bravard County, Florida, which is the home of the space center, so it's another part of the federal government. But if you move outside of the federal government itself, Gingrich's district is number one. They get more federal subsidies than anybody. The biggest employer in Cobb County is Lockheed, which is a publicly subsidized, private profit corporation. They sell commercial planes. But everyone knows, the way the system is designed, technology is developed under the guise of the military, and then handed over to private power when it works. That's true of everything: airplanes, computers, the Internet, you name it. Cobb County is right at the center of it.

He's in favor of being out on your own and fighting in this harsh world? Ridiculous. He's the biggest welfare freak in the country. That's literally true. Except that he wants the welfare to go to very rich people. . . . The way our economy works: take just about any dynamic sector of it you know—at least that I know and have studied—and you find that it's based on massive public subsidies and privatization of profit. The public pays the costs and takes the risks, and private systems make the profit if there is any. Cobb County is just an extreme example of this. . . .

You cannot be a good propagandist unless it's in your bones. It's extremely hard to lie. I think we all know that from personal experience. It's hard to lie to people. Every one of us lies to people all the time, unless we're some kind of crazy angels. But the way we do it—and I'm sure you know this—is, you first convince yourself that what you're saying is true. You're an eight-year-old kid and you steal a toy from your brother. Your mother comes in and yells at you. You don't say: I wanted a toy and he had it so I took it because I'm stronger than him. What you say is: It really wasn't his, and besides, he'd taken a toy of mine, and anyway, I needed it more than he did, so it was right for me to take it. If people haven't had that experience, they're some other species.

That kind of experience goes all the way up to being a hotshot journalist for the *New York Times*. You don't even make it into those circles unless you're already so deeply overwhelmed by doctrine and propaganda that you can't even think in other terms. So when people talk like this, you'll read liberal columnists in the *New York Times* very angrily saying, "Nobody tells me what to write. I write anything I feel like." Which is absolutely true. If people with real power weren't sure that they were going to say the right things, they wouldn't be in a position to say anything they feel like.

How does that work? It starts from childhood, in kindergarten, on television. There's selection for obedience from the very first moment. When I think about my own school experience or any other school experience I know about, there was selection for obedience. I ended up going to fancy colleges like this place. The way I did it was by shutting up. If I thought that the high school teacher was a horse's ass, which I did most of the time, I didn't say so (sometimes I did and got thrown out of class). I learned not to say anything, to say: "Okay, I'll do the next stupid assignment because I know that's the way I'll get ahead and ultimately I'll do this and that." If you have whatever ability it takes to do this kind of thing, and are sufficiently disciplined and passive, you make it through up to the higher echelons.

There are people who don't. . . . They get into trouble. They're called behavior problems, or disruptive, or you stick drugs in them because they're just too independent, and people who are independent are a pain in the neck. They disrupt the system. They're going to be cut off one way or another. . . .

When you watch television, some sitcom, you don't think, "I'm being exposed to the Mohawk Valley formula." But you are. That's the picture of life that's presented, day after day after day.

People have personal problems, but nothing that would bring them together to struggle against the new spirit of the age. When was the last time you saw a sitcom about that? What you get is this stuff that flows out of the PR industry, very consciously. . . .

A major element in the huge public relations propaganda after the Second World War was strictly demonizing labor. And the labor movement knew that.

There was a fairly substantial labor press, even then. As late as the 1950s there were still about 800 labor newspapers which were reaching maybe 20 or 30 million people a week. Not commercial media, but pretty substantial. And they're interesting reading, too. I'm not talking about anything radical, no left-wing press, just labor newspapers, the conservative American labor movement. They were talking about developing antidotes to the poisons of the "kept press," the commercial media, who were demonizing labor at every opportunity and trying to undermine our achievements and glossing over the crimes of the corporate rulers who run the society.

There's a good book on this one, too. This tells you something about American academic life. The first study that I've ever heard of in the U.S. on this major theme of modern history just appeared in the University of Illinois Press, called *Selling Free Enterprise,* by Elizabeth Fones-Wolf. It's kind of apolitical. She doesn't have any special point of view. But the material in it is pretty revealing. . . .

Remember that the U.S. came out of the Second World War pretty social democratic, like most of the world. . . . An awful lot of people in the U.S., too—like maybe half—thought that there ought to be popular control over industry in some fashion. . . . There was enormous support for social programs. That had to be beaten out of people's heads, and fast. The leaders of the public relations industry said, "We have three to five years to save our way of life. We have to fight," and quickly win what they called the "everlasting battle for the minds of men" and indoctrinate people with the capitalist story so fully that they can repeat it on every opportunity.

They weren't kidding around. For example, about a third of the material in American elementary schools was coming straight out of corporate propaganda offices by the early 1950s. Sports leagues were taken over. The churches were taken over. The universities were attacked. It was an across-the-board major effort to try to win the everlasting battle for the minds of men. And it's still going on. . . .

It's particularly harmful to democracy when media systems are in the hands of private tyrannies. . . . Here's this huge system, built at public expense. Most media analysts with their heads screwed on see, and even report, that it's very likely going to end up in the hands of a half-dozen megacorporations internationally. That's worse than the oligopolies that run steel and computers, because here we're talking about a new mode of information and communication being handed over to private power.

We've heard about the Telecommunications Act of 1996, the big legislative achievement of the last Congress, but it wasn't discussed as a public interest issue. It was discussed as a business issue. Most of the reporting was in the business pages. . . . It's not supposed to be a question of public interest whether major systems of information and interchange are handed over as gifts to Rupert Murdoch. The only thing that was discussed was: Do you give it to six corporations or twelve, or do it this way or that way? That's effective indoctrination, when these things don't even occur to people. . . . This is worse than the handing over of decision-making power to private tyrannies, because in this case it's also handing over the things that they're going to use for the control of the public mind. These systems could also be used to liberate people. . . .

This is very much a business-run society. The last figures I saw, about one out of six dollars in the whole economy is spent on marketing. It's an extremely inefficient use of funds. Marketing doesn't produce anything, any public good. But marketing is a form of manipulation and deceit. It's an effort to create artificial wants, to control the way people look and think about things. A lot of that marketing is straight propaganda, advertising. Most of it is tax-free . . . which means, the way our system works, you pay for the privilege of being propagandized, of having all this stuff dumped on you. Those are not small figures. I think it was a trillion dollars a year in 1992. When you've got that much of a commitment to controlling minds and manipulating desires, and doing all the things they talk about in the public relations literature (I'm not making it up; you can read it there) and the social science literature, because this is also standard academic talk—when you've got those stakes you're going to work on it hard. And it's going to be hard to fight against. That's what makes organizing tough. You have to break through a lot of psychic resistance.

The whole history of the labor movement tells you that. This was well understood by mill hands in Lowell 150 years ago. But it's a big battle. And you're not just struggling against somebody who calls it a "right-to-work act." You're struggling against five hours a day of television and the movie industry and the books and the schools and everything else. The scale of the efforts to win the battle for men's minds is enormous. I thought I knew something about this, but when I read Elizabeth Fones-Wolf's book, I was pretty shocked just to see the scale of the efforts, and the frenzied dedication to winning this everlasting battle. It's really impressive. Although if you think of the stakes, it's not too surprising.

The Propaganda Model Revisited

EDWARD S. HERMAN

In *Manufacturing Consent: The Political Economy of the Mass Media*,[1] Noam Chomsky and I put forward a "propaganda model" as a framework for analyzing and understanding how the mainstream U.S. media work and why they perform as they do. We had long been impressed with the regularity with which the media operate within restricted assumptions, depend heavily and uncritically on elite information sources, and participate in propaganda campaigns helpful to elite interests. In trying to explain why they do this we looked for structural factors as the only possible root of systematic behavior and performance patterns.

The propaganda model was and is in distinct contrast to the prevailing mainstream explanations—both liberal and conservative—of media behavior and performance. These approaches downplay structural factors, generally presupposing either their unimportance or positive impact resulting from the multiplicity of agents, and thus competition and diversity. Both liberal and conservative analysts emphasize journalists' norms and conduct, public opinion, and news source initiatives as the main determining variables. These analysts are inconsistent in this regard, however. When they discuss media systems in communist or other authoritarian states, the idea that journalists or public opinion can override the power of those who own and control the media is dismissed as nonsense and even apologetics for tyranny.

There is a distinct difference, too, between the political implications of the propaganda model and mainstream media analysis. For the former, as structural factors shape the broad contours of media performance, and that performance is incompatible with a truly democratic political culture, it follows that a basic change in media ownership, organization, and purpose is necessary for the achievement of genuine democracy. In mainstream analyses such a perspective is politically unacceptable, and its supportive arguments and evidence are rarely subject to debate.

Here I will describe the propaganda model, address some of the criticisms that have been leveled against it,[2] and discuss how the model holds up nearly a decade after its publication. I will also provide some examples of how the propaganda model helps explain the nature of media coverage of important political topics in the 1990s.

The Propaganda Model

What is the propaganda model and how does it work? The crucial structural factors derive from the fact that the dominant media are firmly imbedded in the market system. They are profit-seeking businesses, owned by very wealthy people (or other companies); and they are funded largely by advertisers who are also profit-seeking entities, and who want their ads to appear in a supportive selling environment. The media are also dependent on government and major business firms as information sources; and efficiency and political considerations, and frequently overlapping interests, cause a certain degree of solidarity to prevail between the government, major media, and other corporate businesses. Government and large non-media business firms are also best positioned (and sufficiently wealthy) to be able to pressure the media with threats of withdrawal of advertising or TV licenses, libel suits, and other direct and indirect modes of attack. The media are also constrained by the dominant ideology, which heavily featured anticommunism before and during the Cold War era and was mobilized often to cause the media to refrain from criticizing attacks on small states labeled communist.

These factors are linked together, reflecting the multileveled capability of powerful business and government entities and collectives (e.g., the Business Roundtable; U.S. Chamber of Commerce; industry lobbies and front groups) to exert power over the flow of information. We noted that the five factors involved—ownership, advertising, sourcing, flak, and anticommunist ideology—

work as "filters" through which information must pass, and that individually and often in additive fashion, they greatly influence media choices. We stressed that the filters work mainly by the independent action of many individuals and organizations; these frequently, but not always, have a common view of issues and similar interests. In short, the propaganda model describes a decentralized and nonconspiratorial market system of control and processing, although at times the government or one or more private actors may take initiatives and mobilize coordinated elite handling of an issue.

Propaganda campaigns can occur only when consistent with the interests of those controlling and managing the filters. For example, these managers all accepted the view that the Polish government's crackdown on the Solidarity union in 1980 to 1981 was extremely newsworthy and deserved severe condemnation; whereas the same interests did not find the Turkish military government's equally brutal crackdown on trade unions in Turkey at about the same time to be newsworthy or reprehensible. In the latter case the U.S. government and business community liked the military government's anti-communist stance and open-door economic policy; and the crackdown on Turkish unions had the merit of weakening the left and keeping wages down. In the Polish case, propaganda points could be scored against a Soviet-supported government, and concern could be expressed for workers—whose wages were not paid by Free World employers! The fit of this dichotomization to corporate interests and anticommunist ideology is obvious.

We used the concepts of "worthy" and "unworthy" victims to describe this dichotomization, with a trace of irony, as the differential treatment was clearly related to political and economic advantage, rather than anything like actual worth. In fact, the Polish trade unionists quickly ceased to be worthy when communism was overthrown and the workers were struggling against a Western-oriented neoliberal regime. The travails of Polish workers now, like those of Turkish workers, don't pass through the propaganda model filters. They are *both* unworthy victims at this point.

We never claimed that the propaganda model explained everything or that it shows media omnipotence and complete effectiveness in manufacturing consent. It is a model of media *behavior and performance*, not media *effects*. We explicitly pointed to alternative media, grassroots information sources, and public skepticism about media veracity as important limits on media effectiveness in propaganda service, and we urged the support and more effective use of these alternatives. Both Chomsky and I have often pointed to the general public's persistent refusal to fall into line with the media and elite over the morality of the Vietnam War and the desirability of the assault on Nicaragua in the 1980s, among other matters. The power of the U.S. propaganda system lies in its ability to mobilize an elite consensus, to give the appearance of democratic consent, and to create enough confusion, misunderstanding, and apathy in the general population to allow elite programs to go forward. We also emphasized the fact that there are often differences within the elite that open up space for some debate and even occasional (but very rare) attacks on the *intent* as well as the tactical means of achieving elite ends.

Although the propaganda model was generally well-received on the left, some complained of an allegedly pessimistic thrust and implication of hopeless odds to be overcome. A closely related objection concerned its applicability to local conflicts where the possibility of effective resistance was greater. But the propaganda model does not suggest that local and even larger victories are impossible, especially where the elites are divided or have limited interest in an issue. For example, coverage of issues like gun control, school prayer, and abortion rights may well receive more varied treatment than, say, global trade, taxation, and economic policy. Moreover, well-organized campaigns by labor, human rights, or environmental organizations fighting against abusive local businesses can sometimes elicit positive media coverage. In fact, we would like to think that the propaganda model can help activists understand where they might best deploy their efforts to influence mainstream media coverage of issues.

The model does suggest that the mainstream media, as elite institutions, commonly frame news and allow debate only within the parameters of elite interests; and that where the elite is really concerned and unified, and/or where ordinary citizens are not aware of their own stake in an issue or are immobilized by effective propaganda, the media will serve elite interests uncompromisingly.

Mainstream Liberal and Academic "Left" Critiques

Many liberals and a number of academic media analysts of the left did not like the propaganda model. Some of them found repugnant a wholesale condemnation of a system in which they played a respected role. Some asked rhetorically where we got the information used to condemn the mainstream media if not from the media themselves. (This tired apologetic point was addressed at length in our preface.) For these critics, the system is basically sound, its inequalities of access regrettable but tolerable, its pluralism and competition effectively responding to consumer demands. In the postmodernist mode, global analyses and global solutions are rejected and derided; individual struggles and small victories are stressed, even by nominally left thinkers.

Many of the critiques displayed barely concealed anger; and in most, the propaganda model was dismissed with a few superficial cliches ("conspiratorial," "simplistic," etc.), without fair presentation or subjecting it to the test of evidence. Let me discuss briefly some of the main criticisms.

Conspiracy theory: We explained in *Manufacturing Consent* that critical analyses like ours would inevitably elicit cries of conspiracy theory, and in a futile effort to prevent this, we devoted several pages of the preface to showing that the propaganda model is best described as a "guided market system," and explicitly rejecting conspiracy. Mainstream critics still couldn't abandon the charge—partly because they are too lazy to read a complex work, partly because they know that falsely accusing a radical critique of conspiracy theory won't cost them anything, and partly because of their superficial assumption that, as the media comprise thousands of "independent" journalists and companies, any finding that they follow a "party line" serving the state must rest on an assumed conspiracy. (In fact, it can result from a widespread gullible acceptance of official handouts, common internalized beliefs, fear of reprisal for critical analysis, etc.) The apologists can't abide the notion that institutional factors can cause a "free" media to act like lemmings in jointly disseminating false and even silly propaganda; such a charge must assume a conspiracy.

Sometimes the critics latched onto a word or phrase that suggests a collective purpose or function, occasionally ironically, to make their case. Communications professor Robert Entman, for example, states that we damaged our case by alleging that media coverage of the 1973 Paris Accord on Vietnam "was consciously 'designed by the loyal media to serve the needs of state power' . . . which comes close to endorsing a conspiracy theory, which the authors explicitly disavow early on."[3] The word "consciously" is Entman's, and he neglects numerous statements on the media's treatment of the Paris accords that don't fit his effort to bring us "close to" a conspiracy theory. To say that we "disavow" a conspiracy theory is also misleading: we went to great pains to show that our view is closer to a free market model, with independent entities operating on the basis of common outlooks, incentives, and pressures from market and organizational forces.

The propaganda model explains media behavior and performance in structural terms, and intent is an unmeasurable red herring. All we know is that the media and journalists mislead in tandem: some no doubt internalize a propaganda line as true; some may know it is false, but the point is unknowable and irrelevant.

Chomskian linguistics: Some of the criticisms of the propaganda model have been funny. Carlin Romano, in his review in *Tikkun,*[4] located the problem in Chomskian linguistic theories that allegedly view everything as rooted in deep structures. He was unaware that the rooting of corporate behavior and performance in structure is the core of modern industrial organization analysis, that I had already used it in a 1981 book, *Corporate Control, Corporate Power,* and that I was mainly responsible for the chapter in *Manufacturing Consent* that presented the propaganda model. Of course, whether traceable to Chomskian linguistics or industrial organization theory, the substantive issues are: Are the assumptions plausible? Does the model work? But showing a possible esoteric origin is a form of put-down suggesting remoteness and lack of touch with real media people.

Failure to touch base with reporters: Romano did in fact follow up his Chomskian linguistics irrelevancy with the admonition that we had failed to ask reporters why they did what they did. He implied, without offering any evidence, that the journalistic bias we criticized might have been revealed as for good cause, if we had only asked for an explanation. But, apart from the fact that we did speak with quite a few reporters, the criticism is inane. Are reporters even aware of the deeper sources of bias they may internalize? Won't they tend to rationalize their behavior? More important, if we find, for example, that in reporting on the Nicaraguan and Salvadoran elections of 1984, they asked different questions in the two elections, in exact accord with the propaganda line of the U.S. government, would asking journalists what went on in their minds serve any useful purpose? This line of criticism, like the insistence on inquiry into reporter-proprietor intentions, is a cop-out that essentially denies the legitimacy of a quantitative (or scientific) analysis of media performance.

Failure to take account of media professionalism and objectivity: A more sophisticated version of the last argument, put forward by communications professor Dan Hallin, is that we failed to take account of the maturing of journalist professionalism, which he claims to be "central to understanding how the media operate."[5] Hallin also states that in protecting and rehabilitating the public sphere, "professionalism is surely part of the answer."[6]

But professionalism and objectivity rules are fuzzy, flexible, and superficial manifestations of deeper power and control relationships. Professionalism arose in journalism in the years when the newspaper business was becoming less competitive and more dependent on advertising. Professionalism was not an antagonistic movement by the workers against the press owners, but was actively encouraged by many of the latter. It gave a badge of legitimacy to journalism, ostensibly assuring readers that the news would not be influenced by the biases of owners, advertisers, or the journalists themselves. In certain circumstances it has provided a degree of autonomy, but professionalism has also internalized some of the commercial values that media owners hold most dear, like relying on inexpensive official sources as *the* credible news source. As Ben Bagdikian has noted, professionalism has made journalists oblivious to the compromises with authority they are constantly making.[7] And Hallin himself acknowledges that professional journalism can allow something close to complete government control via sourcing domination.[8]

While Hallin claims that the propaganda model cannot explain the case of media coverage of the Central American wars of the 1980s, where there was considerable domestic hostility to the Reagan policies, in fact the model works extremely well there, whereas Hallin's focus on "professionalism" fails abysmally. Hallin acknowledges that "the administration was able more often than not to prevail in the battle to determine the dominant frame of television coverage," "the broad patterns in the framing of the story can be accounted for almost entirely by the evolution of policy and elite debate in Washington," and "coherent statements of alternative visions of the world order and U.S. policy rarely appeared in the news."[9] This is exactly what the propaganda model would forecast. And if, as Hallin contends, a majority of the public opposed the elite view, what kind of "professionalism" allows a virtually complete suppression of the issues as the majority perceives them?

Hallin mentions a "nascent alternative perspective" in reporting on El Salvador—a "human rights" framework—that "never caught hold." The propaganda model can explain why it never took hold; Hallin doesn't. With 700 journalists present at the Salvadoran election of 1982, allegedly "often skeptical" of election integrity,[10] why did it yield a "public relations victory" for the administration and a major falsification of reality (as described in *Manufacturing Consent*)? Hallin doesn't explain this. He never mentions the Office of Public Diplomacy, the firing of *New York Times* reporter Raymond Bonner, and the work of the flak machines. He doesn't explain the failure of the media to report even a tiny fraction of the crimes of the contras in Nicaragua and the death machines of El Salvador and Guatemala, in contrast with their inflation of Sandinista misdeeds and double standard in reporting on the Nicaraguan election of 1984. Given the elite divisions and public hostility to the Reagan policy, media subservience was phenomenal and arguably exceeded that which the propaganda model might have anticipated.[11]

Failure to explain continued opposition and resistance: Both Hallin and historian Walter LaFeber (in a review in the *New York Times*) pointed to the continued opposition to Reagan's Central America policy as somehow incompatible with the model. These critics failed to comprehend that the propaganda model is about how the media work, not how effective they are. Even the sophisticated and sympathetic Philip Schlesinger calls ours an "effects" model, that "assumes that dominant agendas are reproduced in public opinion," but he immediately quotes our statement that the "system is not all powerful. . . . Government and the elite domination of the media have not succeeded in overcoming the Vietnam syndrome. . . ."[12] Nowhere does he cite us saying anything like his summary of our alleged views on effects. We also stated explicitly with regard to Central America that the elite was sufficiently divided on tactics to allow space and considerable debate. We did stress, however, that the parameters of debate did not extend to fundamental challenges to the U.S. intervention.[13]

By the logic of this form of criticism of the propaganda model, the fact that many Soviet citizens did not swallow the lines put forward by *Pravda* would demonstrate that *Pravda* was not serving a state propaganda function.

Propaganda model too mechanical, functionalist, ignores existence of space, contestation, and interaction: This set of criticisms is at the heart of the negative reactions of the serious left-of-center media analysts such as Philip Schlesinger, James Curran, Peter Golding, Graham Murdock, and John Eldridge, as well as of Dan Hallin. Of these critics, only Schlesinger both summarizes the elements of our model and discusses our evidence. He acknowledges that the case studies make telling points, but in the end he finds ours "a highly deterministic vision of how the media operate coupled with a straightforward functionalist conception of ideology."[14] Specifically, we failed to explain the weights to be given to our five filters; we did not allow for external influences, nor did we offer a "thoroughgoing analysis of the ways in which economic dynamics operate to structure both the range and form of press presentations" (quoting Graham Murdock); and while putting forward "a powerful effects model" we admit that the system is not all-powerful, which calls into question our determinism.

The criticism of the propaganda model for being deterministic ignores several important considerations. Any model involves deterministic elements, making this a straw-person unless the critics also show that the system is not logically consistent, that it operates on false premises, or that the predictive power of its determining variables is poor. The critics often acknowledge that the case studies we present are powerful,[15] but they don't show where the alleged determinism leads to error, nor do they offer or point to alternative models that would do a better job.

The propaganda model is dealing with extraordinarily complex sets of events. It only claims to offer a broad framework of analysis that requires modification depending on many local and special factors; it may be entirely inapplicable in some cases. But if it offers insight in numerous important cases that have large effects and cumulative ideological force, it is defensible unless a better model is provided. Usually the critics wisely stick to generalities and offer no critical detail or alternative model; when they do provide alternatives, the results are not impressive.[16]

The criticism of the propaganda model for functionalism is also dubious, and the critics sometimes seem to call for more functionalism. The model does describe a system in which the media serve the elite, but by complex processes incorporated into the model, involving means whereby the powerful protect their interests naturally and without overt conspiracy. This would seem one of the model's merits; it shows a dynamic and self-protecting system in operation. The same corporate community that influences the media through its power as owner, as dominant funder (advertising), and as a major news source, also underwrites right-wing policy groups like Accuracy in Media and the American Enterprise Institute to influence the media through harassment and the provision of "sound" experts. Critics of propaganda-model functionalism like

Eldridge and Schlesinger contradictorily point to the merit of analyses that focus on "how sources organize media strategies" to achieve their ends. Apparently it is admirable to analyze microcorporate strategies to influence the media, but focusing on global corporate efforts to influence the media—along with the complementary effects of thousands of local strategies—is illegitimate functionalism!

Golding and Murdock criticize the model for its focus on "strategic interventions," allegedly causing us to "overlook the contradictions in the system. Owners, advertisers and key political personnel cannot always do as they wish." Analyzing "the nature and sources of these limits" is a "key task" of critical political economy.[17] The Golding-Murdock claim that the propaganda model focuses on "strategic interventions" is a surprising misreading, as the model's filters are built-in and operate mainly through the internalized recognition and enforcement of constraints and choices based on the structure of power. Strategic interventions certainly occur, but are of distinctly secondary importance.

It is also untrue that the propaganda model implies no constraints on media owners/managers; we recognized and spelled out the circumstances under which the media will be relatively open—mainly, when there are elite disagreements and when other groups in society are interested in, informed on, and organized to fight about issues. But the propaganda model does start from the premise that a critical political economy will put front and center the analysis of the locus of media control and the mechanisms by which the powerful are able to dominate the flow of messages and limit the space of contesting parties. The limits on their power are certainly important, but why should these get first place, except as a means of minimizing the power of the dominant interests, inflating the elements of contestation, and pretending that the marginalized have more strength than they really possess?

Enhanced Relevance of the Propaganda Model

The dramatic changes in the economy, communications industries, and politics over the past decade have on balance tended to enhance the applicability of the propaganda model. The first two filters—ownership and advertising—have become ever more important. The decline of public broadcasting, the increase in corporate power and global reach, and the mergers and centralization of the media, have made bottom-line considerations more controlling both in the United States and abroad. The competition for serving advertisers has become more intense and the boundaries between editorial and advertising departments have weakened further. Newsrooms have been more thoroughly incorporated into transnational corporate empires, with shrunken resources and even less management enthusiasm for investigative journalism that would challenge the structure of power. In short, the professional autonomy of journalists has been reduced.

Some argue that the Internet and the new communication technologies are breaking the corporate stranglehold on journalism and opening an unprecedented era of interactive democratic media. There is no evidence to support this view as regards journalism and mass communication. In fact, one could argue that the new technologies are exacerbating the problem. They permit media firms to shrink staff while achieving greater outputs and they make possible global distribution systems, thus reducing the number of media entities. Although the new technologies have great potential for democratic communication, left to the market there is little reason to expect the Internet to serve democratic ends.

The third and fourth filters—sourcing and flak—have also strengthened as mechanisms of elite influence. A reduction in the resources devoted to journalism means that those who subsidize the media by providing sources for copy gain greater leverage. Moreover, work by people like Alex Carey, John Stauber, and Sheldon Rampton has helped us see how the public relations industry has been able to manipulate press coverage of issues on behalf of corporate America. This industry understands how to utilize journalistic conventions to serve its own ends. Studies of news sources reveal that a significant proportion of news originates in the public relations releases. There are, by one conservative count, 20,000 more public relations agents working to doctor the news today then there are journalists writing it.

The fifth filter—anticommunist ideology—is possibly weakened by the collapse of the Soviet Union and global socialism, but this is easily offset by the greater ideological force of the belief in the "miracle of the market" (as Reagan tagged it). At least among the elite, regardless of evidence, markets are assumed benevolent and nonmarket mechanisms are suspect. When the Soviet economy stagnated in the 1980s, it was attributed to the absence of markets; as capitalist Russia disintegrates in the 1990s it is because politicians and workers are not letting markets work their magic. Journalism has internalized this ideology. Adding it to the fifth filter, in a world where the global power of market institutions makes nonmarket options seem utopian, gives us an ideological package of immense strength.

Further Applications

The propaganda model applies exceedingly well to the media's treatment of the passage of the North American Free Trade Agreement (NAFTA) and the subsequent Mexican crisis and meltdown of 1994 to 1995. Once again there was a sharp split between the preferences of ordinary citizens and the elite and business community, with polls consistently showing substantial majorities opposed to NAFTA—and to the bailout of investors in Mexican securities— but the elite in favor. Media news coverage, selection of "experts," and opinion columns were skewed accordingly; their judgment was that the benefits of NAFTA were obvious, agreed to by all qualified authorities, and that only demagogues and "special interests" were opposed. As Meg Greenfield, *Washington Post* Op-Ed editor, explained the huge imbalance in her opinion columns: "On the rare occasion when columnists of the left, right and middle are all in agreement. . . . I don't believe it is right to create an artificial balance where none exists." But with a majority of the public opposing NAFTA, the pro-NAFTA unity among the pundits simply highlights the huge elite bias of mainstream punditry. It may be worth noting that the transnational media corporations have a distinct self-interest in global trade agreements, as they are among their foremost beneficiaries.

The pro-corporate and anti-labor bias of the mainstream media was also evident in the editorial denunciations (both in the *New York Times* and *Washington Post)* of labor's attempt to influence votes on NAFTA, with no comparable criticism of corporate or governmental (U.S. and Mexican) lobbying and propaganda. The media touted as admirable the puny labor and environmental protective side-agreements belatedly added to NAFTA. Even then, they failed to follow up on enforcement; in fact, when labor tried to use their provisions to prevent attacks on union organization in Mexico, the press ignored the case or derided it as labor "aggression."[18] With the Mexican meltdown beginning in December 1994, the media cleared NAFTA of any blame, and in virtual lockstep they supported the Mexican (investor) bailout despite poll reports of massive public opposition. Experts and media repeatedly explained that the merit of NAFTA was that it had "locked Mexico in" so that it couldn't resort to controls to protect itself from severe deflation. They were oblivious to the profoundly undemocratic nature of this lock-in.[19]

As is suggested by the treatment of NAFTA and labor's right to participate in its debates, the propaganda model applies to domestic as well as foreign issues. Labor has been under siege in the United States for the past fifteen years, but you would hardly know this from the mainstream media. A 1994 *Business Week* article noted that "over the past dozen years . . . U.S. industry has conducted one of the most successful union wars ever," helped by "illegally firing thousands of workers for exercising their right to organize," with unlawful firings occurring in "one-third of all representation elections in the late '80s."[20] But this successful war was carried out on the quiet, with media cooperation. The decertification of unions, use of replacement workers, and long and debilitating strikes like that involving Caterpillar were treated in very low key. In a notable illustration of the applicability of the propaganda model, the long Pittston miners strike was accorded much less attention than the strike of miners in the Soviet Union.[21] For years the media found only marginal interest in the evidence that the majority of ordinary citizens were doing badly in the New Economic Order; they "discovered" this issue only under the impetus of Pat Buchanan's right-wing populist outcries.

In the health insurance controversy of 1992-1993, the media's refusal to take the single-payer option seriously, despite apparent widespread public support and the effectiveness of the system in Canada, served well the interests of the insurance and medical service complex.[22] The uncritical media reporting and commentary on the alleged urgency of fiscal restraint and a balanced budget in the years 1992 to 1996 fit the business community's desire to reduce the social budget and weaken regulation. The applicability of the propaganda model in these and other cases, including the "drug wars,"[23] seems clear.

Final Note

In retrospect, perhaps we should have made it clearer that the propaganda model was about media behavior and performance, with uncertain and variable effects. Maybe we should have spelled out in more detail the contesting forces both within and outside the media, and the conditions under which these are likely to be influential. But having clearly made these points nonetheless, it is quite possible that nothing we could have done would have prevented our being labelled "conspiracy theorists," "rigid determinists," and deniers of the possibility that people can resist—even as we called for resistance.

The propaganda model remains in the late 1990s a very workable framework for analyzing and understanding the mainstream media—perhaps even more so than in 1988. As noted earlier in reference to Central America, the media's performance often surpasses expectations of media subservience to government propaganda. And we are still waiting for our critics to provide a better model.

Notes

1. Edward Herman and Noam Chomsky, *Manufacturing Consent: The Political Economy of the Mass Media* (New York: Pantheon, 1988).
2. Noam Chomsky analyzes some of these criticisms in his *Necessary Illusions: Thought Control in Democratic Societies* (Boston: South End Press, 1989), Appendix 1.
3. Entman's review is in the *Journal of Communication*, Winter 1990.
4. Carlin Romano, "Slouching Toward Pressology," *Tikkun* 4, no. 3 (1989).
5. Dan Hallin, *We Keep America On Top of the World* (London: Routledge, 1994), p. 13.
6. Ibid., p. 4.
7. Ben Bagdikian, *The Media Monopoly* (Boston: Beacon, 1987), p. 180.
8. Hallin, pp. 64, 70.
9. Ibid., pp. 64, 74, 77.
10. Ibid., p. 72.
11. For compelling documentation on this extraordinary subservience, see Chomsky, *Necessary Illusions*, pp. 197-261.
12. Philip Schlesinger, "From production to propaganda?," a review essay in *Media, Culture and Society* 11 (1989): 301.
13. See *Manufacturing Consent*, pp. xii-xiii.
14. Schlesinger, p. 297.
15. It should be noted that the case studies in *Manufacturing Consent* are only a small proportion of those which Chomsky and I have done which support the analysis of the propaganda model. Special mention should be made of those covering the Middle East, Central America, and terrorism. See esp. Chomsky's *Necessary Illusions, The Fateful Triangle*, and *Pirates & Emperors: International Terrorism in the Real World*, and my *The Real Terror Network* and (with Gerry O'Sullivan) *The Terrorism Industry*.
16. In fact, the only attempt to offer an alternative model was by Nicholas Lehmann in *The New Republic*. For an analysis of this effort, see Chomsky's *Necessary Illusions*, pp. 145-48.
17. Peter Golding and Graham Murdock, "Culture, Communications, and Political Economy," in James Curran and Michael Gurevitch (eds.), *Mass Media and Society* (London: Edward Arnold, 1991), p. 19.

18. For a discussion see Edward Herman, "Labor Aggression in Mexico," *Lies of Our Times,* December 1994, pp. 6-7.

19. For discussions of the media treatment of NAFTA and the Mexican meltdown, see Thea Lee, "False Prophets: The Selling of NAFTA," Economic Policy Institute, 1995; Edward Herman, "Mexican Meltdown: NAFTA and the propaganda system," *Z Magazine,* September 1995.

20. Aaron Bernstein, "The Workplace," *Business Week,* 23 May 1994, p. 70.

21. "Lost in the Margins: Labor and the Media," *EXTRA!,* Summer 1990.

22. "Health Care Reform: Not Journalistically Viable," *EXTRA!,* July-August 1993; John Canham-Clyne, "When 'Both Sides' Aren't Enough: The Restricted Debate over Health Care Reform," *EXTRA!,* January-February 1994.

23. See Chomsky, *Deterring Democracy* (London: Verso, 1991), pp. 114-21.

Democracy and the New Technologies

KEN HIRSCHKOP

Social change without a change in social relations—without the pain, conflict, burden of guilt, and sacrifice the latter would entail—has long been the dream of a particular species of social-democratic and socialist thought.

There have always been those who imagine that social life could be transformed by a more efficient husbanding of existing resources, by a more rational administration of the economy or polity, or by simply letting "progress" run its course. In these scenarios, there is no moment of struggle and no moment of loss, for change comes from outside the sphere of social relationships themselves, from science, sociology, or religion. In the latter twentieth century, the "inanimate" world of machinery and technology has assumed the responsibility for curing social ills without upsetting anyone. Proponents of technological transformation have laid claim to the social utopias promised by political radicals, and have promised that they can install them without altering the political status quo. Such postwar visions of the wonders worked by technological white heat have tended to focus on the eradication of poverty and promises of cheap food (as in the so-called Green Revolution), cheap consumables, a more comfortable lifestyle, and steady high wages. With the advent of new kinds of "information technology," however, the stakes have been raised. Technical innovations in the processing and communication of information have been tagged as the keys to not only economic regeneration, but also the transformation of political life, promising greater prosperity and greater democracy in one fell swoop. From Newt Gingrich to Vice President Al Gore, through the Electronic Frontier Foundation down to the not-quite-massed ranks of cyber-anarchists and feminists, the new forms of telecommuting and portable computing equipment are regarded as vehicles of new and more democratic social and political relationships. With a PC and a modem as his or her new mouthpiece, the citizen of the twenty-first century will enjoy a democracy simply inconceivable to earlier generations of the disenfranchised and oppressed.

Mass Technologies?

What are these new information technologies? For the purposes of this discussion, there are two important strands to the technological developments of the last two decades. The first is the creation and development of the "personal computer" and its associated software—in effect, a computer with substantial processing power and memory, designed for mass use (whether at home or at work) and available for purchase as a household item. The degree of technical development embodied in the PC (which, in this context, includes the small computers made by Apple) is evident to all. In the form of a moderately expensive commodity (more than a washing machine, less than an automobile), an individual may now have on hand more computing power than would have been available to a large research institution thirty years ago. Parallel to the development of personal computer hardware has been the industrial development of software also designed for mass use rather than expert usage. The creation of the "graphical user interface" (the symbol-oriented "language" of the Apple Mac System and Windows) and of "user-friendly" programs has made the use of a computer a less technically daunting experience, for which a short course (itself the subject of an industry, naturally) rather than lengthy training is sufficient introduction.

As computer language has been rendered more accessible, so topics of computer "conversation" have broadened, so that now computers can serve a range of entertainment, educational, household, and business functions. The main market for the PC remains the office rather than the home, and many (though not all) models are designed with this in mind. Nevertheless, what was once in effect an item of "heavy information industry" has now been translated into a consumer item, available to the nonspecialist. The second strand is the "revolution" in telecommunications, which has made possible the transmission of new kinds of information in quantities and at a speed which was previously unthinkable. The popular symbols for this transformation are the fax machine, cable television, and the Internet. In tandem with the developments in computing, these have rendered ordinary the transmission of huge quantities of data worldwide virtually instantaneously, and made possible interaction between individually owned and controlled computers. And in this case, the translation of quantity into quality is fairly straightforward: new quantities of data mean new kinds of data, not just figures but complicated text, images, and sounds, as well as the possibility of coordinating all of them.

The transformation of transmission technologies has involved the laying of cable and the development of hardware technologies, but has given rise to a software industry of its own. In combination, these technologies make it possible for a non-expert both to use a computer equipped with the power to manipulate text and images and to communicate with other computers worldwide. Naturally, the economic powers-that-be have no desire to stop there: they would like to integrate computing services with the network established by cable television and telephone, so that the household of the future will mediate all its electronic communication with the outside world through a single, extremely profitable service. No less naturally, there is a sharp economic conflict over the form this integration will take, for here as elsewhere the need for a unified system of telecommunications conflicts with the anarchy of the market.

To take a fairly obvious example, Microsoft, the leading producer of PC software, had guaranteed its dominance in the market by getting computer producers to include its Windows program as part of a basic software package. But when these PCs were hooked onto computer networks, other software, bound to new "network services," came into play and Microsoft had to respond with an aggressive campaign to establish its own network service and its own software. However desirable an integrated system may be, no one is going to sacrifice their market share for it.

The history of this technology is well known and not in dispute: both the software and the hardware associated with the Internet were developed in private and public research institutes depending for the most part on U.S. Department of Defense funding, while the technology of small computers was firmly fixed on corporate needs for the manipulation and transmission of information. No one denies that information technology is firmly embedded in the overdevelopment of the financial services business and the change in organization of production known as "post-Fordism." The new technologies were not designed as a public service, although the Internet was designed as a "state" one. They were and remain the product of either corporate or state-military research and development. Nevertheless, the end result is something that no one quite predicted, with the possible exception of a few science fiction writers.

For the new technologies have in effect "secularized" the use of the computer, making widely available the resources of what had been " high" and expensive technology. While the PC industry has emphasized high-end machines with more power than is appropriate for the "citizen-user," it is nevertheless the case that PCs have come within the range of purchasable goods, and that, however maddening or irritating it may occasionally be, the new style software has made computer literacy also a mass phenomenon. To use a PC and to communicate through the international telecommunications network requires neither extraordinary financial resources nor the equivalent of a university degree. While still a minority interest within even the wealthier industrial nations, access to the Internet and to personal computing resources is a potential reality for the majority in several nations.

But what is this access to? While the much-advertised possibilities seem endless, they break down into two basic kinds of communication. On the one hand, PCs, either in tandem with data encrypted on discs or CDs, or via use of the Internet, provide access to informational and educational resources that have been translated into computer data.

These resources can be composed of texts, sounds, or images, and not the least impressive of modern communicative capabilities is the availability to scan for and track down particular sorts of information, whether these are the record of a debate, a train timetable, or a map of a particular location. A networked computer is effectively a terminal with which one can gain access to computer "archives" of the most varied kinds, which can be upgraded on a daily basis. In terms of access to information, the advertising has a point: the new technologies represent a quantum leap.

The second kind of service is interaction among individual users. Network connections between individual computers and the gradual formation of ever higher level networks of networks have made possible a new kind of written conversation. In its least dramatic form this is represented by electronic mail, which duplicates on an international scale the kind of rapid exchange of correspondence that for an earlier age was the privilege of urban aristocrats. Somewhat more original are the so-called discussion lists and bulletin boards, which constitute a kind of permanently open forum, to which any person with access to a terminal may contribute. These are likewise both faster and more international in scope than anything that would have been made possible in an earlier decade.

But the final and most technologically striking interactivity consists of "real-time" conversations conducted over the screen, where contributions appear instantly and are responded to instantly as well; this represents a new mixture of types of communication, "oral" in time scale, written in form, electronic in range.

Given its novelty as a form of communication, it is not surprising that the last form has attracted the most comment. The possibility of conversation, traditionally the most intimate of forms, conducted on an international scale and with effective anonymity (as speakers are literally invisible to one another) is, depending on your point of view, daring and avant-garde, or a sad substitute for those to whom ordinary conversation is too much of a social burden. Nevertheless, all the forms of interactivity are distinctive in one significant respect: they serve as the basis for so-called "virtual communities," that is, communities founded on the exchange of messages over a computer network. As far as one can tell, the existing network plays host to uncountable numbers of such communities, which range in tone and topic from the utterly puerile to the politically serious. (The description "virtual" is, of course, hyperbole. For once humankind passed the barrier of orality, that is, with the invention of writing, there were plenty of communities founded on something besides physical proximity. Computer networks do not create anything new in this regard, though they certainly make its organization and maintenance easier.)

Online Democracy?

The democratic credentials of the new technologies rest on these capabilities. With a small computer, basic knowledge of the relevant software, and a modem providing access to a telephone line, one can transmit and receive messages, data, images, and sounds, to and from any other international terminal. The possibilities this opens up for political organization were illustrated through the now legendary use of information technology by the Zapatista leader Marcos, who effectively sidestepped the traditional media by sending out his communiqués over the Internet.

As organizing tools, the new technologies are doubtless powerful, rendering international communication rapid, easy, and cheap, and creating the possibility of international bulletins and appeals that make the old telephone trees look rather quaint. But for organizational purposes the technology is politically neutral, for it provides the same aid to those in authority that it provides to those trying to resist that authority. The true political claims for the new technologies lie in the belief that they make possible an access to information, and an international form of interaction that is not politically neutral, which is inherently democratizing. For if informed discussion of a more or less unhindered kind is critical to democratic life, then a technology that fosters it can only work to the advantage of the forces of democracy.

Reading the exclamations of the technologically enthused, however, one senses that what excites them is not what the Internet can do for the sober and responsible citizen, but the dizzying possibilities it opens up for those of a mischievously anarchistic bent. The technology for the Internet was designed as a military command and control system that could survive a thermonuclear attack. By a method known as "packet-switching," scientists found a way to route information that did not depend upon the existence of a central communications facility. This means that there is no central point from which network communications can be controlled or monitored (not yet at least), as if a certain freedom from central constraint were wired into the system itself. The second source of excitement comes from the apparently perpetual insecurity of all software-dependent systems; no matter how hard the great institutions try, they seem unable to keep the determined hacker from penetrating into their systems. The Electronic Frontier Foundation, founded after a concerted government attack on the hacker community, exists to keep this apparent openness of the Internet away from the predations of corporations and government.

Political economists on the left have been quick on the naiveté of would-be cyber-anarchists. They have reminded us that the origins of these technologies lie at the heart of the U.S. military-industrial complex, and that research and development has never been aimed at anything other than commercial and military uses. However heartwarming the generosity of the research network itself (whose tradition of giving away software freely is cited again and again by the techno-enthusiasts), it is a development at the fringe of the new technology, which for the most part is unabashedly devoted to the restructuring of capitalist industry and the maintenance of military control and security. PCs and networks may well be useful for politics; but the form of the network and the structure of computing equipment is determined first and foremost by the needs of the state and capitalist corporations.

Given the sum of money involved, it could hardly be otherwise. The relatively low cost of PCs and modems disguises the enormous costs of computing research and development as well as the laying down and maintenance of a network infrastructure. The money has to come from somewhere, and that somewhere is going to be the federal government and those corporations (IBM and AT&T, for instance) that can look upon it as an investment in future profit rather than the extension of democracy. For corporations, after all, this new mode of communication is also a new mode of exploitation, making possible new kinds of work, new forms of monitoring (as computers can precisely measure the extent and intensity of work done on them), and work from home which can save the employer a great deal in expenditure overheads.

Even as a consumer item, the new technology has clear limits. For while the sums at stake are not large as high-tech goods go, they are not small either, and there is every reason to believe that instead of extending access to the community, the new technology will install a new form of communicative apartheid. While new resources excite the imagination of the better-off, the old informational resources are in the process of being either run down (as in the case of public libraries) or privatized (as with the replacement of traditional broadcast by cable television). When real wages are stagnant or in decline for most of the population, the promise of increased access to information and communication for a fee, however small, is not going to be very appealing.

There are clear limitation, then, on the availability of the new computing and communicative resources, and so long as the new technologies remain the prerogative of the military and the corporate world, this is likely to get worse rather than better. Furthermore, the design of hardware and software will continue to be oriented not to the needs of democratic politics, but to those of new industrial profit.

Information is Power?

Although the criticisms of the political economists are certainly apposite, in another sense they miss the point. For the clear implication is that if all could have roughly equal access to these new resources, then the consequences would indeed be democratic. More information, and easier access to it, would lead to a better informed citizenry; a better informed citizenry could, given the communicative possibilities of the Internet, wield power through more frequent and more thorough forms of consultation (referenda, public hearings, electronic consultation with constituents, and so on).

This equation is the real weak point in the political argument for the new technologies. No one could doubt that access to these technologies means access to information resources, and to the possibility of rapid, even internationalized discussion and consultation. But is the problem with liberal democracies that they lack information, or that voting procedures are too cumbersome? I don't think so. The indefatigable Chomsky once pointed out that seeing through the ideology of the state required neither specialist training, nor access to specialist archives: the information was public and available, all one needs is a skepticism and the desire to root out the facts. The existence of the Internet and the personal computer increases access to information (and theoretically makes "voting" simpler and more immediate), but access to information was not the principal problem in the first place.

Of course, there are plenty of situations where access to information is a problem, particularly where political issues are mixed up with scientific questions (as with, for example, questions about industrial pollution, the safety of commercially produced drugs, and so on). But the fundamental inequity of political power does not rest on inequality of information: those who rule do not rule because they know more (very often they know less, whatever their pretensions), but rule whether they know what they are doing or not. Capitalist corporations may well feed information to political representatives and bureaucrats, but their ability to influence them does not depend "in the last instance" on the quality of the information, but on their ability to give or withhold support for state projects or for particular political groups. Private business institutions and their quasi-public associates have financial power and management structures; the state has juridical institutions and the ability to wield coercive force when necessary.

They certainly use knowledge and require continuous access to information, but this is not itself basis of their power. The rise of the new computing industries, based on "personal computing" and the new software, has confused this issue. Bill Gates, ultimate icon of this kind of capital accumulation, appears as the geek who made good, as if his enormous personal wealth and financial success were testimony to his scientific-technical expertise. But however nerdy his origins, Gates is successful because he has ridden the wave of recent capitalist restructuring so well, with the right combination of financial backing, a product well-suited to changes in business practice, and the ability to force the market into the shape he needs. Even Gates's key product, Windows software, is by all accounts neither original nor particularly impressive, being in effect a watered-down version of the much better Macintosh system.

The same strictures apply to dreams of endless electronic referenda. The absence of popular power in liberal-capitalist democracies has nothing to do with the frequency with which people vote; it stems from the very equation of popular power with the act of voting. Given the shape and limits of the liberal-capitalist state, popular power has to be exercised not only via formal votes (whether for representatives or in referenda) but also in the form of organized demonstrations, industrial action, boycotts, and the like. Those who see a quantitative increase in voting as the solution to democracy's ills imply that the problem with democracy is the fact of "representation" rather than the facts of capitalism. It is the latter, however, which ensure that voting in isolation can at least be legitimate strategies and policies decided on by elites.

It was not a momentary loss of judgment (or the need for a savior in a dark age) that led so many on the left to delude themselves about the democratic possibilities of the new media. Belief in what technology could do depended on a fundamental misreading of the nature of liberal-capitalist states and of political power in the late twentieth century. Thus much of the left was already predisposed to an injudicious equation of knowledge and power, even before the advent of PCs and the Internet. The 1960s critique of "technocracy" quite correctly unmasked the political and economic interests of those who claimed merely to administer capitalism in the most efficient manner possible. But it also set in motion a tendency to see authority as such, as if the state were in effect the RAND Corporation with an army and police force attached. By the early 1980s this tendency blossomed into the "postmodern" equation of science and authoritarianism, according to which any claim to describe things as true or false is inevitably a first step towards the Gulag.

States and capitalist corporations certainly fund and depend upon research and analysis. But one of the defining features of a capitalist ruling class is that it can choose whether to accept or repress the results of research, and can ignore or act upon its findings as its members see fit. Knowledge, scientific or cultural, is not the base of its authority but its instrument, and not its only one at that. In an early editorial, one of the more ambitious techno magazines, *Mondo 2000*, staked its claim to hegemony: "the old information elites are crumbling," it said, confident that it represented something avant-garde and new. There are certainly information elites, and they may well crumble from time to time, but they are not identical with political or economic elites—we do not live in Plato's Republic. The extravagances of the technophiles stem from their belief that once the information is available, political power will fall, or perhaps drift into the hands of the many. But information is for the most part already available, and if power remains centralized, it is because information itself is never enough.

It may appear to be enough to those who depend upon its production for their livelihood. The German essayist Hans Magnus Enzensberger once commented that the distinguishing feature of the middle classes was their interest in innovation, writing, invention, and the creation of knowledge. Lacking the power and wealth of the strictly bourgeois, they devoted themselves to the production of "culture," in the broadest sense of the term. When one reads the current mythic tales of the exploits of computer "hackers," and of the selfless ethos of computing professional who, of all things, give away their software, one cannot help thinking of this. The professional scientist or technician who believes that access to the fruit of his or her own labor is the key to democracy forgets his or her own role in the scheme of things. The hacker only appears as a political character to those who imagine they are at the center of political power rather than on its fringes. It is not, however, the scientists who run IBM but its board of directors, and then only at the behest of institutional shareholders.

Knowledge is a great thing and its pursuit a noble act. But lack of it is not the cause of our undemocratic life, and more of it, whether on the screen or in print, will not make for a more democratic polity. The new technologies are not the driving force of our society, which remains, as before, the imperative of profit. Information technology is currently capitalism's favorite son, but it should not forget that its status is the gift of its parent.

The last few years have been very discouraging for socialists and even moderate social democrats. In the wake of so many reverses and so much disappointment, the idea that capitalism would push a technological bridge too far, and so undo itself, is tempting. Who can resist the poetic justice of corporate power selling its gravedigger to the masses, in inexpensive, high-tech form? But the attraction of poetic justice has always been that, unlike the real kind, one can sit and observe its progress. When the very structure of a society depends upon a lack of democracy, however, democracy will depend upon a fight, and upon social forces with the interests, will, and intelligence to struggle for it. Technology will doubtless have a role in this struggle, but it offers no shortcuts: one cannot buy democracy off a shelf, or download it from a Website. It demands courage, fortitude, and political organization, and, as far as we can see, Microsoft has yet to design software that can deliver these.

Information Technology and Socialist Self-management

ANDY POLLACK

Belief in the possibility of socialism has waned as the so-called socialist countries have reverted to capitalism and as capital has once again expanded the scope and depth of its rule. Yet a self-managed, democratic socialist society has never been more feasible. The material possibility of socialism, as reckoned in the sheer productivity of industry and the availability of masses of goods and services, has existed for most of this century. Now the technical basis for the process of managing those things, i.e., for the process of socialism, has taken huge leaps forward with the advances in information technology of the mid-to-late 1990s.

At the very same time that the postcapitalist bureaucracies were falling, computing innovations were being developed that could put to rest skepticism about purely technical barriers to democratic planning. Just as the socialist countries were rushing back toward capitalism, the explosion in size and use of the Internet—and more generally of information technology (IT)—was providing the technical (and in part the organizational) basis for a truly self-managed economy. Tens of thousands of grassroots social movement organizations around the world can contact each other through the Internet, as can businesses and government and research organizations, with their massive databases and economic modeling tools. Were there to be a revolution in any country in the world tomorrow, the possibility for an immediate transition to democratic and efficient planning using the Internet would put to rest the claims about the unfeasibility of a socialist economy.[1]

Use of IT for self-management assumes, of course, that those things about which IT would store information and analyze would be in the hands of workers, not capital. Information technology is simply a tool for administering power, not a way of seizing it. Media hype about the information age and the way IT can provide a friction-free, democratic capitalism, ignore how and why IT is developed and applied today: as a tool to find new ways of extracting surplus value in an economy still centered on the production of material, not virtual, goods and services. A down-to-earth understanding of the use of IT in today's political economy is a prerequisite for a level-headed picture of how we might get to a self-managed society, which will not come through the click of a mouse but through the tramping of millions of feet, the raising of millions of hands, the use of billions of voices to seize the factories, the mines, the offices—and the computers.

I. Speed, Size, and Access

Alec Nove claims that in a modern economy, in which every day trillions of goods are produced and traded by billions of people, only the market can make the necessary calculations, through its pricing and supply-and-demand mechanisms. Yet every week, there come new reports of increases in size and speed for products at all ends of the computing spectrum. The supercomputers used by Wall Street, the Pentagon, and major university research institutions long ago reached a level sufficient to run the millions of simultaneous equations that would have to be solved to plan a modern socialist economy. What's more, parallel processing and client/server arrays are qualitatively increasing computing capabilities, and at the same time shrinking the size and expense of the hardware on which ever more complex calculations are performed.

The power of parallel processing received wide publicity during the 1995 chess match between Gary Karpov and IBM's Deep Blue. This machine, like others of its ilk, is normally used to predict the behavior of complex systems such as weather changes, ecological shifts, and other systems that are more complex than any economy. Some of these supercomputers and parallel processing apparatuses are already accessible through the Internet. Now government, academia, and business have teamed up to build Internet II: a separate and even faster network (which will eventually be available to the general public as well).

Last November the Cray Research Unit of Silicon Graphics introduced a supercomputer able to perform a trillion calculations a second. A project now taking three months, boasts its inventors, could be done in a few days. Not long after, the Intel Corporation and U.S. Energy Secretary Hazel O'Leary also announced development of a computer that could perform an astounding 1 trillion calculations a second. That smashes the previous mark of 368 billion calculations a second held by Japan's Hitachi Corp. By comparison, it would take every man, woman, and child in the United States 125 years, working nonstop with hand-held calculators, to perform 1 trillion calculations. It's an astonishing achievement, O'Leary gushed over the machine, which was built by connecting 7,264 Pentium microchips of the type found in ordinary home computers. She added, if the machine were Santa Claus it could deliver gifts to everyone in America in less than the time it takes to blink.

The new supercomputer will be reserved for use by scientists working on highly rarefied projects. Intel officials said it will give scientists a tool to simulate everything from nuclear explosions to DNA strands. "It's a baby step toward being able to do a real simulation of the physical world," said Justin Rattner, a chief developer of the project.

And, says the *New York Daily News,* Intel had better look out: IBM is building an even faster supercomputer, capable of 3 trillion operations a second.

O'Leary's Santa Claus analogy may have been tongue-in-cheek, but in fact it reflects accurately the relevance for planning of this new generation of computers. The Santa Claus analogy itself is used in economic theory to model far more complex distributional models. Massively parallel computers can solve in seconds problems involving thousands of carriers with millions of destinations. Such computers—with accurate information provided by grass-roots councils—could solve any of the distributional bottlenecks said to make socialist planning impossible.

Another alleged barrier to socialist planning is the impossibility of keeping track of sufficiently large numbers, of housing in accessible form the sheer quantity of information produced by an economy with millions of producers and consumers and billions of discrete goods and services. Here too IT has already provided the potential to solve this problem.

IBM plans to put 2 million patent filings on the World Wide Web, thus proving, said an IBM spokesperson, that very large data bases can be placed on the Internet and shared by large numbers of people. The company may also put FEC filings on the Web so the public can more easily follow campaign contributions made to politicians, as well as other still unspecified large data bases.

Far bigger databases—those in the financial and commercial sectors—are already accessible on the Web (see below). Now new proposals are being made to universalize access to the Internet that carries them. Although the Net, and computer use in general, are still highly stratified, households online are expected to go from 23.4 million in 1996 to more than 66 million in 2000. One fifth of the 25 million people in the United States between eighteen and twenty-four are already online, and over the next five years the figure is expected to double.

The public library system in New York City has more than 500 computers with Internet access, and in all these libraries there is computerized access to national and world trade data banks, census data on CD-ROMs, etc.

In the computer classes I teach, I've gotten a feel for the expanding access of workers to computers through their unions, and the even greater access enjoyed by their kids, both at school and at home. Even the lab with the most primitive computers (i.e., DOS-based 286s) has been used by students to do spreadsheet calculations on job loss in their industry (health care) and to write essays on the managed care revolution. At my other employer, a 90 percent Black and Latino working class college, there are several labs, with hundreds of computers, many of them online.

Already in most working-class communities there are computers on the street which are tapped into every day by the majority of workers. ATMs connect workers to their banks, while workers place their bets (and lose their money) at state lottery and off-track betting machines. Here we see an apparatus which, in a different kind of society, could be used by workers on an everyday basis to record consumption requests, to register their desires to shift jobs, to vote on production and consumption proposals, etc.

Today junior high school students argue via e-mail with university astronomers about the projected impact of a meteorite hitting Jupiter, and use the mathematical capabilities of the astronomers' computers to bolster their arguments. Every Sunday each New York daily paper lists new web sites for interactive discussion. Weekly alternative magazines report on new electronic chat groups. Each of these are potential sites for decentralized discussion of socialist planning—discussions which, as the junior high school example shows, need not be limited to typing in opinions, but can involve actual exchange of data.

II. Networks: Gateways to Participation

a) Within the firm: Intranets

The potential for self-management within an individual economic unit can be seen by the spread of intranets, that is, internal company networks. Most firms today have, or are setting up, intranets on which employees can electronically send data, correspondence, charts, and even video images to each other. This has led to a lot of hooey in the business press about the potential for new styles of horizontal management—a potential, however, which could be realized under a different system. Technologies now used to monitor and intensify work, to increase the rate of exploitation and profit, could be used for very different purposes.

Back in 1982, a co-worker at Warner & Swasey, a machine-tool manufacturer in Cleveland, showed me how workers could use computers to see for themselves the productivity of their labor and its contribution to the firm's profits. Workers put data into shop floor terminals about the number of the parts they machined, the time it took, which department it went to next, etc. The computer then calculated workers' bonuses, as well as overall plant production. This co-worker used one of these terminals to show me how we were being exploited, demonstrating the difference between what we got in wages and bonuses per piece, and what the company got from each piece as part of the total sales price of the finished machine. That is, he demonstrated to me the theory of surplus value using the company's computer.

The Evil Computer Empire, Microsoft, sells an array of programs sufficient to perform most of the computing tasks that would be necessary for grassroots economic decision-making within a given economic unit: e.g., Project, Team Manager, Access, Excel, Word, and Publisher. Project and Team Manager, perhaps the most important for the decision-making process, enable scheduling and allocation of resources, and constant revision of each. Access is a database, which stores and analyzes relationships between workers, inventories, suppliers, and customers. Excel is used to perform calculations about production and pay. Word and Publisher can be used for memos, newsletters, resolutions, etc.

And the hottest program on the corporate IT market in 1997—SAP/R3, made in Germany—links the database and spreadsheet functions of such programs in a massive multidimensional format, connecting departments in giant firms in qualitatively new ways.

Fierce competition is raging in the software industry over new attempts to link intranets, groupware, and the Internet. Microsoft's strategy switch in the last year from desktop PC software to networking software came partly from a desire to cash in on the consumer rush to the Internet, but even more so from a desire to consolidate its lead in the corporate networking field—first, by advancing the dominance of its Windows NT software (for corporate intranets), and second, by beginning to link that software to Internet programs. Netscape, in turn, reacting to Microsoft's assault on the browser field, moved to enter the market for groupware, which also meant taking on IBM's Lotus division. Netscape execs point to studies projecting that the intranet market will grow to $10 billion by 2000.

Netscape's groupware allows collaboration on documents, and thus the sharing of information within a company, as well as the forging of links to customers and suppliers. Groupware is increasingly being designed to work with "push" software, which automatically retrieves and updates data from the Internet. As corporate hype has it, information finds you, rather than you finding information.

IT developed for internal company use could be used in a self-managed society by workers of a given firm, to plan the mix and number of products or services; to plan work schedules and hiring; and to analyze how to equitably divide the surplus they produce between their own needs and those of society as a whole.

The increased linkage of intranets with the Internet prefigures linkages possible between self-managed economic units—which leads us to innovations in interfirm networking.

b) Planning across firms

The use of computers for ongoing recalculations has become part of the management mania for just-in-time decision-making, to better recalculate flows to and from suppliers and consumers. Wal-Mart has boasted that its computer system allows it to minimize inventory, managing its shelf space to match quickly changing consumer needs. Auto manufacturers use similar systems to tighten their connections with parts suppliers and car dealers. FedEx's Business Link lets shippers build their own Web sites to advertise their goods. Customers can then place orders and tell FedEx to have them delivered—all on-line, through FedEx's Internet links. FedEx executives claimed that they are providing a wide range of integrated information, transportation, and logistics help, including order entry and confirmation, inventory management, invoicing, and service for returns or repairs. One FedEx vice president said the move solves one of the key limitations of electronic commerce by linking the automated order and fulfillment system to the delivery of the product to the end customer.

Now imagine these computers turned over to consumer councils, who would use them to tally the direct registering of consumer desires that have been input into ATMs and home PCs. Those desires could be fulfilled at the point of purchase. The councils could then pass on these figures to production units.

What's more, all of this can be done on an ongoing real-time basis. That is, far beyond ballpark estimates of consumer needs based on a hypothetical basket of goods, the direct input of billions of expressed desires—and the constant recalculation of production and distribution requirements that flow from them—could be transmitted.

I could see the possibility of such constant recalculation years ago, when I was a reservation agent at Pan Am. The company's computerized reservations system was used to readjust the number of flights and their schedules, based on consumers' projected use. The system constantly recalculated fare levels, as it tallied how reservations on each flight were changing the likelihood that it would end up being sold out, thus allowing managers to decide when to end sale prices, to readjust them from among the different sale types, or to add more discounts if sales were slow. Such ongoing changes are a perfect example of the meshing of technical and organizational spheres in the performance of iterative decision-making. (And even at that time many passengers were making their own reservations on-line.)

Advances in this sphere of IT has led to a trend away from reliance on internal computer departments and management information systems, in favor of using outside firms. The technology used by the latter could be used just as well by socialist economic units to develop joint plans. Ross Perot, founder of Electronic Data Systems, first made his fortune by convincing California to let him handle the databases of its government agencies. Now firms like his are bidding to manage state records of welfare rolls, as the states move to comply with the new federal welfare repeal law. General Electric—the company with the largest revenue stream in the United States—draws almost as much revenue from such information management services as it does from its traditional manufacturing base.

Imagine if these companies were taken over and turned into centers for socialist accounting, to coordinate interfirm production, to keep track of and vote on shifts in social service levels, and to decide on changing mixes of services provided by public bodies.

Imagine such programs used by elected planning committees to recalculate continually what they send to and receive from other workplaces and communities. Figures on deliveries of goods and services between units would be checked by members of interunit councils; such figures would lead to updating of decisions on product mixes and amounts, and thus on social priorities. And the savings from decreased distribution cost and time would lead—again, through discussion based on hard data—to further shortening of work time and/or its reallocation to unsolved social problems.

Federal and state departments of labor have long had computer displays of available jobs, and have recently begun listing available jobs on-line. The computers at New York's Worker Career Centers—union-funded employment and retraining centers—could be linked to Department of Labor databases, transforming them from job search centers for hundreds of dislocated, i.e. laid-off, workers, into centers of self-management where the working class as a whole meets to calculate hours worked in each industry, how to redistribute work, and thus how to shorten the workweek.

In April 1997, the AFL-CIO posted a site on the Web in which users can compare their annual income to that of their company's CEO; the program then calculates how many years the worker would have to work to equal the executive's salary. What is now a propaganda exercise could just as easily be turned into a tool to redistribute amounts of both labor contributed and its fruits.

c) Cybershopping: self-management in consumption

The technology and organizational linkages necessary for democratic planning of consumption and reproduction needs have also taken huge steps forward in the last few years.

During the 1996 Christmas shopping season, the media were full of features on the new cybermalls, as retailers put their goods on the Web. And in 1996, 3 million households spent more than $1 billion on purchases online, double the 1995 amount.

These cybermalls could be used by consumers to enter estimates of their consumption needs. Computers that previously registered orders—and projected firms future sales—could now tally the results of consumers' expressed preferences for various goods, and those results could be disseminated to the relevant industries. The latter would then have estimates on which to base their output, estimates which could be continually revised, both by individual consumers and by consumers acting through their councils.

d) Economywide planning

There are already many examples on the Net of macroeconomic analysis and planning tools used by the big stock exchanges, by multinational corporations, and by academia and government. On the exchanges, computers register ongoing changes in the prices of stocks and commodities for tens of thousands of firms, and anyone with Internet access can already view the workings of the exchanges on their PC. Every day, the *New York Daily News* reminds its readers in its business pages that it offers free, up-to-the-minute stock quotes and info on its web site, including earnings, revenue, and high-low pricing.

At least one organization already provides, on-line, an embryonic example of how interactive planning might work. The Economic Democracy Information Network (EDIN) offers an interactive form on its home page, that allows users to see how changing spending for various government agencies affects the federal deficit. The user tells the computer by what percentage she wants to change expenditure by various government departments, and taxes from various social classes. The computer then tells her how much the federal deficit would grow or shrink. She can then e-mail her comments on the process to other participants.

The University of Maryland's Inforum network provides Web access to a set of macroeconomic modeling tools—input-output tables, linear programming, etc.—that socialists long ago claimed could be used to run a planned economy. Since the 1970s, Inforum's EconData program has been responding to such questions as: What effect will reduced military spending have on the airline industry? What would 6 percent growth in the money supply mean for the lumber industry? How would the U.S. chemical industry be affected by a decline in the dollar? And what impact would sweeping changes in tax laws have on employment in various industries?

These questions are answered with the help of input-output tables (first developed by Wassily Leontieff), which portray the flows of goods and services through the whole U.S. economy. Such tables let you see how changes in one industry's production levels affect the others; and to see how these interactions in turn add to GNP, profits, government revenue, consumption, etc. Input-output tables can be constructed for any given length of time, a month, a year, or ten years.

The databases in EconData include a variety of economywide statistics compiled by local, state, and federal governments, as well as the IMF and World Bank. The types of questions that Inforum provides to its business clients using this data are just the sort that would be confronted by worker and community planners. Imagine an expanded version of EDIN's interactive game linked to models like Inforum's, which in turn had real data funneled to it on a continuous basis from an expropriated stock exchange computer system.

Inforum already provides a program to allow users to perform complex mathematical tasks themselves, with only limited knowledge of the math involved. Its PDG program, an econometric regression and model-building program for PCs, allows the user to build and use data banks with thousands of regularly updated economic time series, and perform a whole series of complex mathematical tasks. The United States has millions of working class students taking accounting, business, and economics courses in college—

students who already have far more than the rudimentary knowledge of math and economics needed to use the PDG program.

Millions of workers have already had experience with spreadsheets, which work on similar if more rudimentary principles as input-output tables. It was in fact the ability to handle personal finances and small corporate budgets that first made the personal computer a mass commodity. Millions of households of all classes have already used VisiCalc, Lotus, Excel, Quicken, and other programs to keep track of their personal finances in table form. These spreadsheet programs are the same ones used by the biggest investment banks to do analysis and reports based on the figures generated by the more massive database programs, such as SAP/R3, Essbase, and Oracle.

In a self-managed society such IT could be used for continual mass participation in national and even international planning. And the planning process could be broadcast live over WebTV, allowing individual and council input in real-time into the decision-making process. Mainstream IT pundits boast of the potential of broadcasting innovations to allow electronic democracy in today's society. Such claims have rightly brought forth left critiques that these pundits are talking not about real participation, but at best about mass spectacles with plebiscite-type referenda, allowing elite manipulation. In the context of very different social property relations, could IT instead provide genuine, structured linkages between decision-makers at different levels of society to guarantee socialist democracy? Can we use IT to make lower-level units more than passive producers of data for higher-level decision-makers?

III. IT and Macro-Micro Linkages

Advocates of socialist self-management have always stressed the need for a careful articulation of decision-making, that is, deciding on what level decisions need to be taken, and pushing as many decisions as possible down the chain. Decisions shouldn't be made on a national level that could be made locally; decisions shouldn't be made by industrywide or regional bodies when they could be handled by workers in a particular workplace or residents in a particular neighborhood.

The open nature of the new IT, the range of ways to connect users, the possibility of discussion groups linking up to databases, all make possible the disaggregation of data to the appropriate level. Even further, they make possible ongoing discussion and voting on *how* to disaggregate the data, and how to decide at what level things need to be decided. A democratic socialism must include a process to counterpose different planning models, so workers could assess their relative merits in terms of access to decision-making, decentralization of decisions, and inclusion of an adequate variety of social concerns at each level (i.e. transforming of gender and nationality issues into quantitative forms, etc.).

The real mathematical difficulty in planning socialism is not the tallying of data or the calculation of huge numbers of simultaneous equations, but a method to link such data and calculations with concrete micro- and middle-level organizational decisions, which then would have to flow back into the macro-level, i.e. the iterative decision-making process described by Michael Albert and Robin Hahnel in their *Looking Forward: Participatory Economics for the Twenty-first Century* (Boston: South End Press, 1991). The IT used by brokerage houses—and even more so by the on-line programs allowing individuals to bypass the brokers and interact directly with the stock and commodities markets—are one example of a technology which could handle such a process.

Millions of mutual fund investors already have Internet access, and 32 percent of them have already visited the Web sites of financial service companies. Entrepreneurs are using the latest IT to find ways for the small investor to get access to markets previously open only to the big houses. For instance, after-hours trading on-line, a privilege previously reserved to securities firms, is now available. A reflection of the new importance of such interactive services is Dow Jones's recent embarrassing admission that its on-line services needed massive overhauling—and its subsequent alliance with Microsoft to do the job.

The current run of the stock market through successively higher landmarks—however artificial these landmarks may eventually prove to be—have been facilitated in a technical sense by the proliferation of the brokerage houses, the mutual funds into which they steer investors, and the IT they use. These changes were dramatized by the 1997 merger of Morgan Stanley and Dean Witter-Discover, expected to be a precursor of similar big investor-small investor marriages. Billions of dollars have been poured into mutual funds by middle and working class investors (and by their pension and medical funds). By necessity, the firms that manage these funds have IT that make connections between the databases of national and international exchanges, of huge state pension and health benefit systems, and of millions of individual investors.

Their IT must necessarily provide linkages across the full range of economic levels, from the individual to the macroeconomic.

It is just such linkages that could be used by mid-range workers' councils to ensure an active flow of information across levels of a self-managed society, to keep track of how micro- and macro-level decisions are affecting each other. Under socialism each brokerage house's computer network could be turned over to a regionwide or industrywide council, which could in turn be connected to PCs in homes, union halls, etc.

The stock markets and commodities exchanges themselves could be transformed from gigantic betting pools into measuring devices of real production and consumption changes—changes that could be constantly monitored on millions of PCs, both individually at home and in council offices, using the brokerage house apparatus described above. Decisions made at a national level, and registered through a socialized Big Board, could be disaggregated through the brokerage house IT apparatus into databases appropriate for the kind of decisions which smaller units would need to make.

The New York Stock Exchange announced last December that its ticker would be televised live, each trade being shown on a televised Big Board seconds after being made. Imagine if this ticker registered not private stock prices but numbers of children's shirts sewn, the number of fresh tomatoes brought to market, and so on.

Other examples of the already existing potential for macroeconomic computerized planning come from Washington, where the federal government is shifting its benefit payments to direct deposit, replacing checks with a form of electronic banking. The government currently makes 850 million individual payments a year totaling $1.2 trillion; electronic direct deposits already account for 53 percent of those transactions. Large companies already file around 155 million tax forms electronically. Computer systems capable of handling such massive payments from and to the overwhelming majority of U.S. residents could become a core component of a socialist distribution network.

"Push" software, which got its fifteen minutes of fame earlier this year, is a crass means of forcing advertising onto consumers' screens, designed by corporations to try to overcome the anarchy of information on the structureless Web. It could instead be used by socialist planners to more efficiently disseminate information feedback among councils. Programs could be written that periodically push data to economic units that are approaching preset levels expected to require recalculation of previously entered decisions.

IV. Electronic Cash and Socialist Accounting

In 1996, 9.7 billion transactions were recorded at 122.7 million ATM machines in the United States. And banking transactions from home are swelling, as Citibank and others encourage PC users to go on-line with their accounts. The national clearinghouses that centralize the accounts of banks, stock exchanges, and other financial institutions move trillions of dollars a day electronically.

The following year, Chase Manhattan, AT&T, Dean Witter, Discover, and three other companies announced plans to create a new electronic cash network for U.S. consumers. Several companies are developing software to load cash onto plastic cards through ATMs, over telephones, and soon via the Internet. These cards could be used to make purchases from merchants who have smart-card-reading terminals.

This entire apparatus could be a backup system for socialist accounting. We already register on a continual basis the economic transactions of hundreds of millions of people. A self-managed society could use electronic cash and the computers that record its use to track the accuracy of the decisions made with all the IT described in previous sections of this article. The shadow prices used in postcapitalist societies to gauge the accuracy of bureaucratic planning decisions could find a more concrete manifestation in electronically-generated figures of real economic activity.

V. International Planning

There's no lack of statistics today summarizing worldwide production, reproduction, health, education, etc. International agencies such as the UN, the ILO, the World Bank, and IMF do so all the time. In November 1996, the ILO reported its estimate that 1 billion people worldwide—30 percent of the world's labor force—were either unemployed or underemployed in 1995. (Less drastic levels from 1993 and 1994 were said to represent crisis levels not seen since the Great Depression.) Prior to the 1996 Beijing conference, the UN published global estimates of the billions of dollars in unpaid labor contributed by women around the world, showing that women are doing unpaid work equivalent in size to the formal world GNP. Another, more ghastly global estimate of women's status was made by Amartya Sen, who demonstrated that gender and economic inequities had left the world with 100 million fewer women than should be alive today. Leontieff, of input-output table fame, himself did a study for the UN using international tables, showing how decreases in military spending and restructuring of income and development inequities would reduce poverty in particular countries and on a global scale.

All such databases, tables, statistics, and econometric calculations could become part of a democratic international planning process. However over-rated the current wave of globalization is, there is no question that the international reach of information technology is a brand new phenomenon.

Yet in the existing society the IT sector simply mirrors the unequal international division of labor inherent in the newest stage of imperialism. The Internet's mainstream boosters claim its international character will further the spread of riches and freedom in this "new" era of globalization. But computer hardware (and more recently software) production and assembly is disproportionately concentrated in low-wage neocolonial regions; data input is shifted away from the developed world to the third world (and to impover-ished regions in the first world) for the same reason.

Such disparities are built into the political and economic nature of our system. But the spread of the technology itself shows the potential to redistrib-ute its location and use, once society itself is revolutionized. International grassroots electronic planning to overcome underdevelopment is now techni-cally feasible on a global scale.

VI. IT and the Sphere of Reproduction

I recently read a manual on business networking techniques which argues that those middle layer workers made redundant by the Net could find employment as social workers or childcare workers. It's far more likely that the savings accrued from their firing will end up in the bank accounts of their bosses (and in the accounts of computer moguls). However, a social reassess-ment of priorities and a shifting of resources from manufacturing to services, as part of a restructuring of gender power and roles, could be facilitated by the use of IT under socialism.

The Web, while deluged with advertising from manufacturing and retail firms, also houses home pages from agencies and organizations in the sphere of reproduction. A quick browse with a search engine turns up such sites as the Childcare Administrator, Administrator Software for Windows (designed to meet the needs of childcare centers), American Childcare Solutions, and the federal government's National Childcare Information Center. There's even a websearcher devoted specifically to childcare, the Childcare National Network Gopher. These groups allow users to swap information on types of childcare available, resources and research on childcare, pending legislation, etc.

A socialist accounting system could turn these Web sites into places for parents and children to register their needs on a societywide basis, and to integrate those needs with the production and consumption figures from other sectors of the economy.

In some ways this could be the most fundamental change of all. A self-managed society using IT could prove with hard numbers that the socialist and feminist revolutions can be an indivisible whole.

VII. Who Will Control Information Technology?

Despite the relative newness of the Internet, one can already see several examples of how capital is frustrating its inherent potential. The Internet, and IT more generally, has an openness that drives the corporate world crazy, as they scramble to find ways to secure their business secrets and yet still be able to use the network to boost their marketing potential. Thus the fear of the Net's free flow of information, and the mania to develop software to maintain corporate secrecy.

Communications industry mergers, already happening at a feverish pace, were given a new boost by the recently concluded global telecommunications pact. The expected increases in size and power of these IT titans will further weaken those who would seek to maintain the open, indeed anarchic, nature of the Internet.

What's more, while IT is touted as leading to a leaner and more productive capitalism, it is in the long run leading to a system every bit as wasteful as the precomputer version. The net savings to individual firms, and to the economy as a whole, will not be turned toward increased production of goods or services, or to redistribution of income, but will sink in the hole of capitalist anarchy. The reduced turnover time of capital accruing from implementation of IT will more likely deepen the severity of downturns and depressions.

As we consider the implementation of IT and the purposes for which it is used, we must come back to the question of power, and which social groups wield it. The U.S. left has done far too little during this century to explain how the massive organizational and technological apparatus of existing society could be used in a different way. No other country has produced so many economists, accountants, statisticians, marketing researchers, management information systems analysts, reporters, etc.; in sum, professionals whose job is to plan the affairs of their firm or agency. No country has held so many meetings and conferences, published so many publications, or arranged and rearranged so many complex corporate structures, all to plan business affairs. Thus the left, having done a fairly good job of exposing the waste in our system, faces a new set of challenges and responsibilities. First, showing the potential of the infrastructure of society today to provide conduits for more democratic information flows. Simultaneously, workers who are using those technologies need to know the possibilities they have for manifesting their power today, and for fully realizing a truly democratic society in the future.

Notes

Thanks to Dan Caplin for the insights shared in our discussions of these issues.

1. For further reading on the potential of IT for democratic planning, including concrete estimates of times required to carry out various decision-making tasks using existing computers, see W. Paul Cockshott and Allin Cottrell, *Towards a New Socialism* (Nottingham: Spokesman, 1993).

CONTRIBUTORS

Michael W. Apple is the John Bascom Professor of Education at the University of Wisconsin, Madison. Among his recent books are *Official Knowledge* (1993), *Education and Power* (1995), and *Cultural Politics and Education* (1996).

Nicholas Baran is a former consulting editor for *BYTE Magazine* and currently editor-in-chief of *Windows NT Systems* magazine.

Elaine Bernard is director of the Trade Union Program at Harvard University.

Noam Chomsky, long-time political activist, writer, and professor of linguistics at Massachusetts Institute of Technology, is the author of numerous books and articles on U.S. foreign policy, international affairs and human rights, including *Year 501; Keeping the Rabble in Line; World Orders Old and New; Class Warfare;* and *Powers and Prospects.*

Michael Dawson is the author of *The Consumer Trap,* forthcoming from University of Illinois Press.

John Bellamy Foster is a member of the board of Monthly Review Foundation and is co-editor of *Organization and Environment.* He teaches sociology at the University of Oregon.

Peter Golding is professor of sociology and head of the Department of Social Sciences at the University of Loughborough, UK. His most recent books include *Beyond Cultural Imperialism* (1997); *The Political Economy of the Mass Media* (1997); and *Cultural Studies in Question* (1997). He is co-director of the

Communication Research Centre at Loughborough, and an editor of the *European Journal of Communication.*

Edward Herman's most recent book, with Robert W. McChesney, is *The Global Media: The New Missionaries of Corporate Capitalism* (London: Cassell, 1997).

Jill Hills is professor of international political economy at City University, London.

Ken Hirschkop is a research fellow in English at the University of Manchester.

Robert W. McChesney teaches journalism at the University of Wisconsin, Madison.

Peter Meiksins teaches in the Sociology Department at Cleveland State University.

Heather Menzies is an Ottawa-based writer and adjunct professor (of Canadian and women's studies) at Carleton University. She is the author of seven books, four of them on the social issues of technological restructuring.

Andy Pollack teaches at the Borough of Manhattan Community College and Consortium for Worker Education in New York.

Sid Shniad is research director of the Telecommunications Workers Union, based in British Columbia. He is actively involved in efforts to challenge the telecommunications industry's domination of information technology in Canada.

Ellen Meiksins Wood, an editor of *Monthly Review,* is co-author (with Neal Wood) of *A Trumpet of Sedition: Political Theory and the Rise of Capitalism, 1509-1688* (New York: New York University press, 1997).

INDEX